Education,
Modernity,
and
Fractured Meaning

SUNY Series in Philosophy, edited by Robert Cummings Neville
and
SUNY Series in the Philosophy of Education, edited by Philip L. Smith

EDUCATION, MODERNITY, AND FRACTURED MEANING

*Toward a Process
Theory of Teaching and Learning*

DONALD W. OLIVER
with the assistance of
KATHLEEN WALDRON GERSHMAN

State University of New York Press

Published by
State University of New York Press, Albany

© 1989   State University of New York

For information, address State University of New York
Press, State University Plaza, Albany, N.Y., 12246

Library of Congress Cataloging in Publication Data

Oliver, Donald W.
    Education, modernity, and fractured meaning: toward a process
theory of teaching and learning / Donald W. Oliver with the
assistance of Kathleen Waldron Gershman.
    p.   cm. — (SUNY series in the philosophy of education) (SUNY
series in philosophy)
    Bibliography: p.
    Includes index.
    ISBN 0-88706-941-X. — ISBN 0-88706-942-8 (pbk.)
    1. Education—philosophy. 2. Process philosophy. 3. Curriculum
planning. I. Gershman, Kathleen Waldron, 1943-   . II. Title.
III. Series. IV. Series: SUNY series in philosophy.
LB885.O44E38   88-20990
370 .1—do19   CIP

Contents

PART ONE:

Modernity

Introduction and Overview

Our book begins with the thesis that advanced industrial societies are approaching the end of an age. It is an age in which the unconscious cultural symbols providing our lives with deep meanings are losing their vitality, the passion that drives our love for inventing material things is drying up, and our intimate connection with the natural living world is steadily decreasing. Although awed by the power of our technical achievements, we are nevertheless bewildered by the crassness that increasingly characterizes our personal relationships. The age that is coming to an end we call 'modernity.' Those of us who live in this age, in this time and place in North America, we refer to as 'modern people.'

Our analysis of problems relating to this transition leads off in Chapter One with a passage from Walker Percy's book *The Message in the Bottle*, in which he suggests that the most alarming aspect of the "ending of an age" is our inability to comprehend modernity within the framework of its own ideology. Percy likens us to people who live "by reason during the day and at night dream bad dreams." We would make a distinction between *ideological* confusion and the *paradigmatic* confusion that surfaces during major shifts in culture. In the midst of ideological confusion, a common language will still allow for significant, even violent, communication. (We note the way socialists argue with capitalists, or the way 'born-again' Christians engage liberal humanists, all of whom strive for the material comforts and technical predictability of modern middle-class life.) However, as we become involved in paradigmatic shifts away from older meaning systems, we disassociate ourselves radically from the groundedness of our historic reality, and substitute thin, verbal–conceptual abstractions to support the appearance of continued communication between past and future.

We maintain that the incoherence emerging from this transition is in part a function of efforts to find meaning within the fragments of technical information that have proved useful in creating our modern scientific–materialistic culture in the first place. As modern people we erroneously come to see the problems of our age not as requiring a search for grounded meaning and the renewal of significant symbols but rather as an inability to discover a new piece of technical information. The dying paradigm is then trapped in the circle of its own deficiency: it seeks to find a new technology to repair the machine, not realizing that the limitations inherent in the machine metaphor are themselves at the heart of the problem. Within the modern paradigm we are unable to generate a sufficiently powerful critique to correct our illusions and distortions. At this point, we need, somehow, to move outside the limitations of old patterns of thought and gain a broader understanding of the relationship between our conception of technique and of deep culture.

Chapter Two continues the critique of fragmentation by pointing to the overly optimistic view taken by modern society of unlimited functional specialization as a means of improving the quality of our lives. Progress, from the modern point of view, comes about through the development and application of technical knowledge to improve the efficiency of proliferating professions. In our analysis of specialization, especially as it applies to human service vocations, we distinguish between two kinds of knowing: *technical* knowing and *ontological* knowing. Technical knowing refers to adaptive, publicly transferable information or skills; ontological knowing refers to a more diffuse apprehension of reality, in the nature of liturgical or artistic engagement. In this latter sense, we come to know with our whole body, as it participates in the creation of significant new occasions — occasions which move from imagination and intention to critical self-definition, to satisfaction, and finally to perishing and new being.

We then argue that this fuller quality of ontological knowing requires that we have available a range of living metaphors within culture — not only the machine metaphor that dominates the modern paradigm but also the metaphors of organic life and transcendent dance. We point out that teaching can be interpreted within the framework of any of these metaphors. It can be construed as a mechanistic act in which teacher motivates students to 'learn' predetermined knowledge; it can be seen as an organic interchange, a negotiated settlement of mutual needs and concerns between teacher and student; or it can even be seen as a unitary dance in which participants (teacher and students), knowledge (curriculum), and movement (setting) come together to participate in a common transcendent occasion. A full conception of teaching requires both ontological sensibility and technical competence to bring all of these metaphors into play as appropriate modes of education.

In support of our assumption that a healthy culture is characterized by metaphorical richness and adequate attention to ontological knowing, we offer two sources of evidence. The first is Stanley Diamond's interpretation of anthropological studies bearing on the way preliterate peoples commonly understand and dramatize their immediate social and natural reality; the second is Sorokin's extensive historical–sociological studies comparing what he calls "sensate," "ideational," and "integrative" cultures. Neither of these sources intends to simply romanticize archaic societies. Rather they are intended to point up the biases that diminish modern society's ability to support human potential. We suggest that healthy societies are those whose symbolic roots allow them to cope economically while maintaining an intimate, even warm, sense of organic connectedness *to* and transcendent unity *with* their natural environment.

We then discuss school curriculum within the framework of this critique. First, we point out that curriculum 'development' is currently construed as technique—wherein educators presumably identify explicit learning objectives and then predict in a quasi-scientific way how to manipulate the school environment so as to optimize student attainment of those objectives. In addition, the epistemological emphasis in the content of school subjects (verbal and conceptual knowledge) as well as its organization (unrelated fragments of abstract information) reflect our modern bias toward what is important to study and how it is to be studied. Both conditions, we suggest, tend to prevent teachers, as technically oriented professionals, from gaining any feeling for or understanding of ontological knowing. The risk of being condemned as 'diffuse' or 'fuzzy-minded' is simply too great.

As a final note, it is important to emphasize at the outset that our critique of modernity refers essentially to its culture in the narrower sense of the term—that is, to its meaning system. We understand that meaning (culture), the temperament, strength and diversity of a people, social structures, technology, and the natural environment are all inextricably tied together in the definition of any full-blown social system. We should make clear, here, however, that our major focus, both in the way we use the idea of culture now and our later use of the term 'cosmology,' has to do with clarifying the need for a radical revision in how we imagine ourselves to be—how we *apprehend* and *perceive* the world, the way we *feel* and *dream* and *think*—as a prelude to how we might act within communities of our fellow beings as we approach the next millennium on this planet.

Chapter One

Prologue and Introduction

Prologue: At the End of an Age

The modern age began to come to an end when men[2] discovered that they could no longer understand themselves by the theory professed by the age.

After the end of the modern age, its anthropology was still professed for a while and the denizens of the age still believed that they believed it, but they felt otherwise and they could not understand their feelings. They were like men who live by reason during the day and at night dream bad dreams.

The scientists and humanists were saying one thing, but the artists and poets were saying something else.

The scientists were saying that by science man was learning more and more about himself as an organism and more and more about the world as an environment and that accordingly the environment could be changed and man made to feel more and more at home.

The humanists were saying that through education and the application of the ethical principles of Christianity, man's lot was certain to improve.

But poets and artists and novelists were saying something else: that at a time when, according to the theory of the age, men should feel most at home they felt most homeless.

Someone was wrong.

In the very age when communication theory and technique reached its peak, poets and artists were saying that men were in fact isolated and no longer communicated with each other.

In the very age when the largest number of people lived together in the cities, poets and artists were saying there was no longer a community.

In the very age when men lived longest and were most secure in their lives, poets and artists were saying that men were most afraid.

In the very age when crowds were largest and people flocked closest together, poets and artists were saying that men were lonely.

Why were poets and artists saying these things?

Was it because they were out of tune with the spirit of the modern age and so were complaining because the denizens of the age paid no attention to them?

Or was it that they were uttering the true feelings of the age, feelings however which could not be understood by the spirit of the age?

Nobody wants to hear about his unspeakable feelings. It is only when the feelings become speakable, that is, understandable by a new anthropology, that people can bear hearing about them.

It was not easy to take poets and artists seriously because they often behaved badly, seemed to enjoy their suffering and, though they made fun of the spirit of the age, science, and technology, were as willing as the next man to enjoy its benefits. Has anyone ever heard of a poet who refused penicillin when he got a streptococcus?

But most of all, poets and artists who attacked the spirit of the age had nothing to offer in its stead. If the modern theory of man didn't work, and they said it didn't, what theory did?

The end of the age came when it dawned on man that he could not understand himself by the spirit of the age, which was informed by the spirit of abstraction, and that accordingly the spirit of the age could not address one single word to him as an individual self but could address him only as he resembled other selves.

Man did not lose his self in the modern age but rather became incommunicado, being able to neither speak for himself nor to be spoken to.

A man is after all himself and no other, and not merely an example of a class of similar selves. If such a man is deprived of the means of being a self in a world made over by science for his use and enjoyment, he is like a ghost at a feast. He becomes invisible. That is why people in the modern age took photographs by the millions: to prove despite their deepest suspicions to the contrary they were not invisible.

At the end of an age the theorists of the age will go to any length to stretch their theory to fit the events of the age in the name of science, even if it means that theory is stretched out of shape and is no longer scientific.

What theorists of the old modern age had to confront were the altogether unexpected disasters of the twentieth century: that after three hundred years of the scientific revolution and in the emergence of rational ethics in European Christendom, Western man in the twentieth century elected instead of an era of peace and freedom an orgy of wars, tortures, genocide, suicide, murder, and rapine unparalleled in history.

The old modern age ended in 1914. In 1916 one million Frenchmen and Germans were killed in a single battle.

Future ages will look back on the attempts to account for man's perverse behavior in the twentieth century by the theory of the old modern age as one of the curiosities of the history of science.[1]

Introduction

This book begins with the assumption that Percy's point of departure is essentially correct; that the modern statement of the human condition—its blessings, its problems, and the resolution of these problems within its own terms— is grossly inadequate to explain our contemporary misgivings about how we feel, what we are about, where we are going as modern people. We are at the end of an age, so that its metaphors and symbols no longer explain where we have been nor inform us about what next to do.

In the midst of this incoherence we are here to promote what is perhaps the most painful and hopeful of all dialogues—the conversation that bridges fundamentally different paradigms or cosmological viewpoints. The difficulty with such dialogue revolves around the fact that such differences function at an unconscious symbolic level, where feeling and thought are interrelated with understandings which are apparently not available to rational discourse. Even more importantly, perhaps, we often then pretend that these deeper differences do not really exist, that communication can be established simply as a matter of transliteration of one term into another, trying to persuade ourselves that our wheat is their rice, our coats are their shawls, our Christmas is their Winter Solstice.

Here it is critical to distinguish between paradigmatic and ideological differences. Paradigmatic differences ferment and boil up from unconsciously grounded world views. Ideological differences are much less profound in that ideologies share similar feelings and conceptions about basic metaphysical categories (time, space, causation, force, power, humanhood, and so forth) but place different weights on their relative importance or how they would have them structured. We would consider welfare capitalism and Marxism, for example, as both within the paradigm of modernity. For both, the ethical unit of concern is sensate human happiness and pleasure; for both, the essential quality of reality remains substantial, material being; for both the mode of transformation or change remains the use of force, energy, or power within hierarchy to shape and move material things; for both the methods by which inconsistency or problematics in historical development may be resolved remain those of human technical intervention or the natural dialectic of historical progress. Proponents who debate across ideological boundaries within shared paradigms generate common mediating voices—e.g., similar epithets, prayers, or bombs—to persuade the other side of its folly.

Proponents who debate across paradigmatic or cosmological boundaries lack an adequate experiential or linguistic base for any significant mediation. Therefore, paradigmatic differences are not worked out with language or power or prayers. They require long-term shared experience, which, in turn, requires that one's relationship to all the elements within one's life be altered. We understand that these basic shifts in point of view come about accompanied by epochal historical shifts. There have been, we would guess, at least two great revolutions within the past 10,000 years that have yielded such fundamental differences: The first was the shift from relatively isolated villages to the creation of the feudal or archaic society, which combined two subsocieties: the outlying agricultural village or urban village-neighborhood which paid tribute to and supported the high cosmopolitan culture of nobility, priests, the military, and their retinue. The second revolution has been in full swing for about 400 years and seems to have sprung from the universal application of practical reason within the activity we now call science–technology–professionalism, which is to say the persistent and almost obsessive search for knowledge to make human life a pleasurable, profitable, and progressive adventure through the creation and consumption of products.

Within the past one or two hundred years all three types of society— isolated primitive villages, archaic societies, and technological modern cities—have existed on this planet. Because of this overlap we have some understanding of what is involved in the radical transformation that occurs when one moves from one type of society to another—for example, the transition from village life to modern urban life. Such a transformation requires that we see kinship differently (as temporary rather than permanent personal relationships which disintegrate or substantially reduce in intensity as each person becomes more autonomous); it requires that we see land differently (as a commodity salable for profit rather than as a permanent dwelling place); it requires that we see work differently (as a means of earning money to buy commodities or a way of expressing one's personal inner talents, rather than as the calling of one's family, community or ancestors); and it requires that we see life and death differently (as the beginning and end of our personal reality rather than simply as the transformation of spirit).[3]

But we know by now that the clarity that came with the second revolution—the Benjamin Franklin vision of a rational scientific culture— has rapidly dissolved within the last hundred years into an epochal ambiguity, which impels commentators to speak of "the end of an age." Walker Percy reminds us that we can scarcely avoid a square look at the pathologies of modernity, pathologies that have culminated in a century of incredibly bizarre human behavior.

We have mounted wars of unprecedented scale for the most dubious of reasons. We have made discoveries that mitigate human suffering—the reduction of infant mortality and childhood disease; the release of atomic energy; the development of cheap and abundant foods—and yet we seem unable to deal with the potential disasters that attend these discoveries. Children wither and die of famine; the entire world lives with the quiet certainty of nuclear and ecological mistakes; the earth and air and water are poisoned by the chemicals required to sustain our new-found abundance. We seem unable to raise ourselves above the idolatrous reductionism of the great religions. Moslems kill Moslems because the other is more or less faithful to the purity of their cause. Jews and Moslems kill each other to see which is really the people chosen to occupy the Holy Land. Wealthy Christians, who are born again into the promise of an everlasting life in paradise, build great hospitals where they can transplant artificial hearts to grasp a little more pleasure in this world. The Japanese, with their own brand of Shinto magic, bless new Colonel Sanders fried chicken franchises in the hopes of beating out Burger King down the street.

While one may be hard pressed to identify the particular conditions that have led to such destructive and bizarre events, we are concerned, along with Percy, that the contradictions and distortions which beset the modern paradigm are not interpretable within the framework of its own meaning system. A central illusion of that meaning system, we would assert, is the premise that we need not look at the world or society or culture whole. We need think only about one problem at a time within the various segments of reality into which our lives and consciousness have been divided. If education is problematic, we repair education. If the family is problematic, we fix the family. If poverty is a problem, we increase employment. If one is spiritually starved, one joins a church or goes on a retreat. To raise broader issues which would bring into question the nature of this bits-and-pieces world view is, from a modernist's vantage point, unnecessarily "ideological," theoretically vacuous, and impractical. And it is here, we surmise, that the conversation between those who are searching for a more coherent postmodern cosmology and those who defend the current world view falls apart. Here is the most common point of paradigmatic rupture.

So it is here that our book begins, with the critique of this central premise of modernity—the premise that dealing with reality as a set of technical fragments will inevitably produce moral, aesthetic, and scientific progress for the human race. For it is our experience that cross-paradigmatic dialogue cannot even be imagined until we, as modern people, take seriously the fragmentation that both defines our lives and prevents us from seeing beyond its limitations.

Chapter Two

Modernity, Fragmentation, and Cultural Balance

The doctrine of specialization and progressive evolution.

The fish is presumably the last creature to understand the nature of water. Likewise, most Europeans and North Americans live within a culture we describe as modern, yet we take the lifestyle and many of its beliefs and practices so for granted that we may consciously understand little of its essential nature. One of its central assumptions, for example, is the value, truth, and efficacy of the ideology and social system we call *functional specialization*. We see the obvious analogy between phylogenetic evolution (the progressive evolution of the various species of living things) and human cultural 'progress.'

We see forms of life in the earlier history of the planet as relatively simple and undifferentiated—e.g., the amoeba and jellyfish—and thus denoted as primitive. We associate the development of 'higher' forms of life with increasing differentiation and specialization. (We really don't deal with the fact that many of the earlier, more primitive forms are still around in health and abundance.) Thus, when an animal has separate organs or structures to perform specialized functions, it is described as more efficient, more adaptive, more highly evolved, more modern. This increasing specialization requires, of course, the increasingly complex and centralized systems of information processing and control associated with the nervous system and finally the brain. The organism with the most differentiated structures is the most modern and progressive. The concept of modernity thus takes on a strongly positive tone.

Modern people then carry this evolutionist theory of specialization and hierarchical control into their view of society and culture. 'Higher' cultures are those with complex divisions of labor along with elaborate instruments of management and control. In early archaic and feudal societies, for

11

example, there is the serf and the freeman, the merchant, the artisan, the soldier, the lord, and the king. We see this as more advanced than the 'primitive' society with its simpler division of labor based largely on age, sex, and kinship roles (even though the latter was often less oppressive in many respects than the former).

This crude assumption that specialization and hierarchy are indicators of a progressive culture and society has been transformed into conventional wisdom. We expect modern societies to be differentiated into economic, political, legal, cultural, and health care systems, each run by a pyramidal management structure. Modern schools and universities which prepare people for life and work are commonly organized around these categories. As teachers, we think about education with this 'natural' bias toward delineating the world into highly differentiated functional fields, each governed by technical specialists. So when we study problems of cultural transmission and change—how each new generation learned the modes of adaptation necessary to cope in the contemporary world—we quickly reduce our thinking to key words associated with the specific technical aspects of that function called education: curriculum, teaching, guidance and counseling, remedial education, cognitive education, moral education, socio-emotional development, vocational education, liberal education, and so forth. Once we have accepted education as a separate specific aspect of culture along with the myriad of technical specializations generated within it, our life as educators is reduced to researching, developing, understanding, and practicing a specific set of professional skills. We become legitimate and credible professionals assigned the responsibility for enculturating children, youth, and, increasingly, lifelong clients. We would guess that most school people—administrators, teachers, professors of education, curriculum makers, textbook publishers—consciously or unconsciously believe this dogma of progressive specialization as the normal and right way to maintain and improve the world. Having accepted the notion that modern societies are naturally divided into institutions that perform separate specialized functions, we then need only take the next step of working out policies or priorities for the allocation of resources to the various functions and evaluate the effectiveness or relative success of these actions.

Modern people understand that this policymaking step may require philosophizing—that is, making explicit statements of basic principles and values which must be balanced and compromised. It is at this level that we talk about what we want from education (already assuming it is a specialized function) and where we work out different broad policy postures as bases for choice. (How much do we want basics, the humanities, vocational education, pre-schools, or remedial education? Finally, after these policy decisions we search for technical models to implement the choices made.

Policy becomes a mixture of philosophical reflection interfaced with the practical decisions a society makes and acts upon, both within a specific function (e.g., education) and, in the higher echelons of business and governement, the establishment of choices across functions (guns vs. butter vs. education vs. health care). The social class system in the society is roughly correlated with a hierarchy of people from those who make these more fundamental policy choices down a ladder to those who build technical models to implement the choices, and further down to those folks who tell others what to do or simply do what they are told. But the fundamental assumption modern people make, one rarely questioned, is that working out of a particular field of technical specialization and organizing it hierarchically is the appropriate way to improve quality of life and culture. It is modern. It is progressive. It is efficient.

The parameters of this ideology are well studied. For example, Berger et. al.[1] identify six "themes" that surround it:

1. *Rationality*—not scientific or philosophic rationality, but rather the pragmatic rationality involving problem-solving in everyday life.

2. *Componentiality*—reality apprehended as being constituted by clearly separable components which relate to each other in structures of causality, time, and space.

3. *Multi-relationality*—there is required an enormous variety of relations— with people, with material objects, and with abstract entities—that the individual must hold present in his consciousness when relating to the processes of technological production.

4. *Makeability*—life, including social relations, friends, jobs, or health, is seen as an ongoing problem-solving enterprise.

5. *Plurality*—the capacity to move through separate "multiple realities"; the reality of everyday experience, technical scientific reality, fantasy, and so on. These "realities" need not be related or integrated.

6. *Progressivity*—things can always be improved. There is the tendency to maximize the benefits of any action.

The paradox, of course, is that education has commonly been viewed as the vehicle that will liberate us from ideology. Yet now it is construed as the "subsystem" whose function is to teach us that technical rationality and componentiality in our social and vocational existence is the one appropriate way to understand the world.

From our point of view one must ask: What are the fundamental constraints implied by an ideology that identifies culture with progress and progress with the pursuit and use of specialized technical knowledge?[2] Below we shall discuss two major issues that flow from this question. First is the task of defining an alternative form of "deeper" knowing which we think is necessary to complement technical knowing. And second, there is the task of expanding the unconscious cultural base from which, we would guess, knowing itself flows.

Grounded versus Technical Knowing

Grounded knowing, (or perhaps better, ontological knowing[3]) apprehends the natural history within which events, occasions, or being emerge and become. A human birth, a storm, a conversation are all occasions. Each might be described technically by a gynecologist, a meteorologist, or a sociolinguist. But in ontological terms a birth begins with one's ancestry, with imagination, a courtship, poetry, a first touch. A storm begins with the movement of clouds, subtle changes in atmospheric pressure, wind shifts, the movement of birds and animals. It may include fallen trees and flooded streams and the refreshment of life with the new water. A conversation begins with sounds, language training, experience, mood, and intentionality. Therefore ontological knowing includes feelings, vague sensibilities, and inarticulable thoughts, as well as the more technical description of such occasions as they come into being, as they exist, as they pass on. Ontological knowing is moving, dynamic, and above all continually emergent.

Within grounded or ontological knowing, we feel (usually unconsciously) the many aspects of an occasion evolve into the unity of event, as if out of nowhere. Technical knowing, on the other hand, begins with sharply delineated events, precisely defined. Technical knowing often comes out of highly controlled settings—e.g., the birth of a baby in a delivery room, where the essential truth of the happening is far more profound than the terse technical statement written for the medical file. Likewise, one sees the technical description and tracking of great storms on television, where experts surrounded by computers and radar equipment are asked, in substance, to give final witness to the event, as if, in some sense, their report were to influence what was happening. As this example illustrates, technical knowing is implicitly useful: it makes our lives more predictable, efficient, and adaptive.

It is our thesis that healthy organisms, communities, societies must apprehend a universe/nature/culture that is balanced between these two qualities of knowing. The central quality of ontological knowing is one's feeling for tentative connection—the way in which a novel occasion is to relate, harmoniously or destructively—to the larger world. The salient sense of technical knowing is the resolution of problems that arise for the individual or the group so that it may adapt in order to enhance its own survival, convenience, or comfort. Ontological knowing accepts with equanimity inevitable changes inherent in the emergence of being (birth), concrescence (growth), satisfaction (maturity), and perishing as the way of the world. It understands the craving of being for relationship with other being, since, in the last analysis, all is one. Technical knowing only allows the individual to understand the world at all when the individual separates from it. Technical knowing sees survival of self and extensions of self as the purpose of existence.

Ontological knowing is often expressed through mystical experience, metaphor, poetry, drama, liturgy, dreams or music. Technical knowing is expressed in the analytic/linear explicit language and diagram required to delineate the environment within which one copes and survives. This capacity to break down the environment into its various parts, as well as the hypothetical manipulation of these parts, comprises a major source of human power to manage "nature." One of the unique characteristics of humans is our self-conscious ability to generate, store, and use technical knowing. For most of us the balance between ontological and technical knowing is maintained in some unconscious or fateful way.[4] For humans the delicate balance between ontological and technical knowing (what Redfield implies by the "moral order" and the "technical order"[5]) is commonly in jeopardy because of the often volatile and rapid changes to which human cultures are subject as we generate radical new technology. The problem of balance is expressed in the story of the Faustian seduction. Humans are tempted to seek the technical knowledge which will have the magical power to lift them beyond their destiny: their connection with the undifferentiated ground of universe. At that point technical knowledge assumes an overwhelming importance and the modernist commits to the dogma of progressive evolution. This dogma is associated with the predominant (if not exclusive) use of technical knowing as the means for dealing with the profound and the trivial conditions of life. So we try to determine whether or not abortion is immoral by defining when a fetus is 'human,' as if it were a scientific question. It is obvious to us that we have come to confuse those issues which require the deepest kind of ontological knowing with issues that might be clarified and resolved through technical knowing. This confusion permeates education. We come to see problems of curriculum selection (what is worthwhile knowing and how to learn it) as translatable into a technical field of study through which one can identify the appropriateness of bits of explicit information, or the value of certain skills. This confusion in the selection of modalities of knowing we would call the *technical fallacy.*

AN EXAMPLE OF THE TECHNICAL FALLACY. In April 1984 The National Council for the Social Studies published what it called "a preliminary position statement on scope and sequence for the social studies."[6] The statement turned out to be long lists of goals, knowledges, values, beliefs, and skills. These are refined into other lists that line up with specific grade levels, including different optional contents for various grade levels. Under "developing democratic beliefs and values", for example, there are lists of rights, freedoms, responsibilities, and beliefs. We learn that the individual has the right to life, liberty, dignity, security, equal opportunity, justice, privacy, and the private ownership of property. Under skills, there is a detailed chart (see Table 2.1) which lists well over a hundred items rated according to "suggested strength of instructional effort" cross-indexed with grade level.

Table 2.1 Essential Skills for Social Studies

Suggested strength of instructional effort:
* Minimum or none   † Some   ‡ Major   • Intense

Skills Related to Acquiring Information

Reading Skills

Comprehension

‡ • ‡ † Read to get literal meaning
* • ‡ † Use chapter and section headings, topic sentences, and summary sentences to select main ideas
* • • † Differentiate between main and subordinate ideas
* ‡ ‡ ‡ Select passages that are pertinent to the topic being studied
* † ‡ • Interpret what is read by drawing inferences
* † ‡ • Detect cause and effect relationships
* † ‡ • Distinguish between the fact and opinion; recognize propaganda
* † ‡ • Recognize author bias
‡ ‡ ‡ † Use picture clues and picture captions to aid comprehension
* † ‡ • Use literature to enrich meaning
* ‡ • • Read for a variety of purposes: critically, analytically, to predict outcomes, to answer a question, to form an opinion, to skim for facts

* † ‡ ‡ Keep records
* † ‡ ‡ Use italics, marginal notes, and footnotes
• ‡ † † Listen for information
• ‡ ‡ † Following directions
* † ‡ • Write reports and research papers
* † ‡ • Prepare a bibliography

Reference and Information Search Skills

The Library

† † ‡ ‡ Use card catalog to locate books
* † ‡ ‡ Use *Reader's Guide to Periodical Literature* and other indexes
* † ‡ ‡ Use COMCATS (Computer Catalog Service)
* † † † Use public library telephone information service

Special References

* * † ‡ Almanacs
† • † * Encyclopedias
† • † * Dictionaries
* ‡ † † Indexes
* * † ‡ Government publications
* * † ‡ Microfiche
* † ‡ ‡ Periodicals

Table 2.1 Essential Skills for Social Studies (cont.)

`* † ‡ •` Read various forms of printed material: books, magazines, newspapers, directories, schedules, journals

Vocabulary

`• • † †` Use usual word attack skills: sight recognition, phonetic analysis, structural analysis

`* ‡ • ‡` Use context clues to gain meaning

`* • ‡ ‡` Use appropriate sources to gain meaning of essential terms and vocabulary: glossary, dictionary, text, word lists

`* • • ‡` Recognize and understand an increasing number of social studies terms.

Rate of Reading

`* ‡ ‡ •` Adjust speed of reading to suit purpose

`* ‡ ‡ ‡` Adjust rate of reading to difficulty of the material.

Study Skills

Find information

`* ‡ † †` Use various parts of a book (index, table of contents, etc.)

`* ‡ † *` Use key words, letters on volumes, index, and cross references to find information

`* † † ‡` Evaluate sources of information–print, visual, electronic

`* † ‡ ‡` Use appropriate source of information

`* † ‡ ‡` Use the community as a resource

Arrange information in Usable Forms

`* † ‡ ‡` Make outline of topic
`* † ‡ ‡` Prepare summaries
`* † ‡ ‡` Make timelines
`* † ‡ ‡` Take notes

K-1-2-3 / 4-5-6 / 7-8-9 / 10-11-12

`† † † ‡` News sources: newspapers, news magazines, TV, radio, videotapes, artifacts

Maps, Globes, Graphics

Use map and globe reading skills

`* • ‡ †` Orient a map and note directions

`* ‡ • †` Locate places on map and globe

`* † ‡ †` Use scale and compute distances

`* † ‡ •` Interpret map symbols and visualize what they mean

`* † † †` Compare maps and make inferences

`* ‡ ‡ ‡` Express relative location

`* † ‡ •` Interpret graphs

`* † ‡ •` Detect bias in visual material

`* † ‡ •` Interpret social and political messages of cartoons

`* † ‡ ‡` Interpret history through artifacts

Community Resources

`* † ‡ ‡` Use sources of information in the community

`* † ‡ ‡` Conduct interviews of individuals in the community

`* † ‡ ‡` Use community newspapers

Technical Skills Unique to Electronic Devices

Computer

`* † ‡ ‡` Operate a computer using prepared instructional or reference programs

`* † ‡ ‡` Operate a computer to enter and retrieve information gathered from a variety of sources

Telephone and Television Information Networks

`* † † †` Is able to access information through networks

K-1-2-3 / 4-5-6 / 7-8-9 / 10-11-12

This highly specific mode of curriculum making, we would argue, provides an example of the technical fallacy that is embedded in the fundamental nature of the global culture we have called modernity. We come to see
the world as bits of information relating to discrete problems, which can
be understood through rational analysis. We presume that when problems
are broken into their various minute parts we can deal successfully with one
small, solvable part at a time. It is the position of the authors that the central
creative force for maintaining or building positive culture[7] comes not from
a technical taxonomy-building strategy but rather from a deep, often unconscious experience we call ontological knowing. Langer makes this point
eloquently:

> Sign and symbol are knotted together in the production of those fixed realities
> that we call "facts," as I think this whole study of semantic has shown. But
> *between the facts* run the threads of unrecorded reality, momentarily recog-
> nized, wherever they come to the surface, in our tacit adaptation to signs;
> and the bright, twisted threads of symbolic envisagement, imagination,
> thought-memory and reconstructed memory, belief beyond experience, dream,
> make-believe, hypothesis, philosophy—the whole creative process of ideation,
> metaphor, and abstraction that makes human life an adventure in under-
> standing.[8]

Our premise is that a healthy culture is one which balances between Langer's
"bright, twisted threads" and the fixed reality of facts. We believe contemporary curriculum-making suffers from a regrettable fixation on the latter.
Modern curriculum is built on a technical methodology; it focuses on the
apparent explicitness with which one can fix and order those realities Langer
calls "facts." Perhaps the most influential of contemporary curriculum
schemes are those constructed by Bloom and his associates,[9] who have
organized all knowledge around "cognitive," "affective," and "psychomotor"
domains on five or six levels of complexity. Tasks are then assigned to achieve
learning in the different domains of knowing on various levels of complexity.

The great advantage of this strategy for constructing educational programs in a functionally specialized and professionalized society is that it
transforms what Langer calls "the whole creative process of ideation,
metaphor, and abstraction" from an "adventure in understanding" to a set
of specific technical tasks, tasks which seem to be highly do-able. The purpose of getting to the specific and do-able is to avoid the seemingly wasted
effort of dreaming up visions, sharing these visions with others, and going
through the difficult process of community-building (identifying ontological
connections) that is required for deep and significant mutual understanding.[10]

From Ontological to Metaphorical Balance

Our initial critique of modernity has focused on the unbalanced relationship between what we have called ontological versus technical knowing. At this point it is important to understand that while the major thrust of technical knowing is to describe the texture, contour, and workings of the material world around us in a relatively superficial, sensate way, the commitment of modern people to this mode of knowing appears to be anything but superficial. Paradoxically, modern professionals often exhibit a deeply felt, inarticulable cultural commitment to technical knowing. Along with Langer, we would speculate that the symbolization of ontological stirrings or feelings emerges from our unconscious, where lurks even the image of technique as metaphor. Metaphor provides the sustaining imagery (and consequent language) for what later becomes a conscious sense of culture. Our guess is that the root metaphor for modernity which drives our implicit commitment to the ideology of specialization, efficiency, and technical knowing is the *machine.* The machine as metaphor is a physical palpable instrument, "out there": its parts are knowable through mind and intelligence; it can be taken apart, improved, redesigned with language, drawn in maps, and manipulated in physical experiments. It is seen to have fantastic if not magical powers for controlling objectified nature and humans alike.

Our guess is that once our imaginative energies become locked into a narrow range of metaphors, that is to say, as modern people have come to focus on the machine, qualities of reality which would normally extend beyond the convenience of the single dominant metaphor are inappropriately perceived and understood. Hunger on a worldwide basis, for example, is construed as economic scarcity (we have too small an economic machine) rather than as the result of human greed, exploitation, or thoughtlessness. Paranoid fears between alien peoples are seen as problems to be solved literally with machines—organized armies, weapons of mass destruction—or through conversations between technically trained diplomats and negotiators.[11] Death itself becomes a problem to be solved with life-prolonging measures, even the freezing of corpses for later remediation. As technical persons we lose the capacity for seeing death as a normal condition of being; rather we come to see the body as a worn-out machine.

We might here reconsider how we can carry our understanding of culture beyond the machine. Suppose we speculate that positive culture could begin with a vision in which there is a balance among three complementary metaphors: the *dance,* the *living organism,* and the *machine.* When we imagine the dance, there is no subject or object. There is only motion and pattern, but the pattern cannot be captured or frozen or made into anything substantial. When the dance is over, there is no material object left, only the memory of pattern. The dance is the metaphor of spirit, of transitoriness. It is the metaphor of electromagnetic energy and wave. It is often, literally, the mating ritual. Out of the dance comes new being, the transformation of the dancer, and new reality.

The second metaphor, that of the living organism, is one of self-organization and exchange. We exchange the fundamental substances of life with our environment: oxygen and carbon dioxide; food and water; sperm and egg; minerals and sunlight. We eat the flesh of our prey and we ourselves are eaten. Exchange is intrinsic to the metaphor of the organism, whether it be within the individual, the community, or the universe. Organism is the metaphor of mutuality, reciprocity, becoming, and dying.

The third metaphor, that of machine, technique, artifact and control, is one where living organisms reconstruct nature into useful 'things'—ideas, habits, houses.

The language of the dance is poetry, music, movement, pure science, mathematics, imagination: it is the language of the unpredictable. The language of exchange is laughter and conversation and weeping; it is the language of community, of planting and harvesting, of bonding and living, of giving and taking. The language of the machine is the map, the blueprint, the printout. It is the language of measurement, manipulation, plan, and predictability.

Our thesis is that healthy culture requires that we apprehend, at least in some dim way, a sense of universe/nature/culture that embraces a range and balance of metaphors, metaphors which extend our ontological *feelings* toward reflective conscious meaning. With the dance metaphor one can speculate positively about both beginnings and endings. One need not see death, for example, only as a worn out machine; it can be a transformative beginning. Dance (or spirit) encompasses a state of being which includes a reality that existed before there was life or machine. Within this broader sense of reality what we know as organism, life, mammalian life, primate life, or human life becomes part of a larger unity.[12] Life construed *only* as spirit or dance leads to a kind of empty idealism (or ideationism); life construed only as machine leads to the alienation of humans from nature as well as from one's own humanity. It is this latter construction of organism— i.e., its predominant association with technique and machine, along with our understanding of spirit as mind separated from body—that results in what is perhaps the most dangerous modern illusion of all, what is commonly called *objectification*. When spirit, separated from the experience of palpable ontological connection, becomes simply a human mind or a cybernetic calculator, the natural world 'out there' then becomes only a machine. This machine is dead, so it requires an external being, the cybernetic mind, to run it, to repair it, to give it significance. Herein lies the critical consequence of connection or disconnection among these core metaphors. When spirit or even mind is connected to organism, we have the dance, for we cannot forget that nature is an interconnected whole. When mind stands outside of organism and transforms organism into machine, organism becomes simply hunks of matter. We then lose our apprehension of the whole and nature becomes no more than a mass of locally related parts, technical information. Whitehead calls this the "fallacy of simple location." It is grounded in the world view of Newtonian mechanics. As Whitehead puts it:

> Newtonian physics is based upon the independent individuality of each bit of matter. Each stone is conceived as fully describably apart from any reference to any other portion of matter. It might be alone in the universe, the sole occupant of uniform space. But it would still be that stone which it is. Also the stone could be adequately described without reference to the past or future. It is to be conceived fully and adequately as wholly constituted within the present moment.[13]

When the machine metaphor is dominant, the unit of concern is the individual person, as in the politics of Locke or the economics of Adam Smith. With the passage of time in a highly competitive commercial society, the unit of concern is transformed from person into 'product.' Art, music, peanut butter, drama, science, blood, cancer cures, personalities, business executives, surrogate mothers—all become products; ultimately, the unit of value for the product becomes monetary currency.[14] Our technical, affluent society is thus built on our capacity to abstract, fragment, and separate. We separate nature from humans, humans from resources, resources from machines, machines from work, work from products, products from monetary units. When the human mind is seen to stand apart from natural objects and regards these objects as having significance only insofar as they provide human gratification, the underlying danger of such objectification is twofold. First, the central premise of objectification is simply not true; humans are not separated from nature. The finely tuned cybernetic system humans possess, which is the interaction among sentience, memory, and understanding, evolved in response to the ecosystem of which humans have been an intrinsic part for a million years. We are still embedded within a network of subtle relationships in this ecosystem, no matter how we might deny it. Second, humans, because of the techniques they have invented, hold enough physical power to literally destroy the ecosystem within which they have evolved. As Bateson puts it:

> If you put God outside and set him vis-a-vis his creation and if you have an idea that you are created in his image, you will logically and naturally see

yourself as outside and against the things around you. And as you arrogate all mind to yourself, you will see the world around you as mindless and therefore not entitled to moral or ethical consideration. The environment will seem to be yours to exploit. Your survival unit will be you and your folks or conspecifics against the environment of other social units, other races, and the brutes and vegetables.

If this is your estimate of your relation to nature *and* you have an advanced technology, your likelihood of survival will be that of a snowball in hell. You will die either of the toxic by-products of your own hate, or, simply, of overpopulation and overgrazing. The raw materials of the world are finite.[15]

In this analysis of the post-industrial world, Bell describes the same problem as "antinomianism" or as an imbalance in the relationship between cultural restraint and release:

The antinomian attitude, in fact, is the repeated effort of the self to reach out "beyond"; to attain some form of ecstacy (*ex-stasis,* the leaving of the body); to become self-infinitizing or idolatrous; to assert immortality or omnipotence.[16]

As we pursue our own human self-interest, we destroy the hospitable social natural environment on which our own 'separate' survival depends. This book's hypothesis is that this dualistic 'human mind over nature' understanding of culture distorts our ability to see our relationship to or connection with the whole, or any significant part of the whole. We plunge forward, noticing only "components" of our reality, as Berger says, with little or no thought about how the components relate to each other. We ignore the ontological–technical imbalance in how we come to know; we ignore the limited range of metaphors that provide our world with meaning; we ignore the dangerous process of objectification that comes about when we see nature only as external to ourselves and mind as the only source of meaning and logic which makes nature significant.

Insights toward an Understanding of Cultural Balance

PRIMITIVE SOCIETIES. Thus far, our assumptions about the unbalanced and fragmented nature of modernity have come largely from intuitively developed constructs and distinctions, which are influenced by a broad range of popular, journalistic, and scholarly literature. Beyond this, however, there is a rich literature from anthropology which illustrates the fact that many so-called primitive societies have deeper and more integrated cultures than we commonly find in modernity. Unfortunately, much of the earlier scholarship in this area was generated and interpreted to demonstrate the inferiority of village societies and the superiority of the more 'highly evolved' progressive Western society. In the latter part of the 19th century, Lewis Morgan,[17] for example structured the evolution of societies into three stages: savagery, barbarism, and civilization.

The distinction between 'civilized' and 'uncivilized' has commonly been used as a basis for dismissing any serious comparison between Europeans and the 'primitive' or village people who inhabited much of the world that European colonial nations came to dominate. The English historian Hugh Trevor-Roper notes how "unrewarding" is any serious study of the "gyrations[18] of barbarous tribes in picturesque but irrelevant corners of the globe: tribes whose chief function in history, in my opinion, is to show to the present an image of the past from which, by history, it has escaped."[19] One need only note the extent to which the school subject World History includes (or excludes) material which sympathetically compares the less technically sophisticated but often more balanced cultures of primitive people with those of civilized peoples. History texts generally teach that there was a dark period in the past, called 'prehistory', before humans learned to make cities and write. We learn that such primitive people (either in prehistory or in today's jungles) were and are violent, superstitious, and unpredictable. Much of this image of cruelty and unpredictability has been revised by modern anthropologists, but the mythology of the old Tarzan movies persists. The self-regulating and mutually caring social environment characteristic of most preliterate human life is overlooked. As noted earlier, we associate a highly specialized bureaucratic, legal, judicial, military, and governmental system with progress, little realizing that one can interpret the presence of such institutions in quite the opposite way. Yet the myth of Western civilization persists: the Hebrews gave us our moral law and our God; the Greeks gave us our analytical reason; the Romans gave us government; the Italians, Spanish and Portuguese gave us the New World; the English and Germans gave us technology; and the Anglo-Americans gave us Democracy.

But this prejudice is changing. In North America, especially, a number of anthropologists[20] have come to see native Americans as anything but savages. Diamond[21] is perhaps the most articulate in calling for the importance of comparisons between so-called primitive and the civilized peoples. As he states, "primitive societies illuminate, by contrast, the dark side of a world civilization which is in chronic crisis" (p. 169). Diamond describes what he considers to be the critical features of primitive *social* life, which he maintains lead to a different quality or mode of thinking from that of their modern Western counterparts.

These features are summarized below:

1. Good nurturance. The extensive and intensive psychophysiological contact with a "mothering one."

2. Many-sided, engaging personal relationships through all phases of the individual's life. This is a multi-layered sense and actuality of self which cannot be understood in the one dimensional terms of "ego" psychology. This is the result of a hierarchy of experiences incorporated into an increasingly spiritualized being as maturation proceeds from birth through the multiple rebirths symbolized in the crisis rites, to ancestry of others.

3. Various forms of institutionalized deviancy which accommodate idiosyncratic individuals to the group while permitting unconventional behavior.

4. The celebration and fusion of the sacred and the natural, the individual and society in ritual. Through ritual, life culminates in the form of drama.

5. Direct engagement with nature and natural physiological functions, e.g., slaughtering and harvesting food.

6. Active and manifold participation in culture (as opposed to simply being a spectator).

7. The natural environment is perceived more aesthetically than is commonly the case in civilization. Artisanship is highly prized. Goodness and beauty are not separated.

8. Socio-economic support as a natural inheritance. (pp. 168–171)

From these social and economic conditions come different qualities of thought and different psychological perspectives, which he describes as follows:

> *Primitive (pre-civilized, pre-alienation) existentialism* is evident in: (1) the ritual expression of the primary needs of the person in nature and society. Meanings are questioned and resolved and a literal "being born with others" or co-naissance or "the free abandon of communion" occurs. As Boas puts it: "The readiness to abandon one's self to the exultation induced by art is probably greater [than among ourselves] because the conventional restraint of our times does not exist in the same form in their lives;" (2) the emphasis on existence rather than essence; (3) the responsibility of the individual to self and society; and (4) the lack of concern with analytic modes of thought.

> *Primitive personalism* is revealed in: (1) the web of kinship; (2) the organic community; and (3) the apprehension of consciousness throughout society and nature.

> *Primitive nominalism* is focused in: (1) The emphasis on concrete particulars and contexts; (2) the naming of *existents* in nature and society, in dream and reality; and (3) in the fact that ideas, as such, are not, typically, hypothesized or reified.

Diamond then contrasts these modes of knowing or thinking with the civilized behavior of modern people, which he says are increasingly

> (1) essentialist; quantification becomes etherialized... a political, philosophic, and, finally, a scientific process... (2) abstract and analytic; (3) impersonal and mechanical... (4) collectivized, that is, involved with aggregates of individuals, in pursuit of specialized activities that tend to transform their human associations into technical, or even spatial, arrangements. Personae are substituted for persons. (p. 172)

From Diamond's summary of anthropological evidence there appears to be more commonly a sense of what we have called ontological knowing among primitive people. In what Diamond calls "primitive personalism", for example, there is a deep feeling for the "web of kinship," "organic community," and the "apprehension of consciousness throughout society and nature" which suggest the multiplicity of continuing connections between individual, society, and nature. Diamond argues that civilization must somehow incorporate this deeper ontological quality of experience to balance our own obsessive concern with manifold abstract, technical knowing. In Diamond's words:

> Our illness springs from the very center of civilization, not from too much knowledge, but from too little wisdom. What primitives possess—the immediate and ramifying sense of the person... an existential civilization must selectively incorporate; we cannot abandon the primitive; we can only outgrow it by letting it grow within us. For thousands of years of a cultural development antithetical to ours, man deeply defined his nature; let us make that, which the poets have always known, clear. All notions of progress, and rationalizations about evolution are subordinated today to the dialectical moment we have reached between civilization and the primitive experience. (pp. 173–174)

As literary evidence and a footnote to our own critique of the imbalance between technical and ontological knowing inherent in modernity, we would quote observations made by D. H. Lawrence with special relevance to education:

> We think we are so civilized, so highly educated and civilized...
>
> Wherein are we educated? Come now, in what are we educated? In politics, in geography, in history, in machinery, in soft drinks and in hard, in social economy and social extravagance; ugh! a frightful universality of knowing.
>
> We are hopelessly uneducated in ourselves. We pretend that when we know a smattering of the Patagonian ideal we have insofar educated ourselves. What nonsense!...

What am I when I am at home? I'm supposed to be a sensible human being. Yet I carry a whole waste-paper basket of ideas at the top of my head, and in some other part of my anatomy, the dark continent of myself, I have a whole stormy chaos of "feelings"...

I say feelings, not emotions. Emotions are things we more or less recognize. We see love, like a wooly lamb, or like a decorative decadent panther in Paris clothes: according as it is sacred or profane. We see fear, like a shivering monkey. We see anger, like a bull with a ring through his nose, and greed like a pig. Our emotions are our domesticated animals, noble like the horse, timid like the rabbit, but all completely at our service. The rabbit goes into the pot, and the horse into the shafts. For we are creatures of circumstance, and must fill our bellies and our prockets....

Educated! We are not even *born*, as far as our feelings are concerned....

Man tames himself in order to learn to un-tame himself again. To be civilized, we must not deny and blank out our feelings. Tameness is not civilization. It is only burning down the brush and ploughing the land. Our civilization has hardly realized yet the necessity for ploughing the soul. Later, we sow wild seed. But so far, we've only been burning off and rooting out the old wild brush. Our civilization, as far as our own souls go, has been a destructive process, up to now....

Now we have to sow wild seed again. We have to cultivate our feelings....

Now we have to educate ourselves, not by laying down laws and inscribing tables of stone, but by listening. Not listening-in to the noises from Chicago or Timbuktu. But listening-in to the voices of the honourable beasts that call in the dark paths of the veins of our body, from the God in the heart. Listening inwards, inwards, not for words nor for inspiration, but to the lowing of the innermost beasts, the feelings that roam in the forest of the blood, from the feet of God within the red, dark heart.[22]

In summary, we have been talking about two major types of imbalance in the progressive–functional culture of modernity. The first emerges from its denial (or limited mechanistic conception) of what we have called ontological knowing: what Diamond refers to as "primitive existentialism", what D. H. Lawrence calls simply "feeling." These are the connections all substantial being has with the occasion of emergence, the sense of beings or occasions coming into this world, and the connections each has with other beings which share, in some degree, a common process of what Whitehead calls concrescence, satisfaction, and perishing. It is the connection between differentiated forms that we as humans identify as the world of objects around us and the undifferentiated world of potential, of information and energy that we can only feel taking shape. It is a connection first only felt, then expressed as art, drama, later as story and only later as science or philosophy.

The second imbalance in modernity comes less from an inadequacy in the process by which we come to know than from the content we admit as important, the range of metaphors that connect the deeper strains of feeling to some specific sense of meaning. We suggested the dance, the organism, and the machine as conduits and organizers from such meaning. We assume that genuine culture is necessarily characterized by some degree of balance across metaphors.

SOROKIN'S SENSATE, IDEATIONAL, AND INTEGRAL CULTURE. A third area of imbalance and fragmentation relates to the relative importance we place on different qualities of human satisfaction. We have, for example, various capacities for sensory satisfaction—taste and smell, kinesthetic flexing, sight and sound, and sex. We have the capacity for mental, logical, perhaps even purely aesthetic satisfaction. We have satisfactions that come from spiritual transcendence or the experience of mystical unity. Sorokin has dealt extensively with fragmentation, integrity, and balance across cultures. He describes and documents through historical research two broad types of culture, the sensate and the ideational, each of which is limited by the quality of knowing that it excludes.

> The Sensate form of culture and society is based upon the ultimate principle that true reality and value are sensory, and that there is no other reality and no real value beyond those that we can see, hear, touch, taste and smell.
>
> The whole system of Sensate culture represents mainly an articulation and "materialization" of this ultimate principle in its science and philosophy, its religion, its law and ethics, its economics and politics, its fine arts and social institutions....
>
> Sensate society is successful in technological invention aimed at increasing bodily comfort, but it is less successful in producing supersensory values. It favors the development of materialism, empiricist, positivist, and other sensory philosophies, and it disfavors the cultivation of idealistic, mystical, and metaphysical systems of philosophy. Despite lip-service to spiritual values, it stresses the sensory values of wealth, health, comfort, pleasure, power and fame. Its dominant ethic is invariably utilitarian and hedonistic. (p. 58)[23]

Sorokin then contrasts sensate culture to what he calls "ideational culture," a major example of which is European Medieval Christianity.

> ...this culture believes in God's revelations as the criterion of truth, and disbelieves the testimony of the sense. Accordingly, Ideational culture cares little about scientific study of sensory phenomena or technological invention; since the sensory world is a mere mirage, it is a waste of time to investigate what is only the shadow of reality.

> For this reason, ideational culture is uncreative in the field of science and technology. . .it is creative in the field of religion; theology becomes the queen of sciences and science only the handmaid of religion. (p. 59)

Sorokin argues that the two types of culture yield very different standards for social behavior, artifacts, and so forth. For example,

> Sensate and Ideational cultures have entirely different types of fine arts. . .
> [The object of religious art] is not to entertain or give pleasure, but to bring the believer into a closer union with God. . .
>
> . . .The aim of Sensate art is to afford a refined sensual enjoyment, stimulation and entertainment. For this reason it is sensational, passionate, pathetic, sensuous and incessantly new. (p. 60)

Sorokin maintains that there is a third type of culture he calls "integral," which goes beyond the sensate and ideational.

> Its ultimate principle proclaims that the true reality-value is an Infinite Manifold which has supersensory, rational, and sensory forms inseparable from one another. . .it includes the empirical as well as the super empirical aspects of reality, science as well as philosophy and theology. (p. 60)

These broadly defined types of culture are then placed within an historical context.

> Each of these three types of culture has been realized several times through history; among some pre-literate tribes, in ancient Egypt, Babylon, Iran, China, Greece, and Rome, and in the Western world. In the life of Greco-Roman Western culture and art, the dominant form from the ninth to the sixth century B.C. was Ideational; from the second half of the sixth to the end of the fourth century B.C. it was predominantly Integral; during subsequent centuries it became preeminently Sensate. (p. 60)

Sorokin concludes his historical analysis with a critique of modernity as a disintegrating Sensate culture.

> At the end of the fifteenth century the Sensate type of culture and most of the European fine arts. . .became dominant and so continued until the end of the nineteenth century. Sensate culture achieved unprecedented progress in science, technology, economics, and politics, and created a vast treasury of magnificent masterpieces of Sensate music, painting, sculpture, literature, and drama.
>
> In the twentieth century, the magnificent Sensate house of Western man began to deteriorate. Its crumbling means, among other things, disintegration of its

> moral, legal and other values which control and guide behavior of individuals
> and groups. . .unrestricted egoism (individual and collective) flares up, the
> competitive struggle for existence intensifies, and war, revolution, crime, and
> other forms of interhuman strife explode on an unprecedented scale. (p. 60–61)

In a more positive vein, Sorokin then suggests that modernity is a culture in transition, moving from its limited view of sensate reality to a more holistic understanding of the cosmos. We are, he claims, coming to understand a new integral theory of knowledge in which we have not one but three channels of understanding: sensory, rational, and supersensory-superrational. He sees all three forms as essential for comprehensive knowing, and concludes that:

> The new conception of reality does not deny its sensory form, but regards
> it as only one of the three main aspects. This new conception is incomparably
> richer than the old one, and is at the same time much nearer the true and
> total reality of practically all great religions. (p. 62)

Implication for Education

We would agree with Sorokin that the major challenge in working toward a new and positive conception of culture is not the discounting or casting out of some quality of feeling or understanding, but rather the inclusion of aspects of universe/nature which have tended to be under-appreciated. The problem is finding ways of reconstruing and experiencing the world with greater balance, fullness, interrelatedness. Such integration would include breaking down the barriers between the functional specializations that segregate our consciousness along lines of profession, vocation, and social class. This means, among other things, creating a world of meaning that transcends or undercuts the notion that education is what teachers do, building is what carpenters do, religion is what the clergy does, and so on. Integration includes the deliberate search for occasions in which ontological understanding informs and relates to technical knowing. It includes activities that enrich a broad range of metaphorical sensibilities. In Sorokian terms, it means creating a culture and an education in which there is some balance among various modes of satisfaction, where mind, body, and spirit are not reified as separate qualities of being to be expressed and appreciated in separate times and ways and places. However, we know that the twentieth-century school is the most blatant perpetrator of this separation. We have names for this segregation: physical education, art/music, the humanities, and mental skills such as reading and math (spirit is, of course deliberately excluded in our public schools as unconstitutional).

In short, we need a new cultural paradigm to inform a broadened conception of education.

Reforms in schooling and curriculum have been and are construed within the modern paradigm: how do we remove the oppressive obstacles of our feudal past, e.g., slavery, racism, autocratic government, unequal chances in life; how do we improve the liberal democratic state as the central institution of governance; how do we make work more efficient and rewarding in the factory and office building; how do we prepare the individual to be a discriminating consumer of products? Framed in these ways, education is a specialized function, its problems technical problems.

We argue here for a reconsideration of this piecemeal way of viewing modern educational change, seeing it not within the limited framework of our progressive functionalist ideology, not simply as part of a machine that is to be analyzed, improved and made more efficient, but rather within the broader framework that emerges when we consider the full evolutionary potential of the human species. This requires us to take as seriously the first million years of human history—as best as can be reconstructed—as we take the last five thousand years of 'civilized man' or the last four hundred years of 'scientific-technological man.' We would then see the human record as considerably more than an evolutionary climb from savagery to barbarism to feudalism to the modern industrial state. We might then discover human cultures and systems of belief which suggest creative and positive ways by which the unbalanced and fragmented qualities of modernity can be reconsidered.

This requires that we work toward a sophisticated theory of deep knowing and being that will raise the most general questions about the quality and destiny of the human species, of nature, and of human participation in nature. It is at this point, for example, that the distinction between the various academic disciplines must break down. For the study of such questions requires that we be able to move between and interrelate the fields of physics, biology religion, history, and poetry in a single conversation.

Such questions require that our commonplace assumptions about 'fields' of knowing be explored in terms both of explicit knowledge and the underlying metaphors and modes of feeling or subconscious expression that inform them. For example, one might ask: Is the Cartesian view of the universe as a disembodied mind viewing the finished machine a reasonable model of knowing , feeling, being? This exploration must be directed at the content of our world view, as well as at the modes of knowing and communication that provide its basis. We would note here, for example, the provocative work of Marshall McLuhan, who wrote about the experiential qualities evoked by various media—print, radio, movies, television—and the differential influence of various media on our conception of reality. We must also, therefore, be willing to consider alternative paradigmatic viewpoints, not simply within finely honed and explicitly elaborated verbal modes but also as they express themselves through music or story or dance or ritual or craft or vocation.

In short, we need a reformulated educational content with a broadened philosophical and metaphysical base[24]; with a broadened statement of the human cultural record; with a reconsideration of the central importance of more integrated and balanced apprehensions of experience—beyond the mechanistic analytical quality of thought that now dominates schooling and curriculum making.

The remainder of this book is an effort to reach toward that new educational content. We are doing this not by going through a taxonomical exercise—listing topics and methodologies that all students should know—but with a critique of the idea of listing itself, and, more fundamentally, of the misguided idea of the functional separateness of education and schooling from the broader culture.

From this vantage point a central question becomes: How does one begin to see cultures and meaning systems with sufficient breadth and depth that we can move toward a comparative cultural understanding, some sense that our lives as humans stretch across more than one paradigmatic perspective? Where does one find broader categories of thought and understanding that might lead us toward these questions? In the next chapter we begin such a search.

PART TWO:

Cosmology

Introduction and Overview

In Part One we argued that modern people tend to resist seeing various aspects of their world as a single interrelated system, because the modern paradigm itself conditions them toward a deep distrust of more holistic styles of understanding. They are then unable to understand the misgivings they may feel over their loss of connectedness with a more integrated vision of reality, for such a vision would require them to give up their faith in one of the central premises of modernity: that a high quality of life is developed and maintained through one's capacity to divide the world into separated technical–professional specialties.

Part Two (Chapter Three) begins, however, on a different note. It concedes that there exists, in the academic world at least, comprehensive categories of knowing. These categories or fields of study include 'culture,' 'philosophy,' 'metaphysics,' 'science,' 'religion,' 'theology,' 'history.' When we look more carefully at these subject areas, however, we find that they tend to be narrowed, even trivialized, as pressures toward technical knowing shape the definition and quality of 'respectable' scholarship. We propose here to reclaim a relatively unused category—one that implies a broader quality of knowing than other academic or vocational terms used currently. This is the term *cosmology*, used early on by Whitehead and Koestler and more recently by Toulmin. (We assume, of course, that the word can be rescued from its narrower use by modern physicists and astronomers who see it as denoting only a scientific description of the natural history of the universe.)

In Chapter Four we present some possible implications of using cosmology as a basis for reconceptualizing the current state of curriculum theory. We begin by pointing out an important ambiguity in the term. On the other hand, it can mean the specific meaning system—stories and myths, science and religion—of a single culture or tradition (the way fundamentalist Christians, for example, may see *The Holy Bible* as providing the basis for their cosmology). But it can also mean universalistic, abstract, analytic, and critical models of the cosmos (the way Whitehead, for example, uses the term). We then discuss the paradox that results from this ambiguity: one's confidence in the authenticity of a universalistic meaning system probably requires intimate experience that grows out of sustained involvement with a particular culture. Thus, our confidence in an objectively defensible cosmology may well depend upon a personal history of parochial groundedness. This ambiguity in the term may, however, be its strength, for it points to the likelihood that every significant system of abstractions must rest on the ground of an existential living world, and every specific living occasion searches for its place within some universalistic vision.

In Chapter Five we move to a discussion of how one might actually use the idea of "cosmology" as a basis from which to develop curriculum. We do this in two ways. We first give three examples of more abstract analytic literature which illustrate what it means to think within the broader framework of several cosmologies. These are from the fields of systematic philosophy (Brumbaugh), feminist literature (Griffin), and contemporary social theory (Coates). It is clear, however, that our examples extend beyond the comprehension of a beginning cosmologist, since all assume that our potential student not only has a grasp of the substantive cosmologies being compared, but also that she or he is already in tune with cross-paradigmatic or cosmological thinking. To use cosmology as a realistic basis on which to build curriculum, we suggest that at least two ingredients are needed: first, vivid descriptions of interesting specific cosmologies; and second, questions to provoke students to compare and contrast the cosmologies so as to demonstrate their usefulness in interpreting general issues of lasting human concern. To clarify how this more descriptive approach might be worked out, we elaborate with an example. We present brief scenarios of four cosmologies (Platonism, Judeo–Christianity, modernity, and the world view of the Hopi Indians, describing how each imagines the universe and world to have come into existence and the role that humans are expected to play within the order of that universe.

We conclude the section with a discussion of what seems to us the most serious challenge for a comparative cosmology curriculum. It stems from the fact that cosmologies are inextricably tied to deep images and metaphors which influence not only *how* we describe the world with language but even *what* we actually apprehend, perceive, and thus bring to conscious expression. To clarify and document this issue, we refer to the work of Whorf and his comparison of the English and Hopi languages. While the English language assumes a subject-acting-on-an-object posture as the essential structure of experience, the Hopi are able to see the world simply as dynamic states of being, and their language easily allows for this construction of reality. We then describe the theories of Whitehead and Barfield, who insist on the more radical position that we must begin thinking about human experience on a *prelinguistic* level—as interactions among electronic particles that participate in the dynamic states of "being" which characterize the physical world as well as in the process by which humans come to apprehend these states of being. Barfield supports his theoretical speculations by referring to the experience of preliterate peoples who actually seem to participate in this domain of micro-reality.

We might note here that Part Two (as does this book generally), reflects a continuing concern over the complex problems associated with efforts to communicate across cultures and, more importantly, across cultures that represent different underlying paradigms. We are convinced that these problems are underestimated and poorly appreciated by modern people. This is, in considerable degree, attributable to our implicit faith in the primacy and communicability of seemingly universal conceptual knowledge, which, in turn, leads us away from questioning inadequacies in the way each of us actually senses, apprehends, and perceives (connects with) the immediate world around us. The inability of contemporary Americans, for example, to take seriously the great mystery of why so many native Americans have not/cannot/will not adapt or accommodate to the European cosmology and underlying metaphysics brought to this continent some 400 years ago is, we believe, an unattended mystery of the greatest magnitude. We suspect that the absence of any sensibility by modern people of what members of these native cultures perceive, feel, and understand about the cosmos is a particularly catastrophic loss to humankind at this precarious point in our planet's history. For it is this fundamental issue—the richness and quality of human experience, if not the survival of the planet itself—that we think might possibly be addressed by our cosmology-based curriculum.

Chapter Three

Categories of the Whole

Categories which denote various domains and qualities of knowing tend to lead us to academic people, academic fields, and academic words. This is no less true when we search for broader or more holistic kinds of knowing. Anthropologists, philosophers, scientists, literary and religious scholars, and historians, among others, commonly study some aspect of inner human experience or the world 'out there' that seems more comprehensive than what we have called technical knowing. For the anthropologist there is the broad construct called 'culture.' For the physicist, the whole is called the 'physical' or 'natural' world, and the venture by which she or he approaches this world is called 'science.' For the philosopher, the field of concern over what is to be considered part or whole is commonly called metaphysics. For the theologian, it is theology or, more broadly, religion.

Simply listing these broad academic fields within an implicitly comparative framework, however, gives us considerable pause. On the one hand it suggests that we should treat the meaning and history of each category as well as its comparative relationships to other categories with comprehensive and scholarly care. Yet we are clearly in danger of such a venture becoming self-defeating, for by the time we have fully elaborated and developed one academic construct, the reader will have lost sight of the way it relates to the next, and the next, and so forth. In short, we may well get lost among the trees searching for the forest.[1] However, we feel compelled to discuss, briefly and admittedly superficially, the meanings of some of these terms as possible candidates for a lexicon which might allow us to talk more coherently about the broader and deeper qualities of understanding discussed in the last chapter.

Culture

While a prime candidate to describe deep and comprehensive knowing is certainly the construct *culture*, we find on closer inspection that the term has a somewhat mixed and ambiguous history. In one sense it has been associated with the idea of 'civilization' which connotes a higher form of human society than 'primitive' society, usually referring to the lifestyle lived by the upper classes in urban places. Culture, in this sense, connotes literacy, wealth, formal manners, and privileges. More recently, the term has come to mean the patterns of behavior and meaning associated with discrete societies, generally as interpreted by well-heeled academic anthropologists and sociologists. From the point of view of the people within a culture, the term constitutes the self-evident truths of everyday life. It provides not only the map for routine behavior, but answers questions of basic meaning. How and why are humans to be born? How are they to marry? How are they to eat, play or work? What is the meaning of death?

When immersed in culture, a person does not question its prescriptions and meanings. As a society undergoes rapid change, or as it comes into contact with other societies with different cultures, its members suddenly find their sense of culture-as-self-evident-truth violated; they then face the new problem of justifying their belief system. That they can even engage in such cultural comparisons illustrates a basic fact: humans have, to a considerable degree, an indeterminate nature. Different societies live out different patterns of behavior and give these patterns different meanings. We do not, however, have infinite choices; we have only a range of choices. Tart describes this ambiguity in human nature:

> By the simple fact of being born human, having a certain type of body and nervous system, existing in the environmental conditions of the planet earth, a large (but certainly not infinite) number of potentials are *possible* for you. Because you are born into a *particular* culture, existing at a *particular* time and place on the surface of the planet, however, only a small (perhaps very small) number of these potentials will ever be realized and become *actualities*. We can think of a culture as a group of people who, through various historical processes, have come to an agreement that certain human potentials they know are "good," "holy," "natural" or whatever local word is used for positively valuing them, and should be developed. They are defined as the essence of being human. Other potentials, also known to the culture, are considered "bad," "evil," "unnatural." The culture actively inhibits the development of these potentials in its children, but not always successfully. A large number of other human potentials are simply not known to that particular culture, and while some of them develop owing to accidental circumstances in a particular person's life, most do not develop for lack of stimulation.[2]

A central concept implied by the idea of culture is 'potentiality.' Humans are born with tendencies and possibilities, only some of which come to be expressed.

While many human needs are universal (humans must be loved and cared for in early life much as other mammals), there is also a range of freedom. Languages may have an underlying universal grammar, as Chomsky maintains, but there are important and substantial differences from one language to another which often express important cultural differences. For example, whether one calls the children of one's mother's brother 'sisters and brothers' or 'cousins' is significant.

Our genetic inheritance lays down a set of possibilities and our social experience then proceeds to choose some over others. In Geertz' terms:

> We are, in sum, incomplete or unfinished animals who complete or finish ourselves through culture—and not through culture in general, but through highly particular forms of it: Dobuan and Javanese, Hopi and Italian, upper-class, and lower-class, academic and commercial. Man's great capacity for learning, his plasticity, has often been remarked, but what is even more critical is his extreme dependence upon a certain sort of learning: the attainment of specific systems of symbolic meaning. Beavers build dams, birds build nests, bees locate food, baboons organize social groups and mice mate on the basis of forms of learning that rest predominantly on the instructions encoded in their genes and evoked by appropriate patterns of external stimuli: physical keys inserted into organic locks. But men build dams or shelters, locate food, organize social groups, or find sexual partners under the hunting lore, moral systems, and aesthetic judgments: conceptual systems molding formless talents.
>
> . . . the boundary between what is innately controlled and what is culturally controlled in human behavior is an ill-defined and wavering one. . . . Our capacity to speak is surely innate: our capacity to speak English is surely cultural. Smiling at pleasing stimuli and frowning at unpleasing ones are surely in some degree genetically determined (even apes screw up their faces at noxious odors); but sardonic smiling and burlesque frowning are equally surely predominately cultural, as is perhaps demonstrated by the Balinese definition of a madman as someone who, like an American, smiles when there is nothing to laugh at. Between the basic ground plans for our life that our genes lay down—the capacity to speak or smile—and the precise behavior we in fact execute . . . lies a complex set of significant symbols under whose direction we transform the first into the second, the ground plans into the activity.
>
> Our ideas, our values, our acts, even our emotions, are, like our nervous system itself, cultural products—products manufactured, indeed, out of tendencies, capacities, and dispositions with which we were born, but manufactured nonetheless.[3]

Early social experience to some degree 'fixes' behavior in the sense that photographic film is fixed. Even the most enlightened or culturally liberated person is surely grounded to some degree in the culture fixed in his or her childhood.

As we indicated in Chapter One, however, a great revolution has taken place over the past 5,000 years, especially over the past 400. The revolution began when humans created urban places where cultures lost their isolation. It accelerated with human mobility around the planet and even more as we came to invent technology which accelerates rapid social change. Fundamental sexual taboos, for example, can no longer be maintained in the private steel enclosures of automobiles or in the impersonal environment of the hotel. Technology creates options that can bypass established culture. The idea of choice itself, based on practical pragmatic considerations, becomes an explicit aspect of the culture—or, perhaps better, the metaculture—we have come to call modernity.

So what we term the grounding of the culture, its core habits and beliefs, becomes shallower; its roots do not go so deep. The set ways of doing things are not so set as they once were. As the grounding becomes shallower, one invokes another funadmental rationale for human action—practical reason. What results is a dialectic between culture and practical reason as two forces that shape patterns of human behavior. Sahlins tells us we must decide

> whether the cultural order is to be conceived as the codification of man's actual purposeful and pragmatic action; or whether, conversely, human action in the world is to be understood as mediated by the cultural design, which gives order at once to practical experience, customary practice, and the relationship between the two.[4]

The question raised by Sahlins is central to the integrity of the term culture. Are humans always so deeply enculturated that even our sense of practical reason takes place within a framework of unconscious order and meaning? Or can culture, conceived as the subconscious conditioning of our early life, be replaced by a logic of utilitarian reason which can calculate benefits and losses independent of these irrational vestiges of the past? In some sense, the continued use of the idea of culture depends on the plausibility of the assumption that it provides us with a deep and comprehensive identity whose significance is rooted in some purpose beyond the immediate survival of the individual or society.

Freilich discusses this issue, presenting with considerable clarity the argument that culture is simply a mechanism for passing on successful practical solutions for problems of adaptation and survival. He calls practical knowledge "the smart" and cultural knowledge "the proper."

> From within this viewpoint, culture has two rather contradictory jobs to do: 1) to solve *external*, adaptive, problems that demand smart solutions; and 2) to solve *internal*, self-awareness problems, which demand the creation of a new phenomenon—properness and goodness. The basic human dilemma—

to be smart and survive, or to be proper and feel good—was solved by modern man (Homo sapiens) quite ingeniously: *The smart was transformed into the proper.* Behaviors defined as "smart" became "good" when they had "proved" their adaptability, effectiveness, and efficiency to the satisfaction of community members. . . . Today the smart still get transformed into the proper and this manufacturing process is often referred to as *institutionalization.*[5]

From this perspective, the more basic quality of knowing is the practical, the "smart." Rituals and myths are built to make sacred or to 'fix' those smart and adaptive practices that work. The smart and proper conflict with each other when institutionalized practices become obsolete as a result of changing geological, ecological, or technical circumstances.

One must challenge Freilich's functionalist theory, however, to explain artistic, religious, playful, or bizarre activities, which apparently have little or no survival value. Such questions often provoke long and convoluted explanations—demonstrating, for example, that play is really preparation for work, or that religion has its basis in taboos or emotional responses that promote survival (dietary laws that protect one from unclean food, or marriage arrangements that protect the society from negative gene loads).

Recently, more phenomenologically oriented anthropologists have sought to explain culture in terms other than simple survival or adaptation. For people like Douglas or Foucault, the symbolic–expressive dimension of culture becomes a separate domain of human activity explainable in its own terms. To one reviewer of such research, Wuthnow:

> . . .one of its chief aims is to identify empirical regularities or patterns in this dimension of reality and from these regularities to specify the rules, mechanisms, and relations which must be present for any particular symbolic act to be meaningful. The subject matter of cultural analysis is readily observable in the objective acts, events, utterances, and objects of social interaction. The appropriate level of analysis is the patterns among these artifacts of interaction, rather than efforts to reduce culture either to internal states of individuals or to the material conditions of society.[6]

We would certainly agree with Wuthnow that it is preferable to search for symbolic–expressive regularities or patterns in our attempt to understand more fully what a culture means, rather than reduce this behavior to the functional requirements for survival and adaptation. We would like to point out, however, that even here the anthropoligist is playing the dualistic role of scientist, standing outside the culture and treating others as instances of objectified behavior. Staying within the constraints of the internal regularities of symbolic–expressive behavior may not be reductionism, but neither does it extend one's perspective by asking broader, more ethically sensitive questions; for example, What are authentic and balanced symbolic systems for a culture? Do these symbols allow the culture to have an interdependent view of a larger ecological planetary and universal reality?

We would contend that whether reducing culture to institutionalized 'smart' behavior (i.e., adaptive practical behavior), as does Freilich, or treating the expressive–symbolic quality of culture as having integrity and regularity in its own right, as does Wuthnow, both men ignore or underestimate their own deep engagement in the ideology of objectification out of which the observations are being made.

Both view culture as machine: Freilich as the machine that more or less successfully adapts to conditions of practical (economic) survival, Wuthnow as the machine that has certain rules or a logic to its internal working parts. One might ask, from either perspective, for example, why the Hopi Indians perform rain dances. The practical functionalist might suggest that it is to reduce the Hopi's anxiety over the shortage of rain, to maintain interpersonal cohesion, to make production more efficient. It is proper behavior, and it is also smart. The symbolic structuralist might look for some connection between the myth that seemingly motivates the dance and the specific choreography of the dance itself. But neither type of anthropologist is provoked to ask: Why cannot I, the sober, scientifically disciplined anthropologist, dance like this, with this sense of hope and cultural groundedness? Why has my modern art, my music, my dance, my ceremony, my science lost its connection to the whole of my life? For once such questions are asked, we immediately note that the implicit dualism—the we-they, the anthropologist observing primitive people–makes us feel uncomfortably self-conscious. Almost all modern science contains this dualism—the scientist stands outside the phenomena that she or he is observing. For the most part, this objectification is not noted. But for the social scientist, who presumably makes a host of unconscious cultural judgments about the subject matter he or she studies, the denial or avoidance of experiencing the dualism seems intrinsically corrupting. For we are objectifying ourselves when we objectify others; we make ourselves into the instruments of data collection and into the logic machine that codes the data.

What might well prevent this from happening is a greater sensitivity to the problems shared both by the modern educated academic and those less educated observed partners in the investigation. The most profound of such shared concerns may well be the meaning of the transformation from parochial/primitive or village culture to the vocationalized or professional (functionally differentiated) culture in which the units of humanity become rational, egocentric individuals rather than kinship sets and communities. These shared concerns in the more personal sense have to do with the forces of modernity which have overtaken the social scientist in his or her academic training, and which have often overtaken the 'subjects' of study in what is commonly the recent transformation (or even destruction) of their way of life. Diamond's comments on this narrowing and fragmentation of anthropology in the interest of 'science' are instructive:

> Paradoxically, as civilization increases in depth and scope, anthropology proliferates, but it becomes increasingly professionalized. The urgency of the central question is lost sight of; it is even denied and the question is repressed *because* of its urgency and the risks we must undergo in attempting to answer it. The very circumstance, then, that leads to the deepening need for the anthropological search, that is, the expansion of civilization, also converts anthropology into a narrow discipline with mechanical techniques and trivial goals. It may even come to pass that the central question—what part of our humanity we have lost and how and why we have lost it—will cease to be of concern to anthropology. Perhaps, significant statements about man will no longer be made by anthropologists, just as most sociologists no longer say anything very compelling about society, or political scientists about politics, economists about economics, and so on, precisely because these fields, reflecting the larger division of labor in our culture and its increasingly analytic attitudes, have grown further and further apart.[7]

Rarely can the social scientist bear to mix, for example, ethical, metaphysical, and spiritual insights within the study of culture, for this may jeopardize his or her academic reputation as a scientist. She or he continues the fiction that the scientific–technical perspective can describe culture more accurately when the full depth of one's own being is suppressed or 'controlled.' This means that many of our own intuitive and deeply felt reactions about ourselves, the nature–universe within which we are embedded, the culture within which we live, the 'outside' cultures we study, and the connections among all of these must remain unstudied.

Science and Metaphysics.

As suggested above, the term 'culture' has gone through a series of changes. As a more general construct, it presumably describes the patterned 'stuff' in the life of a people—in a specific society, group, clan, or family—as well as how these people make sense or meaning out of this 'stuff.' Within this framework we speak of 'high' culture and 'low' culture with clear evaluative connotations, but the underlying breadth of the term remains the same. More recently, as suggested by Diamond, the term has been narrowed for the convenience of the scientist who seeks a more focused and plausible arena for study. So we find that one who describes culture from the viewpoint of a casual observer or participant gives the term greater breadth and depth than one who uses it for scientific study. This is presumably because anthropology as science generally seeks to uncover regularities in human behavior that transcend the specifics of a single culture and are universally true within limited and specified circumstances.

Anthropology, as does all science, seeks to discover and describe the universal. Metaphysics, like science, seeks to reveal or expose metacultural regularities and meanings through systematic observation, rational-logical contemplation, and reflection. Unlike science, however, it is willing to make more speculative assumptions regarding, for example, the nature and existence of a God. Both science and metaphysics, however, can presumably lift us out of cultural prejudice into a realm of universal human judgment, or, at least, into a realm based on comparative cultural judgment. This requires, as we saw with the academic anthropologist, that we stand apart from our culture and nature, as if we could become objective spectators.[8]

We believe the distinction between science and metaphysics is one of degree—that is to say, the degree of speculative risk one is willing to take regarding assumptions and premises from which one begins to describe the 'truth' of the cosmos. Metaphysics is clearly the more general and risky enterprise. In Whitehead's terms, metaphysics "is the endeavor to frame a coherent, logical, necessary system of general ideas in terms of which every element of our experience can be interpreted."[9] In short, it is the search for some kind of interrelated unitary view of our natural and cultural universe. Kaplan describes its breadth:

> The unity sought is that which would disclose the commonalities and continuities between fact and value, science and religion, prudence and morality, utility and beauty, and so through a whole range of conflicting dualities. The questions Kant formulated two centuries ago still perplex us: What am I? What should I do? What may I hope? For Kant these questions depended in turn on the traditional ones: Is there a God? Does man have free will? Is the soul immortal? Metaphysics aims at resolutions of these perplexities.[10]

From a holistic perspective, we must applaud metaphysics' breadth of concern and search for unifying principles. However, one of the major difficulties with metaphysics is the weight it places on the verbal-conceptual mode of knowing. While the idea of culture assumes a diversity of communicative expressive possibilities in what we have called the 'stuff of life,' metaphysics begins and often ends with the linguistic clarification and elaboration of dichotomies, ambiguities, predicaments, and queries: permanence-change; cosmos-chaos; culture-nature; matter-life; plant-animal-human; life-consciousness; body-mind; mind-spirit; free will-determinism; good-evil; God-man-matter; religion-science; science-mysticism; thought-action; theory–practice. Our Western philosophical–analytic bias suggests that these dichotomies–trichotomies or seeming contradictions can be clarified, if not resolved, in a world dominated by some kind of verbal–conceptual mode of inquiry. Popper calls this intermediary domain, which presumably exists between personal sense experience and objctive reality, "world three."[11] It is, Popper claims, a "real world" inhabited by problems and intellectual structures that have an existence in their own right.

Much of Western thought has been concerned with filling the storehouse of "world three." Popper identifies two variations of this world. There is the Platonistic tradition of the essentialist, who posits a world of pure concepts, pure ideas. Those who pursue this tradition assume that by getting the ideas (and words) just right, basic metaphysical problems can be resolved or substantially clarified. From Popper's point of view, it is more fruitful to see "world three" as containing largely hypothetical statements, the theoretical problems of human construction. Viewed this way, science and social science become subclasses of metaphysics, differing only in that they describe phenomena in limited ways so that the possibility of demonstrating empirical regularity, confirmation, or replication is more likely.

In practical terms, however, the separation between science and metaphysics has become more profound over the past hundred years as the scientific enterprise has increasingly specialized and merged with countless new fields in engineering and technology. Technology and technological knowledge are certainly more than "world three" —more than statements. They constitute millions of bits and pieces of highly predictable events. Here, theories are valued for their heuristic power or elegance, but such theories are so commonly altered as new bits of information are discovered that it is folly to take them in any way as permanent. An interesting case in point is the field of genetics. While the perennial debates on Darwinian evolution still make headlines in the popular press because of their metaphysical implications (e.g., are humans the divinely inspired creatures of God or are they random events?), the academic and business worlds are much more involved in and excited by microbiological knowledge and techniques which hold the promise, through genetic engineering, for manufacturing cheap beer, protein, insulin, and interferon.[12]

It is, perhaps, easier to plot a continuum from metaphysics to social science in the field referred to generally as social theory. Here one might include the work of psychologists such as Freud, Jung, James, Allport, and Maslow; the work of sociologists such as Marx, Durkheim, Weber, Sorokin, Reisman, Bell, and Berger. These scholars are willing to make broad and comprehensive claims about culture, society, and quality of life, yet their claims are based less on the homely examples or hypothetical problems suggested by philosophers and more on systematic case studies, using historical and statistical evidence. This kind of scholarship attempts to merge the comprehensiveness and depth associated with metaphysics with an effort to marshall evidence in the systematic manner of the scientist. Social theory shares with both metaphysics and science a single-minded commitment to verbal–conceptual, definitional, and explanatory schema as ways of knowing and communicating.

If metaphysics works toward comprehensiveness and unity in the way it construes experience or knowing; if science works toward more focused empirical claims about material regularities, requiring "public" evidence to support them; and if social theory falls somewhere between these efforts at making general meaning and systematically justifying suppositions, we can say that all embrace a similar conceptual methodology, one which uses the abstract structure of number, logic, and language we associate with classical Greek philosophy as the highest medium through which one might construe human experience. We then must deal with the disquieting sense that the 'stuff' that people do and think and feel in daily human intercourse and the meanings they experience in the midst of such 'stuff' seem richer and deeper than the operational or instrumental language of data and scientific schema, or the logical and rational language employed in metaphysics and social theory. For culture, as noted earlier, is expressed in a great variety of ways that transcend the human capacity for expository verbalization; the caressing associated with loving and bonding; dance; sports; storytelling; gesture; painting; sculpting; singing; ritual; worship; meditation; prayer; and even the style with which one performs such common coping tasks as cooking, walking, or making love. (We should note, however, that all of these fields are now studied 'scientifically' and 'academically.') So we are provoked to ask: Is it possible that the most general understandings about truth, beauty, justice, and knowing which come out of science, metaphysics, and social theory describe a reality that is somehow less 'real' than the inarticulable stuff of culture which those who make such rules implicitly carry with them—in their very language, habits, behavior, celebrations? For example, astronomers may discover and describe (within limits) the qualities and regularities of celestial bodies, but the description of the phenomena themselves, as in the term "celestial mechanics," reveals an unconscious metaphor informed by the culture out of which the description comes. Moreover, the behavior these men exhibit in studying celestial mechanics is set within a context of telescopes, computers, and corporate bureaucracy.

In short, as modern people, we associate the generality associated with mathematical and conceptual–verbal knowing as a higher or truer form of understanding, yet the obvious fact is that this kind of technical knowledge is still connected, on some level, in some way to broader and more fundamental qualities of cultural experience. And beyond this the question is not necessarily What are higher or lower ways of knowing? or Can we separate the higher ways of knowing (science) and keep them pure, uncontaminated from the lower ways (unsubstantiated intuitions and metaphors)? The question may rather be: How can we keep these ways of knowing together, so that culture and experience are apprehended in deeper and more expansive ways? The history of modernity is one of increasingly separating out different domains of knowledge and then being forced to make judgments about which is more fundamental, more true.

Historically, the problem is not new. We find points of separation in Western thought between what are termed mystical, non-rational, or intuitive bases for cultural meaning and rational–metaphysical–scientific methodologies. Within the past 400 years, we see a sharp separation between science, technology, and social theory on the one hand versus the continuing tradition of metaphysics, theology, and religion on the other.[13] Within an even broader framework a distinction can be made between the more expressive and less theoretical–conceptual cultures of the Eastern and Southern hemispheres of the globe (Hindu, Buddhist, Mayan, Aztec, and so forth) and the highly articulate, verbal, conceptual cultures of the North and West. For example, a major study by F. S. C. Northrup undertaken some 40 years ago, attempted to integrate these two modes of cultural meaning-making.[14] Northrup saw the roots of a major world conflict (which is still with us) as emanating from two fundamentally different ways of construing reality. The solution, he maintained, was not the domination of one over the other, but rather some new form of integration:

> ...the ideal society must return to the primitive intuition of the past with respect to its aesthetically grounded portion and advance to the sophisticated science of the present with respect to its theoretically based part. This has one very radical consequence for Westerners. It means that the traditional Western tendency to regard the primitive as inferior or evil must be rejected with respect to the aesthetic component in culture. A people leaves the primitive aesthetic intuitions of its past at its peril. It must move forward to the scientific theory of the future, taking along the primitive aesthetic intuition of the past. (p. 459)

Little seems to have changed in the thinking of modern people since Northrup published this injunction. Technology–science or even technology–science embedded in more general philosophical statements about the meaning of our contemporary human condition (e.g., various forms of humanistic or dynamic psychology) are seen as somehow 'truer' than creative, artistic, or intuitive statements in the form of music, games, movement, painting, story, poetry and craft, which are now generally considered as entertainment and recreation. More expressive, less affluent cultures are still seen as invidiously primitive. The argument boils on. For example, contemporary philosophical–literary efforts, many of them associated with an approach called *deconstruction,* attempt to rescue the notion that literature or "story" may express a deeper or fuller sense of the groundedness and meaning of a culture than its philosophical conceptual apparatus. Norris puts it thus:

> Deconstruction begins by questioning the deep laid assumption that "philosophy has to do with certain kinds of truth which are not to be found in "literature." At its simplest and most prejudicial, this attitude takes the form of Plato's belief that poetry was a kind of irrational seizure, exempt from all the curbs of wisdom and reason. [On the other hand, Shelly argued] that poetry was the source and inspiration for every great advance in human society, since even science and politics had to partake of the imaginative vision if their efforts were to benefit mankind.[15]

As Northrup and Norris suggest, the great problem for the fragmentary abstract modern academic is to move away from considering different modes of experience, thought, and communication as separate or even competing aspects of knowing and rather consider that experience or knowing is *one integrated process.* While it is possible, as a matter of practical convenience for a specific time or purpose, to reduce our world to fragmentary literary or scientific qualities of knowing, we need not pretend that the world is actually made of such unrelated fragments that can be legitimately studied *only* in this way—in the library, in the laboratory, in the "field"—or must be taught in this way in the classroom.

Religion and Grounded Culture.

It should be clear by now that we are really talking about two dimensions of holistic knowing and understanding. The first is the scale or comprehensiveness with which one views the universe. One can, for example, experience, connect, and relate the facts of one's micro world (e.g., oxygen being transferred between the air in one's lungs and the blood in one's veins and bodily tissues) to broader macro events (e.g., to the heaving of the chest with the intake of air, and even to the earlier cosmic events out of which air was formed—the initial creation of heavier elements such as carbon and oxygen, which presumably occurred during the expansion of the universe after the hypothetical 'big bang'). In modern physics, one can ponder the relationship between fields of virtual particles and our obsevation of physical energy, or the relationship between energy and its transformed existence as matter. In these instances, one is relating that which is smaller and more discrete to a larger context. As humans we have the natural vision of our eyes, but we also have the perspective of the cosmic dreamer (and now a telescope to go with it) as well as a curious concern for that area of reality where something comes from nothing—which we imagine to be very small. The latter we now search out in traces made by particles in the cyclotron and in images photographed by an electron microscope or traces made on light-sensitive film.

A second dimension of holism has to do with the depth or richness with which one apprehends the world. For someone grounded deeply, the culture which represents that experience speaks profound truth. This depth, however, is not generally expressible in language and logic. It is more expressible in the actions of one's life, one's feelings, and as these feelings are transformed into art, movement, music, poetry, work, and craft. Sherrard, an Eastern Orthodox theologian, makes an eloquent statement about the distinction between the sense of *grounded culture*, where language and symbols are linked to a deeper, more connected experience of reality, and that of *relative culture*, where culture is presumably constructed by the logic of conscious—or, perhaps, unconscious but mechanistic—human choice, persuasion, and manipulation. Sherrard talks about the "creative vitality" that characterized communities that were presumably integrated by some kind of grounded spirituality. He then states:

> . . .Whether there have been such communities is difficult to say. But when from the inhuman proliferation of our modern cities we go, notebook in hand, on various journeys of escape or research to centers of vanished or vanishing cultures: to Sicily, to Mexico, to Tibet, or China, to India; when we stand before Chartres Cathedral, or in St. Sophia, or at Stonehenge or Delphi, or in the caves of Lascaux, or watch a dance in southern India, or the dancers of Bali, or listen to a lament sung by a peasant woman of Andalusia or of the Greek mani or by a Negro; or when we see Etruscan funeral urns or Minoan frescoes, then we know that we have lost some crucial grasp of life and that this is not without consequence for us.

> What is this grasp, and why have we lost it? Here at once we come up against a difficulty. The art of those vanished or vanishing cultures in which we recognize the presence of some quality that now eludes us, is a religious art. . . .

> . . .Its purpose is to make as coherent as possible the nature of the principles and of the laws which, issuing from them, govern man's life and that of all creation. It is to aid man in what is the central concern of life, that to which everything else is subordinate: his search for communion and harmony with these principles. For when what is to be realized and experienced through such communion and harmony is regarded as the source of all vitality and significance, of all inspiration and beauty, what, in fact, alone is actually real, then not to make that the central concern of life would be to show a curious lack of judgment. . . .

> . . .Those myths that lie at the base of the cultures in which we recognize the presence of some quality that now eludes us are for the people of such cultures not mere decoration, but symbols and images making possible a direct and constant intercourse with the universal principles of life; and if these people occupy themselves so much with such symbols and images that they not only fill their rites and their places of worship with them, but also paint them on their pottery, weave them into their clothes, sing them in their songs, dance in obedience to them, lay their fields out after their pattern, score them on rock and tree, and even cut them into their own flesh, that is because they recognize how on that intercourse depends their very existence, the existence of the culture of which, as of a living organism, each of them is a part. And yet it is impossible to interest the vast majority of the modern world in any such images and symbols. A whole language of the soul, a whole spiritual science, has been lost to us, and what this means is that we have destroyed our capacity to participate in the reality of which it is the expression.[16]

Sherrard's observations about the quality of an experience which he would denote as "religious" seem, as he himself acknowledges, gnawingly anachronistic.

More recently, academics both in colleges and the lower schools have come to construe 'religion' simply as subject matter, as 'religion studies,' rather than as the basis for a more deeply grounded integrated experience. And although some ten years ago it became trendy for a number of schools to strengthen or add more integrative curriculum offerings, such as religion and anthropology, there was always the sensitive concern that they might not have the bounded legitimacy of conventional disciplines, such as history, philosophy, and the social sciences. In the words of a recent complaint:

> Contemporary religious studies has two striking features. One is that, like minority studies, women's studies, Judaic studies, it is a new discipline. Child of prosperity and eager to bring a good return to those who have a stock in its future, it has been diligent in the pursuit of its tasks. Thus it has worked hard to expand the breadth of both its sources and its subject matter: it has drawn its ideas from philosophy, theology, anthropology, and sociology, literary criticism, psychology, and political science; it has attended to every area of the inhabited earth and to epochs, from prehistoric times to the current cults. The second marked feature of this discipline is that it is not yet a discipline.[17]

We would, of course, applaud this academic direction —the search for breadth. At least there is an area of concern, unfettered by archaic academic traditions, where one can roam the planet without fear of losing one's disciplinary credentials. Wiebe, however, draws precisely the opposite conclusion.

> The challenge to religious studies is to become an accomplished discipline.
> The first step in this direction is to identify promising theories of religion . . .
> There is also a second step, and that is to institutionalize the best of these
> theories. (p. 362)

We find the most interesting aspect of religion studies to be the fact that
its proponents do *not* focus on the opportunity to create a more integrative
experience, one which would unite, not bifurcate, our sense of grounded
experience and the abstract way we conceptualize knowing. Rather than
merge imagination and scientific fact, religious studies proponents seek a
focused discipline.

As noted above, high schools and elementary schools have also shown
increasing interest in teaching *about* religion or religious studies—strictly
as an academic subject. *Social Education* published a section on "teaching
about religions in the public schools" in December 1969 as well as a special
issue on the same topic in January 1981. The topic was revisited in
November/December 1987. The general thrust of 'religion studies' as social
studies professionals see it can be summarized in two sentences:

> Curriculum content brings together four structural factors: ideas, values, infor-
> mation, and skills. In religion studies, as with any other academic content,
> the relative merit of each for young learners requires consideration.[18]

In short, religion or religion studies is to become another academic subject
in which the teacher apparently seeks to objectify religion and give it the
firm reality of ideas, actions, facts and even skills, that stand outside the
student, to be dissected, labeled, and understood in an academic way, much
as the crayfish or the frog is killed, objectified, and dissected in the biology
lab. Although few academics seemed to acknowledge the import of his
insight, Smith, ten years earlier, presented this issue with persuasive clarity:

> The external observer's awareness is different from that of the *engagé* partici-
> pant. A relationship of which you stand at one, with your whole personality
> and perhaps your eternal destiny at stake, and at the other end stands, God,
> crushingly overwhelming in his majesty and frightening in His imperious
> demands and yet utterly winsome in his unfrustratable love and concern for
> you as a person—this is a very different matter from those relationships that
> you may write down in your notebook as you observe other people's exotic
> behavior, or even that you may infer from a careful study of other's symbols
> which, even if you finally come to understand their meaning, do not reach
> out and take hold upon your life. It is this latter complex to which the term
> "a religion" "the religions," and the names of the various religions, have come
> to refer.[19]

As we have noted with anthropology, religion studies becomes another academic enterprise with an apparent stake in objectifying or placing itself outside the intimate concerns of those who study it. The notion is that one somehow understands things—nature, humans, God, the world, culture— better when one is on the outside. From Sherrard's point of view (where one is concerned with understanding how ground permeates all perception and conception) the academic outlook seems outlandish. Or in Smith's terms,

> The observer's concept of a religion is beautifully suited to ignore it. The participant can see very clearly that the outsider may know *all about* a religious system, and yet may totally miss the point. The outsider may intellectually command all the details of its external facts, and yet may be—indeed, as an outsider, presumably must be or demonstrably is—untouched by the heart of the matter.

> There is a difference between knowing a doctrine of salvation, and being saved.[20]

History

If "religious," in Sherrard's sense, is the quality of depth we apply to an integrated or whole culture, it is necessary nonetheless that this quality be set within a contextual frame. This frame is commonly called 'history.' Cultures often describe their beginnings, their course, and usually their destiny. Judeo-Christianity is an obvious example. The Old Testament describes the beginning of the world, the circumstances and reasons for its creation, and the story of the rise of the Hebrew peoples. For Christians, the New Testament describes the turning point in that history, wherein all humans were promised redemption, first by Jesus alone and later within the framework of the Church.

Other branches of history—intellectual, social, and cultural history— are inventions of modernity, composed in the spirit of scientific descriptions and interpretation within the framework of an empirical methodology—using documents, previous histories, and oral corroboration as an evidential base for statements. The writers of such history, as other social scientists, stand outside their subject and attempt to correct for their own cultural bias. Gone is the sense of prophetic revelation in Genesis, the poetry of the Psalms, or the wonder and mystery of Homeric poetry and song. Such historical-religious statements are now seen as superstition or allegory, rather than the specific context of a deep and integrated culture. What were once comprehensive statements describing the context and grounding of a culture has now been fragmented into a variety of genres. We read a history which is seemingly only religious (the Holy Bible, the Koran, the

Bagavadgita); history which is credible literature (academic and 'popular' history); history which is quasi-fiction (literary inventions based on historical events—e.g., Kenneth Roberts, Gore Vidal, James Michener); history which is social science (chronologically limited monographs using carefully gathered documents and statistical corroboration); and history which is textbook (mainly superficial gleaning from academic history and the social sciences).

Conclusion

We have given a brief sketch of various terms—culture, metaphysics, science, religion and history[21]—which tend to connote comprehensive and deep ways of knowing. Sorting through these categories, one would note the tendency for their domains to be increasingly fragmented. (One could easily imagine the opposite tendency if, by chance, we were moving from Sorokin's sensate phase to a more integral phase of societal development.) The term 'culture,' for example, begins as a naturalistic phenomenon: it includes the patterns of language, habits, and beliefs that provide an underlying stamp to the life of a specific people. We next encounter a split between culture and practical reason, and find that culture may be considered only the vestigial adaptive habits and symbols institutionalized in the past. Then we find a split between the functional view of culture versus the symbolic-expressive view, the latter often employing complex structural schema as sources of explanation. We find decreasing concern with the search for normative criteria to describe genuine or authentic culture induced from observation of specific cultures, as in the work of Sorokin. The term is preempted by anthropologists who tend to see it strictly as a construct within their scientific discipline, rather than as a key term at the intersection of science, ethics, and metaphysics.

Metaphysics analyzes the relationships between specific cultural claims and plausible universal claims (e.g., Is ultimate being more like spirit or matter or both?), but within the limits of a narrow logical/verbal–conceptual methodology. When metaphysics moves toward poetry or fantasy or drama, as in the work of Camus, Heidegger, or Ingmar Bergman, we give it a different name—existential philosophy or simply literature and film.

Religion (or religion studies) is no longer seen as having a grounded or transcendent quality that permeates all of a particular culture (its art, its work, its family life) as was suggested by Sherrard. It is rather only one separate aspect of culture, like economics, or politics, or the kinship system, which can be studied as an academic discipline only in a somewhat more eclectic way.

We wonder whether or not it would be possible to develop a field of study, an attitude toward knowing that would push us toward constructing bridges *across* these fields, rather than carving them into smaller separate domains of knowledge. Could we begin, for example, with a metaphysical problem (e.g., Does the quality of spirit permeate all being?) and add to that a religious or grounded sensibility (a sense of awe, reverence, and celebration for the connectedness among beings that we experience as spirit—the spirit of a friend, the spirit of a friendly tree). Then we might add the quality of scientific inquiry which searches for the most productive context within which to study the nature of living personality: Is that most productive context of understanding within individual organisms, within species, within ecosystems, or even within the whole planet? We would certainly find that dealing with such issues requires various degrees of specialized knowledge, but we would also see that testing the relevance of statements in science or metaphysics or religion would call for a breadth of understanding that would, of necessity, include the other fields as well. The effort would be to raise and deal with issues of fundamental human concern within a comprehensive context—one that would include both technical and ontological sensibilities; one that would provoke synthetic as well as specialized analytic speculations; one that would not rule the more imaginative questions "out of order."

Our sense is that such questions are rarely dealt with in schools, and that to do so would require a profound change of heart and mind for modern educators. For we surmise that the pursuit of highly specialized, focused questions in all fields of academia is driven by an unconscious faith in machine imagery which suggests that the precise definition and description of many small parts will add up to some kind of meaningful vision of a whole (although it is conceded that no person can now imagine what that whole might be). And to ask academics to work within a curriculum in which the relevance of bits of knowledge may seriously be brought into question is to risk the most devastating insight of all—that the emperor may really have no clothes. The questions that many, if not most, academics ask of their students may, in fact, not only be specialized and technical; they may often be trivial.

Chapter Four

Cosmology

We have now arrived at the central theme of this book. It is the search for a conception of education which would move us to generate imaginative scenarios of positive culture, whole visions which might direct us both to feel and critically examine the depth and breadth of human experience—qualities of becoming, qualities of being; qualities of knowing; qualities of participation and connection. We see the essential flaw in modernity as its inability to generate such visions in the midst of the fragments of its incredibly successful machines. The crisis of modernity arises from the fact that while it continues to create ever more bits of specialized knowledge, ever more sophisticated technology and material products, its members perceive no way to stand outside of the cycle of products that move from factory to shopping mall to home to town or city dump and ask what it all means.

Taking cultural visions and imagination seriously requires a radical new mindset, one that is willing to try on different lenses, to add and subtract them in combination without fear of losing the identity or integrity associated with 'owning' or understanding one particular lens. The universe is then more like the shifting patterns in a kaleidoscope than a complex machine. The prisms of glass shift and vary the frequencies of light which pass through them; while one sees different and changing patterns that dance before the eye, at a single moment there is a unitary pattern which is both inside the mind, inside the eye, and in the world. And there is at that moment the search for what mind and eye and pattern mean as an interrelated unity.

What might we call such a venture that would embrace the various fields of knowing—metaphysics, science, religious intuition, the arts, history? We would propose the word *cosmology*[1] after Whitehead, who was, perhaps, one of the first modern thinkers to use the term and deal systematically with these issues.

In Whitehead's terms:

> It must be thoroughly understood that the theme of these lectures is not a detached consideration of various traditional philosophical problems which acquire urgency in certain traditional systems of thought. The lectures are intended to state a condensed scheme of cosmological ideas, to develop their meaning by confrontation with the various topics of experience, and finally to elaborate an adequate cosmology in terms of which all particular topics find their interconnections. Thus the unity of treatment is to be looked for in the gradual development of the scheme, in meaning, and in relevance, and not in the successive treatment of particular topics. For example, the doctrines of time, of space, of perception, and of causality are recurred to again and again, as the cosmology develops. In each recurrence, these topics throw some new light on the scheme, or receive some new elucidation. At the end, insofar as the enterprise has been successful, there should be no problem of space–time, or of epistemology, or of causality, left over for discussion. The scheme should have developed all those generic notions adequate for the expression of any possible interconnection of things.[2]

One need not believe Whitehead's optimistic claim that all philosophical issues will somehow be connected at the end of an adequate cosmological treatise to experience the excitement inherent in such a venture, for it clearly transcends science, religion, metaphysics, aesthetics, and so on. And while the term cosmology sounds rather cold and analytical, at other points Whitehead discusses passionately this philosophical enterprise as an effort to integrate what we have called grounded experience and rational analysis:

> Philosophy frees itself from the taint of ineffectiveness by its close relationship with religion and with science, natural and sociological. It attains its chief importance by fusing the two, namely religion and science, into one rational scheme of thought . . . Religion is an ultimate craving to infuse into the insistent particularity of emotion the non-temporal generality which primarily belongs to conceptual thought alone. In the higher organisms the differences in tempo between the mere emotions and the conceptual experiences produce a life-tedium, unless this supreme fusion has been effected. The two sides of the organism require a reconciliation in which emotional experiences illustrate a conceptual justification, and conceptual experiences find an emotional illustration.[3]

As we see it, the field we call cosmology not only includes the various domains of the universe (e.g., the macro world of the heavens, the 'normal' world of human sense experience, and the micro-world of molecules, atoms, and smaller particles), it also implies that these various domains are somehow interrelated and connected. It refers not only to various facets of knowing—to the existential moment of the present, to the scientifically determined repeatable events in nature, to the conclusions of metaphysical logic, and the sense of groundedness of religious intuition; it refers also to the fact that these various ways of knowing and kinds of knowledge are all different aspects of a common reality. None is supreme; none is exclusive; none is discounted.

The Judeo-Christian cosmology provides a familiar example of the plurality and oneness we are talking about. In the Christian cosmology there is a God, a heaven, a subheaven with spirits and angels, a natural world, purgatory, hell. One sees the universe as a single entity. There are various qualities of insight and science by which we come to know this universe; there is also a biblically revealed history which describes and gives significance to these different domains. There are different metaphysical qualities to these different domains. Time, for example, means one thing in a timeless heaven and another thing in hell where time exists without end. The various domains have different characteristics of permanence and change, different characteristics of suffering and happiness. But for the Christian or Jew, while there may be multiple domains, there is a single unitary reality, a single cosmos, a single cosmology.

Cosmological thinking bears a characteristic stamp. It describes in a factual mode the various aspects of the natural world, as does science; yet it speculates about the origins of life, and why things are created and perish, as do historical and religious thinking. Cosmological thinking describes appropriate relationships between humans and the natural world, between humans and other humans—i.e., the nature of the good society. It distinguishes between the ideal and the real, but treats the ideal as an essential ingredient of reality. It is, at least in tone, non-relativistic. One may say that the Hopi believe this and the Navaho believe that, but that is more culture talk. The anthropologist notes apparent contradictions and inconsistencies as well as regularities within a system of cultural beliefs because she or he is speaking as an outsider. The cosmologist speaks from the inside, showing how beliefs are plausible, how inconsistencies can be resolved. The sympathetic posture of the cosmologist toward his or her subject stems from his or her own personal search for an adequate cosmology. The cosmologist is involved in much more than a scholarly appraisal of what other individuals or cultures believed. She or he is an artist working on the adequacy, comprehensiveness, and coherence of his or her own meaning system.

In short, the cosmologist or cosmological point of view is involved in an effort to integrate reflection, a broad historical philosophical perspective, with personal commitment, meaning, and prudent action. The cosmologist understands that one is involved in a process of immanent creation—the creation of oneself in an interrelated universe of which we are part. We are *in* each new pulse of creation; we are not outside the process. The cosmologist cannot accept the dominance of the machine metaphor—that we must somehow always stand apart from the machine that we seek to understand and control—because this limited conception of our being would grossly distort our view of some larger whole. There is no philosopher, scientists, priest, or teacher 'here' and a world or universe 'out there.' Reality always includes the observer.

The cosmologist is searching—as is the scientist—for an accurate, descriptive, non-dogmatic statement of the universe, but he or she is willing to take speculative risks in beliefs about which the disinterested scientist, with a narrower technical focus, cares little. The cosmologist seeks to understand and resolve (if possible) basic metaphysical questions (e.g., is the essence of actuality characterized by permanence or change) but not in the spirit of disinterested inquiry. Rather, his or her search is in the spirit of existential urgency, since the understanding will have immediacy and importance in one's daily affairs. The cosmologist sees cosmology as a statement of ultimate understanding and commitment, as does the committed religionist, but the 'ultimate' is always permeable to contemporary claims for truth and understanding that seriously challenge one's existing world view. Like the religionist, the cosmologist seeks to create and institutionalize art, ritual, and meditation that will expose the human mind to 'deeper' experience.

Cosmology, Modernity, and Education

Underlying this discussion of various terms which describe aspects of human meaning systems—culture, metaphysics, science, social theory, grounded knowledge, history, and cosmology—is an effort to open the way for a consideration of deeper and more holistic conceptions of education. For it is our thesis that humans are, in fact, part of all life, that life is part of nature, that nature is one domain within a broader universe, and that unless we feel—in a deep ontological way—these connections, we, as humans, tend to build destructive illusions of grandeur, to dream Faustian dreams of ultimately controlling all life, nature and universe. Our assumption is that without some intuitive sense of these connections cultures and social systems lose their homeostatic balance between the separateness and the unity of being. The consequence of this loss of balance is a mixture of arrogance, as we seek to dominate a nature that stands outside ourselves, and the loss of our inner spiritual will, as we lose the feeling for what it all means.

There is nothing novel about this phenomenon. Historical commentators who have documented the rise and fall of societies have commonly included this blend of arrogance and alienation. Our modern circumstance, however, is unique because of the immensity of its scale. Modernity is driven by a massive global economic–technological system which is transforming local 'deep' cultures and societies all over the planet. There seems little likelihood that this global transformation will be geographically or historically contained. Peoples everywhere experience a tremendous sense of incoherence as local cultures atrophy and change into centers of urban production and consumption. The center of gravity shifts from a concern for the quality of life in village and community, the continuity from ancestors to progeny, and the sense of a 'way of life' to be preserved to private hedonistic choices and the individual purchase and use of products for profit.

Halpern describes the profound consequences of this transformation:

> That underlying revolution which we have neglected —the revolution of modernization—is not a peculiar burden carried temporarily by the underdeveloped, but is history's first common, world-wide revolution.
>
> Change in the modern age is historically unique in its quality. For the first time man and all the political, social, economic, religious, intellectual, aesthetic and psychological systems by which he has so far organized his life, are persistently being rendered incoherent. Elements are being destroyed and the linkages between them disconnected. Specifically, the connections that are being broken are those links between individuals, groups, and concepts, which give men capacity to cope simultaneously with continuity and change, collaboration and conflict, and justice. My hypothesis is that this breaking of connections, and therefore, the destruction of the capacity to deal with the most basic issues of social life, is the persistent and permanent challenge of the modern age. Since our perceptions and actions have not yet caught up with this new quality of change, most of the breaking is unintended and uncontrolled. If this be the nature of the modern age, we have two alternatives. We can live with the incoherence—and with the apathy, repression, and normless violence which usually accompany it . . .or else, we can seek to create an enduring capacity to overcome persistent incoherence and to take creative advantage of the opportunities that arise from the breaking of established connections.[4]

THE PARADOX OF GROUNDED CONTEXT AND UNIVERSAL COSMOLOGY. One possible response to this incoherence, especially for teachers, is that we should forthwith set up curriculum committees to work out an intelligible vision, a cosmology, that we could safely and in good conscience pass on to the coming generation. Quite obviously, the problem is not so easily resolved. The most serious difficulty comes out of the relationship between cosmology and grounded culture. There is an ambiguity in the term 'cosmology' which has to do with the generality with which cosmology speaks, and, likewise, the level of concreteness that characterizes grounded cultural experience. If we look, for example, at the meaning system of a particular culture, such as European medieval Christianity, we can say that it has a cosmology. The medieval Christian may know that Syrian Moslems or French Jews have a different cosmology but she or he does not attempt to rationalize or transcend inconsistencies among these more specific cosmologies by synthesizing a new and more general one. There is simply a cosmology that goes with a specific culture. From this perspective, other people's cosmologies are either in error (illusions and distortions), or, if seen relativistically, may be appropriate for others but not for us. We would call these *cultural cosmologies;* they are *seen* (from the inside) as universal, but are grounded in cultural practices, in the context of the culture of a specific time and place.

There is another cosmological enterprise. In this approach we look at the cultural record of humankind, at the 'facts' of science, at the speculations of philosophers and metaphysicians, at the artistic and religious statements and practices of deep cultures, and finally seek to create a general statement that will take into account all of these experiences. We would call these statements universal or metaphysical cosmologies. There is, then, an ambiguity for the members of a specific culture who truly believe in the universality of the cosmology of that culture. Christian missionaries, for example, spread the Judeo–Christian cosmology across the globe because they believe it to be the universal truth of humankind. Much of what we call the Western philosophical tradition has spent its energy placing either the Judeo–Christian cosmology or the modern scientific–technological cosmology within some broader, more intellectually defensible position.

Here we come to the somewhat paradoxical relationship between the two kinds of cosmology. Cultural cosmology, by its very nature, is grounded in specific context, a primal intuitive experience which connects it to a sense of the sacred, which implies universality. The quality of religiosity in what we have called ontological knowing gives humans an experience of universal connectedness (with other forms of life, with nature, with the creative qualities of being and becoming, with the sense of oneness we often call God). The quality of experience associated with connectedness has the feeling of universality precisely because of one's deep grounding in a specific context, a grounding in the sacredness that evolves from experiencing the uniqueness of one's ancestors, or one's prayers, and food, and dance, and music, and work. But while the experience of groundedness or universal connectedness emerges from a specific culture, when one tests these cosmological 'feelings' against the intuition of other cultures or more worldly fact (e.g., modern science), the cultural cosmology may be found woefully limited or deficient. From a universalistic or rational–scientific point of view it is simply not plausible that Christians or Jews or Moslems are 'the' chosen people, that their histories are 'the' one authentic history of the world. So there arise fundamental inconsistencies between the authentic ontological experience associated with local cultural cosmologies and the more abstract intellectual understanding associated with universal cosmologies. (And we need not construe these on only two levels—universal vs. cultural.) The general point is that we come to feel the validity and depth of cosmological understanding as it is associated with a specific context in a specific time, place, history, kinship net. One might think, for example, of Thoreau's affection for Walden Pond, the Concord River, the fields and woods around his native Concord. His critique of modernity emanated from his affection for these places. Within the limits of one specific context, however, it is difficult to extend one's imagination and create a more general critique of the *content* of a cosmology. Thinkers such as Whitehead, Sorokin, and Northrup cast back through the historical and cultural record of humankind in search of a seemingly reasonable and plausible way of looking at positive, adequate, or authentic cosmology. Once having done this, however, we face the fact that we have been sorting the dry bones of 'other people's' deep meaning. And the transformation of what appears to be a scientifically, metaphysically, aesthetically, or theologically more plausible cosmology into a 'living' cultural cosmology involves a process about which we know little or nothing. We are then faced with the great crisis which has been evolving ever since the ancient Greeks began their sophisticated cosmological probings 2,500 years ago. We can often understand much more than we can *feel* or *experience* or *do.* Our technical knowing races ahead of our ontological knowing.

One may deal with this paradox in several different ways. One can assume that the specific tribal contexts within which cosmology is first learned should be considered as only a passing developmental phase, to be later outgrown by all or integrated into a more abstract and universalistic cosmology. This is the modern developmental position, supported on a societal level by thinkers such as Parsons and Inkeles and on a psychological level by educators such as Fenton and Kohlberg. Or else, one can argue (as presumably Plato did) for a stratified society in which an intellectual elite, initially grounded in the culture of the people, is educated to look at the world in a more universalistic way, uncontaminated by the cultish pietism of the common people. In this kind of feudal society, the individual is caught in a dialectic between the narrower but more deeply felt commitment by the common people to a parochial context-bound cosmology and the effort of a more circumspect, objective, and passionless elite to present an 'accurate' comprehensive view of the universe. In a modern society served by mass electronic media and compulsory education, one can reduce the tension of such a dialectic by creating the illusion of deep specific contextual symbols to which literally millions of people will feel a personal, familial, or communal attachment. (One may obtain the same feeling of personal intimate loyalty and legitimacy by brushing with Crest toothpaste as one does by using the baking soda recommended by one's grandmother. Or one may feel loyal and positive about eating at MacDonald's or Pizza Hut because one has seen friendly, neighborly people raving ecstatically about their food on television.) The plausibility of creating an illusory context-based cosmology, with its intuitive sense of groundedness, in an impersonal mass society was demonstrated by Hitler's Germany. Within this model, it is presumably possible for an elite to generate deeply felt tribal symbols on a mass basis which would be consistent with a more universalistic cosmology. The dangers of this way of teaching cosmology are self evident, for here the context of commitment is not a tribe or community or family of specific people for whom one has affection and love; it is messages on an electronic oscilloscope or in mass rallies of strangers in a stadium. We assume that adequate and authentic cosmologies can evolve only within relatively intimate cultural and natural settings which reflect the interdependence of the human condition—interdependence with earth, air, other living things, friends, kin, and home.

A third response to the paradox under discussion (the requirement that authentic cosmology be grounded in the context of tribal community to have depth and personal connectedness yet have a cross-cultural or universalistic capacity for imagination and critique) seems to us most defensible yet most difficult, given the conditions of modern global society. This response would posit a highly decentralized or confederate society and set of societies. Cosmologies would evolve out of the historical and cultural conditions that characterize specific neighborhoods, cities, or geographic regions. Yet there would be some larger national and global effort to critique the quality and authenticity of local cultural cosmologies. How to create the political, diplomatic, and educational structures for such a bi-level or tri-level global society is beyond the scope of our speculation at this point. Our proposal is, however, similar to what is actually undertaken now in bicultural education in bicultural communities. Bicultural education programs attempt to maintain the language, kinship structures, commitment to geographic community, sense of space and time, and the special feelings children (or adults) have about food, music, dance, games, work, craft, and the like, while at the same time recognizing that one must cope, at least part of the time, economically and politically within a semi-alien metaculture. Bicultural societies without grand designs of culture hegemony sometimes handle this model fairly well (e.g., Quebec), while those in which the dominant group is grounded in racism and a feeling of cultural superiority handle it least well (e.g., South Africa). The historical experience of the United States is mixed, but we have little experience with the kind of serious bicultural education for which some Native Americans and Hispanics now press.

Our position that meaningful cosmology is found not in an ideological commitment to some abstract philosophical 'truth' but rather within both the groundedness of communal roots and the search for authentic universality that informs these roots should reassure readers who assume we are searching for some grand new religion for all. In short, there must be a balance among individuality, community, and universality. Vaught, in his study of the nature and conditions of wholeness, summarizes the parameters of cosmological search in terms with which we essentially agree.

> ...The quest for wholeness involves a delicate interplay between the individuality we express and the communities in which we participate, and it is the harmonious interconnection between individuation and participation that those who undertake it must attempt to achieve. However, in the final analysis, the quest requires that we move beyond the finite order and that we stand face to face with what is ultimate and unconditioned. As the word itself suggests, the quest for wholeness is a quest for salvation; but what can salvation mean apart from a source of power and meaning that can sustain our existence? This source of significance can be symbolized by the communities of which we are a part, and it can be made relevant to our particular condition. But the ground of existence transcends the human community, and it can never be reduced to the uniqueness of the individuals within it. Though the quest for wholeness spreads outward toward the whole of humanity, and though it reaches down to the particularity of the individuals who undertake it, it also seeks a source of meaning that lies beyond the human realm. In doing so, it generates a three-dimensional space in which human beings can live.[5]

We are arguing, in short, for an educational dialectic which includes the concreteness and groundedness of significant family, community, and microcultural experience but at the same time allows members of the community the broader search for the fundamental, universal, and even transcendent aspect of meaning. This position calls for two major social–educational programs. First, it requires an effort to rebuild and strengthen cosmological thought within family and community life—to give local context significance beyond the replication of signs and symbols flashed on TV screens and viewed in textbooks, periodicals, and classrooms. Second, it requires the integration of the traditional academic subjects and vocational categories so that the search for authentic and persuasive cosmologies is not only permitted but encouraged within the educational settings that people normally inhabit. Our next chapter provides illustrations of what we call comparative cosmological thinking as well as an example of the content and questions that might flow from this approach to curriculum and teaching.

Chapter Five

Cosmology as Curriculum

Thus far we have undertaken a critique of certain aspects of modernity's meaning system: its cosmology; the fragmented view of reality emanating from its functional–structural social system; its emphasis on utilitarian technical knowledge, disconnected from deeper ontological sensibilities; its limited range of metaphorical imagination; its repression and rejection of the experience of 'being in nature' which primitive people cultivate and dramatize in their daily lives; and the separation of abstract conceptual knowing from its grounded source, which then leads academics to restrict their use of those categories which might encompass a broader range of reality.

It is clear to us that modernity, despite its great achievements in the enhancement of human physical power and practical intelligence, has a flawed if not pathological cosmology. We would then ask: How do we educate ourselves and our children to generate more balanced and authentic cosmologies? How do we come to see more clearly the missing dimensions of our modern cosmology? How do we begin to think across cosmologies, comparing whole systems of meaning, one with the other? The answers to these questions suggest that we must experience the feeling that time and space, substance and causation, art, spirit, and God—as well as other significant categories of meaning—have a comprehensive and coherent intelligibility within at least two different paradigms. Our premise suggests that experts who become knowledgeable only within one narrow technical area of modern Western thought may well be miseducated. This would certainly apply to those whom we now consider as professionals: engineers, physicians, lawyers, administrators, and so forth. It would also apply to those who are more 'holistically' educated but exclusively trained in a Western vocation—e.g., Christian theologians or analytic philosophers. From this point of view, most universities are, in considerable degree, miseducative institutions, and it is the universities that largely generate and legitimate the content and meaning systems passed through to the lower schools. As we noted earlier, the fragmentation characteristic of modernity begins in the way we select curriculum for children and young people—as a list of categories related to the presumed functional requirements of a confusingly complex society.

But simply to indict leads nowhere. Where to turn for another approach? First, we might ask: What occasions provoke us to think in terms of whole cosmologies or even across cosmologies? It seems to us that such experience comes less from any systematic scholarship—which, by its nature, tends to focus on narrow questions—than from a general intense curiosity, a reaching out to understand the myriad of beliefs, dogmas, slogans, and preachings that flow through our daily lives. It may happen when the humanist turns on the TV during the Sunday morning broadcast of a fundamentalist Christian worship service and moves into the mood and spirit of the occasion. It may happen when the Christian probes empathetically the humanistic skepticism of a friend or neighbor as she or he proclaims that his or her body is ultimately nothing but manure, food for worms. It may happen when we test with a degree of semantic intensity what academics, politicians, or business people mean when they use strong metaphors like "conquest": conquering space, conquering disease, winning the war on poverty, conquering illiteracy, and so forth. In short, the world is filled with cosmological statements reflecting a mixture of fact, feeling, and imagery, which reveal implicitly the way we all apprehend becoming and being, knowing and doing, perishing and regenerating, power and justice. So the first step in cosmological thinking may well be for us to become sensitive to the mixed qualities of knowing embedded in everyday language and to the fact that our statements are always connected to broader, deeper meaning systems.

This leads to a second quality of cosmological thinking: the requirement that we make the effort not only to see through the puzzling differences, inconsistencies, and seeming irrationalities in the facts, feelings, and images that surround us but also to sort them into some kind of meaningful wholes. Sometimes this sorting has already been done for us by those who have worked out a coherent and comprehensive cosmology—e.g., the Hari Krishna, the humanistic philosopher, or the radical Christian. But often, as with many modern people who proclaim themselves to have a more pragamatic or eclectic view of the cosmos, one must piece together another's operational paradigm, which rests at a deeper implicit symbolic level. In this kind of paradigmatic detective work, one must allow for space or 'cracks' between cosmologies. Most of us undoubtedly live both with dominant cosmologies as bases for meaning and order in our lives and with fragments from other cosmologies or simply emerging or dying pieces of old cosmologies.

Our premise in this kind of curriculum-making should be clear and explicit, however. We believe that it is important at this transitional point in our history for humans to operate with a guiding search for comprehensive meaning (not necessarily permanent or dogmatic), which relates integrated qualities of knowing to underlying qualities of being. We assume that such whole meanings (cosmologies) are constantly in transition — as philosophical abstractions, as literary statements, as lived culture — but that there is (and should be), at any point in time, a broad understanding of nature, culture, and the human condition.

Therefore, as individuals and as cultures we are constantly in the process of 'composing' cosmologies. These compositions may contain only fragmentary outlines or they may be a comprehensive statement of a whole cosmology. Nonetheless, we are advocating here that greater attention be given to identifying, composing, and comparing whole cosmologies — the exercise of learning to think holistically and comparatively rather than within isolated pieces of understanding, disciplines, skills, problems, or lists.

Creating and Comparing Cosmologies

The media and genres by which one undertakes cosmology-making are varied and many. For example, B. F. Skinner, in *Walden Two*, paints a very concrete picture of two contrasting cosmologies, including a good deal of reflective commentary about the positive and negative aspects of each. Anthropologists have, over the past fifty years, described a wide range of meaning systems associated with what modern people have come to call 'primitive' or preliterate societies. Such studies have sometimes included cultural comparisons, especially since Ruth Benedict's ground-breaking *Patterns of Culture*. Reisman's broad-gauged study, *The Lonely Crowd*, makes a profound distinction among traditional, early entrepreneurial, and modern, "other directed" corporate societies by showing correlations among historical, economic, social, and psychological aspects of cultural systems.

Much of this work of thinking across paradigms has been done within a philosophical mode in which the speaker assumes that the audience is already familiar with the cosmologies being discussed, so the major effort is given over to comparisons rather than descriptions of the cosmologies themselves. Systematic philosophy and social theory have been about this business for any number of years. In the remainder of this chapter we shall present four illustrations of what we call comparative cosmologizing. The first three come from the work of individual writers who show through their particular quality of inquiry the ability to think in the comprehensive style we are advocating. In the fourth illustration we present brief overviews of four diverse cosmologies and suggest how they might be used to raise significant questions about the nature of our contemporary world. It is this last example that we think illustrates the potential for a full-blown curriculum.

BRUMBAUGH'S FOUR PHILOSOPHICAL FAMILIES OF THE WEST. An illustration of perhaps the most abstract and comprehensive mode of cosmologizing is represented in the work of Brumbaugh[1], who attempts to organize and summarize the major insights of Western philosophy within a four-fold scheme.[2] He presents his conclusions diagramatically in roughly the following way (pp. 6–7):

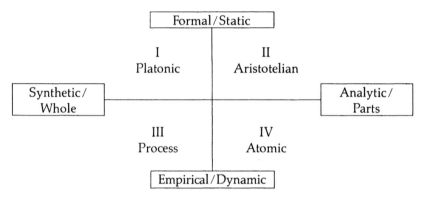

The categories in the chart are summarized as follows:

> . . .an atomist seeks indivisible, distinct elementary parts in his search for reality. (These parts may, of course, be material or psychological or linguistic "atoms.") . . . .Democritus, Epicurus, Hume, and the young Bertrand Russell, all fall into this family.

> Platonic systems are committed to a formal direction and a synthetic method of explanation. The attempt is to grasp a timeless form—a determinate defining pattern in an abstract field of logical space. But in the field, each form is defined by its relation to the other structural parts and to the whole. The general pattern is one of formal hierarchy. Explanation then must order formal parts hierarchically, indicate a relevant vertex, and study the participation by which structures ingress into and determine history and fantasy.

> Aristotelianism represents a third system . . . [which has] a formal explanatory direction, but an analytic method of explanation. Thus where a Platonist has logical hierarchies in a continuous field, an Aristotelian has rather a cabinet of natural kinds, species, types, in separate compartments. But science remains a study of species, for knowledge is of the universal. However, Aristotle's forms come in discrete units here, just as the atoms do in the atomic theory. Causality can be read either as teleological or blindly mechanical or both. It is probably correct to say, as is often done, that the Aristotelian world-view is the one

that would occur naturally to a biologist or a doctor, who studies not just health and humanity, but health, normalcy, and humanity in individual patients or specimens, each running more or less "true to type."

The fourth pair of commitments to physical direction and synthetic method is characteristic of twentieth century process philosophy. It had its classical ancestors—Heraclitus and Anaxagoras come to mind . . . poets and mystics have held this metaphysical position continuously, but the tendency has been to treat it as alternative to any "properly philosophical" view until recently. Process philosophy sees the world as a continuous, dynamic field, with new entities and values emerging with the advance of time. Forms or species are abstractions; explanation depends rather on intuition, on an appreciation of concrete individuals. Where the elements of an atomic theory are separate and static, the single field of process philosophy is continuous and dynamic. Some students of systems call this fourth family "Bergsonian," some "Whiteheadian," and both names are appropriate. (pp. 5–6)

While one can feel a certain excitement over the comprehensive and generality of Brumbaugh's analysis, it reveals a serious difficulty as an initial basis for curriculum precisely because of its generality. The problem is that as we search for all-inclusive philosophical schemes on increasingly higher planes of abstraction, we tend to lose sight of the fact that our appreciation of the scheme itself depends upon an intimate understanding of specific cosmologies. And that understanding, in turn, requires some actual immersion in the cultural milieu from which any cosmology has been abstracted. Thus, when we think of selecting curriculum to teach cosmological frameworks, we must take into account the power of abstractions as a way of seeing a multiplicity of relationships across meaning systems as well as the implicit understanding that comes from the texture and tone of the visceral feeling that overtakes us in our momentary life experience. The cosmologist's challenge is to see both horizontal connections across broad domains of reality (as Brumbaugh does) and the connection between the stuff of immediate experience and elements of the more abstract scheme.

When we perform some homely act like that of raking leaves, for example, we may feel excited by the smell and the sight and the touch of the experience—the dry deadness of the leaves, the moisture of the earth which reaches up and clings to the leaves, the random, disorderly way the leaves lay across the lawn or field. But we might also consider what raking leaves means for us in more abstract terms. Do we put the leaves neatly into plastic bags and have them hauled away to a dump, so that we will not be reminded of the death and disorder they brought with the changing season? Or do we lay them in a garden place so that they can participate in a rebirth to follow in the spring? The power of cosmological thinking is essentially that it provides context and meaning for the details of life, and the details provide challenge or confirmation for the context.

So on the one hand there is the ability to move abstractly with great breadth through two or more cosmologies, as Brumbaugh's work illustrates, but with minimum feeling for the texture and specificity of the actual stuff of life or the cultural imagery from which the cosmologies have been abstracted. On the other hand one might be able to 'feel' one's experience shaped and influenced by unconscious images and metaphors, yet be unable to explicate in any comprehensive or precise way the broader basis of such feelings. Our underlying feeling for a clean and orderly world may incline us to reject the dead and disorderly fallen leaves. Yet a deeper sense of our own organic connection with the earth may incline us toward identifying with a more positive image of the leaves as both they and we participate in the perennial life–death drama of planetary existence. The major goal toward which we should move within our cosmologically oriented curriculum is between the concrete and the abstract — to feel for ourselves, and to have our students feel, the breadth and power of abstract schema yet always be informed by the grounded immediacy of the sensuous imagery that gives life to each microsecond of our existence.

GRIFFIN'S LITERARY APPROACH. An example of comparative cosmological thinking which has less the lofty abstract quality of Brumbaugh (and also less the systematic comprehensiveness), but much more a sense of integration with the concrete and the immediate, is the work of Susan Griffin.[3] Griffin clearly carries with her deep experiential scars of a male-dominated world, which give an emotional tone to her descriptions of Platonic, Christian, Modern, and postmodern cosmologies. She uses dramatic language and imagery (e.g., shadows cast on the wall of the cave by the firelight; the soul as the cause of all movement; peeling away fact to reveal number) that give us a sense of involvement with our own inner stirrings. Below are four selections to illustrate the power and quality of this kind of cosmological thinking.

The first excerpt apparently evolves out of a Platonic–Christian view of nature, wherein pure thought is considered higher, closer to God, than the physical or sensuous, which is construed as debased nature. The reader is given to undertstand very well that the connection between purity, abstraction, and truth is the construction of a male-oriented meaning system.

It is decided that matter is transitory and illusory like shadows on a wall cast by firelight; that we dwell in a cave, in the cave of our flesh, which is also matter, also illusory; it is decided that what is real is outside the cave, in a light brighter than we can imagine, that matter traps us in darkness. That the idea of matter existed before matter, and is more perfect, ideal.

Sic transit, how quickly pass, *gloria mundi*, the glories of this world, it is said.

Matter is transitory and illusory it is said. This world is an allegory for the next. The moon is an image of the Church, which reflects Divine Light. The wind is an image of the Spirit. The sapphire resembles the number eleven, which has transgressed ten, the number of the commandments. Therefore the number eleven stands for sin.

It is decided that matter is passive and inert, and that all motion originates from outside matter.

That the soul is the cause of all movement in matter and that the world was created by God: that all other movement proceeds from violent contact with other moving matter, which was first moved by God. That the spheres in perpetual movement are moved by the winds of heaven, which are moved by God, that all movement proceeds from God.

That matter is only a potential for form or potential for movement.

It is decided that the nature of woman is passive, that she is a vessel waiting to be filled.

It is decided that the existence of God can be proved by reason and that reason exists to apprehend God and Nature.

God is unchangeable, it is said. *Logos* is a quality of God created in man by God and it is eternal. The soul existed before the body and will live after it.

And it is stated elsewhere that Genesis cannot be understood without a master of mathematics.

That there are three degrees of abstraction, each leading to higher truths. The scientist peels away uniqueness, revealing category; the mathematician peels away sensual fact, revealing number; the metaphysician peels away even number and reveals the fruit of pure being. (pp. 5–6)

The second selection from Griffin describes the universe according to the Newtonian paradigm—a somewhat peculiar amalgamation of the clockwork machine and a deterministic version of the Christian God:

It is decided that matter is dead.

That the universe acts as a machine which can be described by describing the actions of particles of matter upon the particles according to immutable mechanical laws.

That the secret of the universe may be revealed only through understanding how it works. That behind the material "how" may lie the first cause, which is immaterial.

That the particular (like parts of a machine) may be understood without reference to the whole.

That the "celestial machine is to be likened not to a divine organism but to clockwork."

And it is discovered:

That the weights of two bodies are proportional to their masses.

That every body perseveres in its state of rest or uniform motion in a straight line, except as compelled to change that state by impressed forces.

That change of motion is proportional to the moving force impressed and takes place in the direction of the straight line in which such force is impressed.

That reaction is always equal and opposite to action.

Inertia is named.

And it is said that the maker of the universe was skilled in mechanics.

And it is discovered of light that the sines of the angles of refraction and incidence bear a true ratio and it is argued "was the eye contrived without skill in optics?"

And it is discovered that the heart circulates the blood through the body like a hydraulic pump.

And it is said that just as a king is the foundation of a kingdom, so the "heart of animals is the foundation of life, the sovereign of everything within them, the sun of their microcosm, that upon which all growth depends, from which all power proceeds."

And it is decided that the moment of death occurs at the moment the heart stops beating.

And it is determined that air has weight. That its volume is proportional inversely to its pressure.

That a heavy weight and a light weight falling reach the ground simultaneously.

That God is skilled in gravity.

And the parabola is discovered as a result of continuous horizontal movement and inexorable gravity.

And the ellipse is discovered to be the path of the planets.

Everything in the universe, it is perceived, moves according to the same laws: the earth, the moon, the wind, the rain, blood, atoms. (pp. 18–19)

The third selection moves from the scientific insights of the sixteenth and seventeenth centuries described above to the nineteenth century doctrine of Western progress, the natural laws of Darwin's "great discovery," and the use of both conceptions to bolster an ideology of domination and death as positive images.

Through evolution, "All corporeal and mental endowments will tend to progress toward perfection," it is written "The brain stands vertically poised on the summit of the backbone. Beyond there is no progress." (p. 25)

1859, Charles Darwin publishes *The Origin of the Species.* 1864, Navaho tribe forced from the Canyon de Chelly by the U. S. military and marched to a reservation. 1864, Contagious Disease Act in England requires all women suspected of prostitution to register as such. 1872, Married Women's Property Act, giving married women the right to own property, repealed. 1872, Alexandre de Lodyguine makes lamps with short, straight carbon filaments. 1872, Battey performs the first clitoridectomy in America. 1894, at the official academy of art in London, women are finally admitted to life drawing classes, but only when the model is partially draped. 1913, Emmeline Pankhurst's first hunger and thirst strike at Holloway Prison.

And it is said that without the male, "civilization would be impossible."

That mankind has evolved away from the bestial and closer to the angel . . .

That all animals are merely fetal stages of man, it is decided.

It is declared then that man is an animal, and he is the most perfect animal.

That according to the laws of survival . . . "the stronger and the better eqipped . . . eat the weaker and . . . the larger species devour the smaller."

And it is stated that if women were not meant to be dominated by men, they would not have been created weaker.

(That woman is as far from man as man is from the forest monkey's it is reflected.)

That the able survive.

As for instance the wolf who is swiftest and the slimmest.

That nature has selected this wolf and his offspring to live.

That stags have horns and cocks spurs

Because among males it is always the victor who is allowed to breed.

That the species is shaped by death. (pp. 27–28)

In the fourth and last selection from Griffin we move away from the older 'modern' cosmology, which celebrates 'man's' discovery of fixed natural laws and his consequent use and control of physical forces as symbols of divine progress, toward the dramatic new insights in postmodern science wherein a more creative and unpredictable process-centered universe is described.

The meson is discovered, the lambda, the sigma, the eta, the muon, pion, cascade, kaon, are discovered.

Thirty kinds of elementary particles are discovered.

It is suggested that the elementary particles may not be fundamental. Man's notion of nature is again threatened. Her face is changing, it is said. And it is suggested that a structure invisible to measurement is beneath particles.

But it is also argued that there are no elementary particles.

Every question about the essential nature of things, it is said, leads to another question.

Of the nature of earth, rock, river, cloud, light, wind, breath, flesh, of mules, of horses, of birds, of the body of woman, womb, breast, vulva, hair, it is acknowledged these are still unknown.

It is written that we are both spectator and part.

And time does not flow universally. The universe is amorphous, without fixed design, always subject to change. There is no absolute space. Time and space are one.

We are the rocks, we are soil, we are trees, rivers, we are wind, we carry the birds, the birds, we are cows, mules, we are horses, we are Solid elements, cause and effect, determinism and objectivity, it is said, are lost. *matter. We are flesh, we breathe, we are her body: we speak.* (p. 46)

The power of Griffin's work lies in her capacity to select quasi-historical language that poetically expresses comparative and contrasting world views and to stand, in some way, both inside and outside of these views. It is striking when, for example, we compare two such statements as:

That there are three degrees of abstraction, each leading to higher truths. The scientist peels away uniqueness, revealing category; the mathematician peels away sensual fact, revealing number; the metaphysician peels away even number and reveals the fruit of pure being... (p. 6)

We are the rocks, we are soil, we are trees, rivers, we are the wind, we carry the birds, the birds, we are cows, mules, we are horses, we are. Solid elements, cause and effect, determinism and objectivity, it is said, are lost. matter. We are flesh, we breathe, we are her body: we speak. (p. 46)

We can feel the power that comes with the insistent apprehension of contrasting paradigms. It is not that our sense of universality and abstraction in the first statement is more or less authentic than the grounded texture and organic imagery expressed in the second. The point is simply that Griffin seems able, through the use of graphic metaphors to move through the chambers of a house and to feel and express the underlying basis of being that inspires a different response to the size and color and resonance of each separate room—i.e., each separate cosmology.

COATES' THEORY OF MODERN AND POSTMODERN SOCIETY. A third example of comparative cosmologizing is summarized in the following chart, reprinted from Coates' *Resettling America*.[4] The thrust of the book is consonant with much that we have been saying here, suggesting that modernity is undergoing an historical transition between what it calls an industrial paradigm and a metaindustrial paradigm. The chart is sufficiently comprehensive and detailed that it needs little or no comment.

Table 5.1. Changing Definitions of Reality

	INDUSTRIAL PARADIGM	METAINDUSTRIAL PARADIGM
Progress and History	The belief in the inevitable, linear flow of time from a primitive, archaic, and savage past toward an advanced, modern, and civilized future. Newer is, therefore, better. Since the past is seen as inferior to the present, and the present inferior to the future (in material terms), a suggestion that we return to any technology or practice of the past is seen as a regression and a rejection of the ideology of progress. Through other civilizations may have experienced a cyclic rise and fall, the modern world is seen as proof that our scientifically based, technologically advanced civilization will remain forever young. But this belief requires that we sacrifice in the present to achieve even greater happiness in the future.	While some aspects of life have shown improvements, it is not axiomatic that history is a one-way, positive flow from the worse to the better. It is believed that history is a spiral, a progressive movement of recurring cycles of emergence and expression, growth and decay, rather than a linear model of time. You can't return to the past, since your world and images of reality have continually shaped and been shaped by the unfolding of events in time, but there are both necessary and inevitable organic and circular rhythms to the pulse of the individual life as well as the collective biography we call history. To deny and to resist this is to be out of step with time, and the consequences can only be negative. To sacrifice human dignity, freedom, and joy in the present as a means toward some future day of release is, at best, a suspect proposal.

Table 5.1. Continued: Changing Definitions of Reality

	INDUSTRIAL PARADIGM	METAINDUSTRIAL PARADIGM
Technology and Industrialization	It is believed that machines are value-free (only their use determines if they are good or bad) and that industrialization is both necessary and inevitable (it is the vehicle of progress), as well as good. If a technology or institution exists it is because it is more efficient than what it replaced, since technology is seen to evolve according to the natural "laws" of evolution such as "survival of the fittest." Large-scale, centralized organizations and machinery, and the sub-division of labor into increasingly specialized roles is the symbol, cause, and outcome of the evolution of society. While we might regret what has been lost, we must accept the verdict of evolution and history. What is, is what is best for humanity in the long run.	Technology is viewed as a language of social action. Built into the structure of various tools and techniques are certain values and assumptions that determine the personal, social, and political outcomes of their use. As the projection of human consciousness onto nature, technology can be either destructive and parasitic or constructive and symbiotic. We can unilaterally impose our will on the landscape or we can enter into a dialogue with climate, slope, and soil to co-create a humanized world. Human beliefs and values shape the nature of the tools and techniques used. The current technologies are neither necessary nor inevitable since they were consciously created to serve the socioeconomic and political needs of the power-elite of a particular form of culture. If we can alter how we think we can alter our technologies. Urban-industrial society is viewed as a failed experiment an evolutionary cul-de-sac.
Science and Knowledge	Science, as a rational logical, experimental system of inquiry is the *only* real way of knowing and experiencing the world. All other forms of knowing, such as myth, dream, intuition, and poetry are merely subjective. The ideal of all realtionships with other people or the natural environment is a cool,detached,	Science, as one among many modes of inquiry and ways of knowing, is viewed as potentially useful and good. But the view that "objective consciousness" and personal detachment are the only legitimate forms of knowledge is rejected as being hyper-rational and destructive. There are

Table 5.1. Continued: Changing Definitions of Reality

	INDUSTRIAL PARADIGM	METAINDUSTRIAL PARADIGM
Science and Knowledge	objective observation, an *I-It* relationship. All other expressions of relatedness represent a potentially regressive return to superstition, magic, or worse. Maturity demands objectivity and emotional control.	many realities and each has its appropriate way of knowing, including ways that require a "participative consciousness" and active concern for the subject. The goal is to establish an *I-Thou* relationship with all sentient beings and things. *I-It* relationships, like violence in general, should be undertaken with caution and regret.
Expertise and Power	Growing out of the views on science, it is believed that technically trained, rational, scientific planners and other certified experts, who know more about every aspect of the world than the common man, can and should hold positions of authority and power, and should direct the movement of society (planning *for* people). To introduce democratic principles into the management and design of a technological society is inappropriate and risks the breakdown of society. Ideology and politics should be entirely removed from the world of science and technology.	Given the doubts about the limits of science and scientism and given the respect held for all persons, it is believed that the role of scientists, professional planners, and experts of all kinds should be carefully constrained. To usurp the rule of the people in the name of expertise is to replace democracy with social science. Not only is it wrong but it won't work. Nonexperts are more knowledgeable, as "clients," about the nature of the problems and the effects of the solutions on their lives. To deny this kind of knowledge is to fail to address the problem. The goal should be planning and design by a dialogic, mutually beneficial process (planning *with* people). People can and should assume responsibility for their own lives.
Nature	It is believed that the domination of nature is both necessary and desirable, since nature is just so much undeveloped raw "stuff" to be used for human	The human domination of nature is seen as an epistemologically false, morally bankrupt concept. The earth and the cosmos are not merely made of

Table 5.1. Continued: Changing Definitions of Reality

	INDUSTRIAL PARADIGM	METAINDUSTRIAL PARADIGM
Nature	ends. Human beings are the end and purpose of evolution, and only people, as self-conscious beings, can be considered fully alive. A moral concern for other sentient beings (rock, soil, plants, and animals) is seen as an atavism from prescientific ages. (Nature is a commodity to be used.)	dead matter drifting through the voids of timeless space. They are whole and integrated, complex and alive. We belong to and participate in the life of this being, earth, and in the ordered life and rhythm of the universe. (Nature is a community to which we belong.)
The Individual versus the Group	In any conflict between the individual and the group, the interests of the group *must* take priority over the individual (the person exists for the company, not the company for the person). Society is like a machine. In order for it to run smoothly, all friction in its parts (individuals) must be eliminated. The group must shape the individual to fit its needs. It is believed that society is inevitably and necessarily repressive of the natural instincts and conditioned tendencies of the individual. Whether through overt power or behavioral engineering (it depends on your views of human nature), society must remake the person in its own image.	The primary purpose of any social organization, formal or informal, is to promote the growth and psychic development of the person. Society is viewed not as a machine, but as a complex web of emotionally charged, intimate, and diverse patterns of relationships rooted in shared space and belief. The nature of any group does and should grow out of the interactions and character of its members. Individual persons must participate in the process of shaping society to the needs of the self (not the ego). Society is an organic whole.
Human Nature (the Self)	Since the ideologies represented by industrialism include both capitalism and socialism, as well as liberalism and conservatism, human nature is variously defined as basically good or bad, improvable or not. What links this spectrum is the belief that production	While the ideologies represented by meta-industrialism vary considerably, the basic assumption is that, properly nourished in a healthy cultural milieu, most people will behave cooperatively rather than competitively and will transcend their small and limited egos. To

Table 5.1. Continued: Changing Definitions of Reality

	INDUSTRIAL PARADIGM	METAINDUSTRIAL PARADIGM
Human Nature (the Self)	consumption and the improvement of the material conditions of life are the goals of both the individual and the society. You are what you consume, and the more you possess the more you are a success. Happiness, the goal of human existence, is a function of the acquisition of people, goods, and power. The society that succeeds in maximizing these needs of human nature is the best society.	realize this potential, the culture must provide both techniques and opportunities for psychic development. Since the goal of human existence is self-transformation, material goods must be kept to a minimum to avoid breeding attachment. You are what your being is.
The Meaning of Work	The purpose of work is twofold: 1) for the organization it is to maximize profit and productivity (for the state or the shareholders, depending on ideology and socioeconomic form); 2) for the individual it is to make the maximum money for the least effort, or if you are a "professional" to make the most money while providing the greatest service to humanity, advancing your career, and so on. Of course we all work to create more leisure time for which we then spend our money *having fun*. The ultimate end of work is to escape from work into a world of impulse release and fantasy.	The purpose of work is to maximize the welfare of the worker, the productive organization, and the broader community. In producing goods and services the goal should be to serve others while minimizing harm to naturally occurring ecosystems. In assuming responsibility for his or her actions, the worker learns to temper selfish impulses and in so doing promotes his or her own good. The reward for work is not leisure, it is play. Leisure is empty time and space that requires work to fill up. Play is a spontaneous enjoyment of creation that itself is the outcome of right livelihood.
Size, Centralization, and Growth	Big is better. Large, centralized, formal organizations are natural outcomes of an evolutionary process. They are more efficient because of the economies of scale and they are more effective because they exercise more power and control	Small is not only beautiful, it is usually better. Although large scale, centralized organizations can be appropriate to some tasks (for example, administering and managing a public utility), large organizations with widespread geographical and

Table 5.1. Continued: Changing Definitions of Reality

	INDUSTRIAL PARADIGM	METAINDUSTRIAL PARADIGM
Size, Central- ization, and Growth	over their internal and external environments. Growth in the size of enterprises (whether economic, governmental, or social), like economic growth in general, is necessary and good. You must grow or collapse. "What's good for G.M. is good for the country," and so on. Small, informal groups, such as clans, neighborhoods, and extended families are archaic, inefficient, and inhibitive of the growth of progressive, modern, rational, formal institutions. While such primary groups may continue to exist due to the inertia of custom and habit, in the future they will necessarily decrease in extent and importance. Many of our current social problems and political abuses can be traced to the persistence of ties to blood and soil.	political power should be avoided. They are difficult to control, often impersonal, and frequently insensitive (cybernetically speaking) to feedback from the environments they affect. Since it is well known that there is an appropriate economy of scale for every technology, there is an appropriate size for every enterprise. (Bigger is not necessarily better.) And since many goals besides task efficiency must be achieved by human groups, what's good for profit in the production of automobiles is not necessarily good for the ecology or the country. Small, informal, face-to-face groups are and have always been the substance and foundation of effective and healthy collectivities. Communal organizations, such as families, clans, and neighborhoods should be strengthened, and informal groups within large enterprises should be encouraged.
The Impor- tance of Place	Like local societies and other remnants of the past, the uniqueness, character, history, and texture of particular places is more often than not a hindrance to progress. The best kind of space is a flat, empty universal plane that can accept people, buildings, highways, and other "improvements" with minimum alteration. Universal, modern architecture	The homogenization of place and culture have proceeded hand in hand with industrialization. Like any healthy ecology, an alive, human ecology should aim at maximizing the diversity of landscapes and regions. Architecture and planning should enhance the particular and unique character of localities, creating a symbiosis of nature and culture, earth-

Table 5.1. Continued: Changing Definitions of Reality

	INDUSTRIAL PARADIGM	METAINDUSTRIAL PARADIGM
The Importance of Place	with a uniform year-round microclimate is both a symbol and means toward greater wealth and human betterment. Reduced costs and the promotion of industrialization result from the standardization of building parts and local sites.	scape and mindscape. The outcome would be a humanized nature that would represent an acceleration of evolution.

In these three examples we have a philosopher, literary artist, and social theorist who present contrasting world views which allow them to move across a varied landscape of ideas and to make comparative statements out of what might otherwise seem to be relative intellectual disorder. Assuming we take seriously this capacity for more comprehensive thinking, we then come to the question of how to approach the specific *content* of a cosmologically oriented curriculum. Certainly we cannot *begin* with the high-level abstractions reflected in the Brumbaugh and Coates illustrations or the sophisticated weaving of specific historical and literary allusions in Griffin's work. These show, rather, where one might *arrive—at the end of a good deal of careful study and questioning of cosmological descriptions.*[5] Our task now is to search for descriptive materials appropriate for the *initial study* of cosmologies and to explore what kinds of questions might be raised within the framework of such a curriculum.

Cosmologies and Questions

TOWARD A CURRICULUM FRAMEWORK CONSTRUCTED FROM SPECIFIC COSMOLOGIES. The following example is intended to provide only a glimpse of a more systematic alternative to the current fragmentary basket-full-of-topics found in most humanistic courses of study. Our example begins by raising the metaphysical question: *How did the world/universe begin and what place is human life to occupy within such a world/universe?* Our approach to this question comes from the perspective of four varied cosmologies which have imaginative and culturally significant things to say about these issues: the Platonic vision (as best that might be reconstructed); a Judeo–Christian vision; the contemporary world view, which we might refer to as humanistic modernism; and the cosmology of the Hopi Indians of the American southwest. In our hypothetical curriculum, we would present brief statements of each of these world views and then move into detailed and focused comparisons. A very brief sample of descriptive material and questions raised by this material is presented below.

FOUR PERSPECTIVES.

The Platonic vision. The Platonic cosmos envisions three very different domains of reality. We have the perfect realm of forms, the realm of nature, and the city-state of humans. The world of form is true, perfect, unchanging and everlasting. It is a motionless world of eternity. There is a second realm that we know as the universe of the heavens and the earth. This realm arose in the transition from disorder to order under the influence and power of spirit—one might call it a god or a demiurgos. Before the demiurgos intervened, this earth was in a state of disorder, chaos, a domain of brutal necessity or aimless causality, not subject to purpose or direction. But the demiurgos gave this planetary system, including the earth, a certain degree of intelligibility. The demiurgos has a world-soul from which has emanated the many forms of matter and life in the world. And all this world is in motion—material objects are constantly being created and changed; mountains rise from the sea and erode away into plains; what we know as species of plants and animals struggle to be created, struggle to survive, and finally give way to new forms of life.

Humans are part of the world of nature. They are like animals, except that they have varying degrees of intelligence and can vaguely penetrate the logos of the perfect formal realm. The true representation of the forms is, however, never available to humans. The demiurgos has created particulars patterned after the perfect forms, but they are imperfect copies. Humans, like other animals, first apprehend reality with their raw senses but then, unlike animals, give meaning to that reality. Our human understandings of logos or form—call them myths—are partly true and partly illusion.

The world, then, is actually a debased or imperfect version of the realm of perfect forms. It is at this point that we can see the function of human culture as it evolves in the city-state. It is here that the more intelligent humans who have some dim comprehension of the realm of perfect forms can attempt to correct or improve upon the mistakes originally made in the creations of the demiurgos.

The Judeo-Christian world view. One might compare this Platonic scenario of the beginning of our human domain with that of the Judeo-Christian cosmology. Here we begin with one God, an unmoved mover, existing totally outside any creation with which we humans are familiar. The world is created as a loving act of God to please Himself. Humans are, initially, the crowning achievement of this God. But one particular gift to the human is unusual: it is the freedom to *choose* obedience to God as opposed to obedience to one's own egocentric desires. Humans do, in fact, choose to disobey God, to sin, and are then destined to the everlasting punishment of a difficult and harsh struggle for survival on this planet. There comes, however, a major turning point in human history. God sends to earth his Son, Jesus Christ, in human form. The example and message Jesus brings is that salvation, victory over suffering and death, is possible through God's grace and through the special significance of Jesus' life. God (and so Jesus, also) is willing to sacrifice His only Son to cleanse and wash away the sins of the humans themselves.

Within the meanings of the Platonistic and Christian cosmologies, both of which are, in all likelihood, embedded within our Western consciousness, we can make some interesting comparisons. For the Platonistic cosmology there is a world of perfect forms but no personified ultimate divine being. Neither is there any ultimate power of goodness and grace intervening in the affairs of humans to save them from their own folly. Both cosmologies do, however, share the assumption of a bifurcated reality. There is the world of nature and the world of perfect being. Both see humans as caught in some peculiar way between these two domains. The way out (if there is one) for the Platonist is through self-purification by means of reflection and intelligence. The way out for the Christian is through a life of devotion to the body of Christ (the Church) and the loving spirit of God.

Both meaning systems also see 'nature' on this planet as a somewhat debased version of a higher perfection. For the Platonist, the inferiority of nature is a consequence of mistakes committed by the demiurgos; for the Christian it is simply in the scheme of things that there is a hierarchical order in the universe—a great chain of being from God to the archangels to the angels to the humans to the beasts to the plants to inert matter. Both the Platonist and the Christian see humans as superior to 'lower forms of being,' as having a unique quality of mind or soul or intelligence. But the Christian sees this essential quality as given for a particular purpose: to understand and to know God so that humans may someday return to heaven and be at home with God and Jesus and the Angels.

The modern humanistic vision. For the modern humanist, the universe began, as twentieth century astronomers and physicists tell us, with the big bang. (Whence came the initial matter–energy that expanded during the big bang remains an embarrassingly unanswered question.) Herein, however, is the most profound difference between the Platonist/Christian and the modern humanist. For the latter the central focus of concern is on the one natural universe. From the big bang to the time of our contemporary world has taken, it is said, about twenty billion years and been characterized by a process of continuous change called 'evolution.' Evolution is the natural movement within a single universe, in which higher forms of life are explained in the same terms as other changes, —e.g., the formation of the stars and the planets. All evolution is simply the consequence of the laws of nature working themselves out. The implications for humans living in this single realm of nature is that the destiny of the species is tied to its own ability to cope and understand in greater depth and comprehensiveness the laws of nature—what some observers now call 'co-evolution.' Nature, instead of being a debased representation of perfect form or a lower form of God's creation, provides the resources and the setting within which humans are to constantly improve this planet, if not the reaches of outer space.

We might point here, also, to the profound difference in the way humanists, versus Christians, see the concepts of history and time. The Christian lives within the temporal framework of The Holy Bible, which describes the circumstances under which humans will be saved from toil and death. For him or her, there is a single true history, both for the past and the future; at some point, time will come to an end. For the humanist, there is a continuing sense of time often associated with the *progressive development* of the human condition. It is assumed that within the one realm of the universe, we will come to understand the secrets of nature and be able to control with increasing certainty our own destiny.

The Hopi Way The story of the Hopi begins with a solitary creator, Taiowa. All is endless space; the infinite, in the mind of Taiowa. Taiowa first creates a male being, Sotuknang, who makes the infinite manifest—solids, water, wind. Taiowa then creates a female being, Spider Woman, to help Sotuknang. Spider Woman creates from the earth trees, bushes, plants, flowers, and all kinds of seed-bearers to clothe the earth. And likewise she creates the various birds and animals, as well as the forms of humankind. The Hopi people then pass through three worlds, each of which is eventually destroyed because of the pride and arrogance of the humans. Finally, there is an emergence into a fourth world and Sotuknang tells humans that it is the World Complete. It is not a beautiful land, easy like the previous ones. It has everything to choose from, but what the people choose will determine if, this time, they can carry out the plan of creation or whether it must in time again be destroyed. Noteworthy in the Hopi cosmology are both its similarities to and differences from the Christian story. Like Genesis, it begins with an 'infinite person', a conception or idea before the substantive world; and likewise we have the problem of human arrogance and disobedience to the point where the world is actually destroyed and recreated (much like the story of Noah). But unlike the Christian world view, the Hopi do not set out two realms of being between which humans are somehow caught. There is only a single world of nature where humans belong, where they can live in peace and be at home. And as the story continues, it is clear that humans have no special claim to this world. They are to coexist in unity with mother earth, the father sun, the earth-corn, the sky, the winds, the rain, and the other living things who are always to be their neighbors. Unlike the Platonistic vision, the earth is not a debased set of flawed particularities that represent forms or ideas existing in another perfect realm. The earth is a friendly, congenial place, where life may at times be hard but where there is to be an underlying wholeness and harmony among all of its inhabitants. The constant concern for and living with this sense of universal relatedness is called by the people themselves The Hopi Way.

Comparisons between the Hopi and the modern humanist are also interesting. While both see themselves living within a single natural universe through a possible infinity of time, the scientific–technological humanist imagines a world in continuous radical change, transformed through the ingenuity and intelligence of the human mind—the heavens and the earth and the waters are simply resources, to be used to enhance the favored human position on the planet. For the Hopi, on the other hand, the application of technology to the material world is a relatively minor aspect of one's relationship to the universe. For beneath the manifest world is an unseen quality of reality which reveals itself in dreams and song and and dance and ceremony. Within this less obvious aspect of reality one must constantly search for ways to remain in touch with the totality of the natural world, every part of which has a significant place within the whole. The major adaptive technique for the Hopi is thus 'right thinking..'

THE SIGNIFICANCE OF COSMOLOGICAL COMPARISONS. These cosmological illustrations suggest, perhaps, in a more concrete way, the kinds of questions one can raise within the framework of a curriculum consisting of diverse holistic meaning systems or cosmologies. The approach is clearly normative; a central purpose is to search out more and less authentic or positive aspects of the ways humans may come to construe the universe. Moreover, it makes an explicit effort to correct our underlying bias, which celebrates almost exclusively the particular achievements of the contemporary Western way of life. Rather than seeing human history within the traditional Western paradigm—as a progressive movement from the primitive 'savage' to the 'successful modern'—we look for both strengths and deficiencies in the various meaning systems that constitute the legacy of our collective human memory. In short, we would stress the fact that modernity has its shortcomings as well as its achievements. The scientific evolutionary story, for example, which begins with the big bang and proceeds to intelligent life on earth, reveals not only great scientific ingenuity and insight; it commonly reveals the arrogance of a pseudo-vision. For it suggests that the naturalistic description of how human life evolved here on this planet also explains the underlying purpose and meaning of that life. In this sense we modern people exercise a kind of stubborn denial of the limitation (which Plato accepted) in our capacity for knowing the ultimate value of our own humanness.

Likewise, the widely accepted Western view that there is to be some miraculous escape out of this flawed planet into a paradise or new Jerusalem—inherited partly from Plato and the Biblical prophecies and partly from science fiction and NASA—may well be a disastrously problematic cosmological notion for the future of the planet. The Hopi conception of the future may, in fact, be more authentic—that we are, indeed, already in a fourth and last world from which there is no escape, and thus we have to learn to live in harmony with the other forms of being here and now. This may be the gift of a very wise culture, albeit one that is relatively primitive in material technology.

The Limits of Communication Across Cosmologies Based on Underlying Differences in Language and Perception.

While we are arguing from our brief example above that one can gain broad and significant insights by comparing and contrasting whole cosmologies around perennial metaphysical issues and that this justifies developing a curriculum which moves in such a direction, there is a deeper issue that must be addressed. In many cases, a valid comparison of the underlying qualities of radically different cosmologies may not be possible when they are expressed by radically different languages. Cross-cosmological understanding may require even that we undergo prelinguistic changes in how we actually perceive and apprehend reality. From this perspective, understanding differences among the Platonist, the Christian, the modern humanist, and the Hopi is very likely beyond the reach of education as we now understand it.

We would maintain, for example, that a major source of *mis*understanding in comparing and contrasting cosmologies lies in our materialistic assumptions about the underlying nature of reality and the particular structure of thought and language used to describe and communicate that reality. Thus, in our modern cosmology, the speaker stands outside the 'subject matter,' treating it as an object of consideration. This dualistic subject–object style of thinking carries with it a pervasive bias which inevitably colors the way we come to understand any cosmology. Whorf describes and documents the plausibility and importance of this thesis:

> Every language binds the thoughts of its speakers by the involuntary patterns of its grammar. . . Languages differ not only in how they build their sentences but in how they break down nature into the elements to put into those statements. . . .
>
> For example, English terms, like "sky", "hill," "swamp," persuade us to regard some elusive aspect of nature's endless variety as a distinct *thing*, almost like

a table or chair. Thus English and similar tongues lead us to think of the universe as a collection of detached objects of different sizes. . . Thus as goes our segmentation of the face of nature, so goes our physics of the cosmos. . . . (p. 153)

Whorf then gives an illustration of his point in a comparison between the English and Hopi languages. He says:

> We are constantly reading into nature action-entities, simply because our verbs must have substantives in front of them. We have to say "It flashed" or "A light flashed", setting up an actor, "it" or "light", to perform what we call an "action", "to flash." Yet the flashing and the light are one and the same! The Hopi language reports the flash with a simple verb, ri-pi: "flash (occurred)." There is no division into subject and predicate, not even a suffix like -t of Latin tona-t ("it thunders"). Hopi can and does have verbs without subjects, a fact which may give that tongue potentialities as a logical system for exploring and understanding aspects of the universe. Undoubtedly modern science, strongly reflecting western Indo-European languages, often does as we all do, sees action and forces where it might be better to see states. On the other hand, "state" is a noun, and as such it enjoys the superior prestige traditionally attaching to the subject or "thing" class; therefore science is exceedingly ready to speak of states if permitted to manipulate the concept like a noun. Perhaps, in place of the "states" of an atom or a dividing cell, it would be better if we could manipulate as readily a more verb-like concept but without the concealed premises of actor and action. (pp. 155)

Here Whorf is presenting us with the possibility of building into our notion of being the dynamic process of becoming. An atom or cell is not, in fact, in a static state; rather Whorf suggests that we might well collapse the ideas of movement or process within the idea 'being' or 'state'. The basic point is clear: there is a critical interaction between the way we perceive, apprehend, and then actually experience the world and the communicative structures used to express this experience. To use a common communicative structure across radically different cosmologies may well misstate or understate distinctions between cosmologies.

But this is only half the problem. There is also the relationship between language and the underlying qualities of perception or apprehension that occur prior to language. The cosmology of a culture (especially a preliterate culture) might well be understood not through language but through perceptions experienced as a result of living through powerful, dramatic ritual. Christianity is an interesting mixed case, since it places great importance both on written text and ritual sacrament. Even Christianity, however, in its English-speaking institutional expressions of the church, operates out of a subject–object framework. There is God 'out there' and humans 'here';

there is nature 'there' and humans 'here'. God acts upon humans; humans act upon nature. There is the structure of experience and language in which a subject acts upon an object.

Suppose, however, we should undertake to describe a particular cosmology in which perception itself is altered—one that actually sees the world differently from the standard subject–object modality common to our modern experience. (The Hopi, according to Whorf, is probably such an example.) Obviously, the communicative structure must be changed to accommodate the perceptions. This is, in fact, the case that Barfield[7] makes in his discussion of some preliterate peoples' understanding of nature.

Barfield begins his thesis with a distinction among four different qualities or operations of human thought. The first is the unconscious sensory process in which the neutral structure of the sentient being interacts with what he calls "the particles out there," that is, the micro-electronic events that physicists assert are the underlying 'beings' which together constitute the larger macro world most familiar to our casual human experience. Such an interaction produces, in the more complex aggregated stages, figures or 'objects' in the world, as opposed simply to the underlying micro events in the human nervous system. The most basic unconscious interaction, between the dynamic particle world of nature and the particle world within the sentient body, Barfield calls "participation." The second level of apprehension, where humans collectively name figures in the world (Whorf's slicing up of nature), is called "figuration". On a third level, Barfield asserts, one "thinks *about* the figures" in the world. And, on a fourth level, one can "think about what it means to think about the figures" in the world— which is what we do in psychology or philosophy.

Barfield suggests that some preliterate peoples actually experience the processes of "participation" and "figuration" in ways that radically differ from our conventional modern subject-object world. According to Barfield, early anthropoligists assumed as a matter of course that primitive peoples (i.e., surviving groups of preliterate peoples with whom Westerners came into contact) perceived and structured reality much as did their anthropological observers. Their 'bizarre' beliefs and actions were ascribed to an inadequate or incorrect knowledge of the material world. Native people's experiencing of spirits or their intimate feelings for mountains, rocks, lakes, trees, and animals as sharing a common lineage or even common souls was seen simply as evidence of intrapsychic projections of unconscious material, or as pre-scientific modes of explanation. Barfield brings into question these earlier conclusions, refering to subsequent observations by Levy-Bruhl and Durkheim, which suggest another interpretation, namely, that primitive peoples actually engaged in a fundamentally different perceptual process of "coming to know." Levy-Bruhl calls this the "law of participation." Barfield then elaborates what he means by "participation," including a quotation from Durkheim:

> 'Participation' begins by being an activity, and essentially a communal or social activity. It takes place in rites and initiation ceremonies resulting in "collective mental states of extreme emotional intensity, and which representation is as yet undifferentiated from the movements and actions which make the communion towards which it tends a reality to the group. Their participation in it is so effectively *lived* that it is not yet properly imagined."

> This stage is not only pre-logical, but also premythical. It is anterior to collective representations themselves, as I have been using the term. Thus the first develoment Durkheim traces is from symbiosis or active participation (where the individual feels that his ancestors were the totem, that he will be when he dies, etc.). From this symbolic apprehension he then arrives at the duality, with which we are more familiar, of ideas on the one hand and numinous religion on the other.

> This extra sensory participation of the percipient in the representation involves a similar link between the representations themselves, and, of course, between one percipient and another. 'Mana' or 'waken' (which *we* can only translate by abstract terms like 'totemic principle,' 'life principle' or—since it is also present in inanimate objects—'being') is anterior to the individuality of persons and objects; these, (says Durkheim) are rather apprehended by the very primitive as 'stopping places of mana.'[8]

In short, Barfield maintains that there may be a preconceptual process in which the micro world of humans interacts with the micro world of nature, and only at a second stage is this set of unified interactions transformed into a dualistic subject–object world of human observer *here* and materials things and figures 'out there.' Moreover, through cultural conditioning it is presumably possible either to sense one's participation in this 'unconscious' initial stage of perception or to defend oneself against any apprehension of its existence—the latter being characteristic of non-superstitious or 'anti-occult' modern people. Thus Barfield is suggesting that cultures exist and have existed in which humans perceive the sense of unitary participation in this micro world, first on an individual level and then as a collective representation of that group's experience.

Our point should now be clear. Given two cosmologies with very different perceptions of and experiences with nature which consequently have language structures that reflect these differences, one must ask how there can be any significant communication across such world views. The modern scientific materialist, for example, sees the world as ultimately consisting of visible-touchable-hearable objects, moved or changed only by 'natural'—i.e., palpable, material—forces. For the Hopi, on the other hand, the world consists of visible and invisible forms, both of which are vividly experienced and connected—a world in which human self and nature cannot be sharply separated; a world in which thoughts and songs speak as importantly to and equally affect, for example, the sprouting of a corn seedling as do the more obvious material things such as the sun in the sky or the moisture in the soil.

So the problem of comprehending cosmological comparisons is not solved simply by the careful study and analysis of different world views. It requires that we take seriously the possibility that our perceptions and the communicative expression of these perceptions may distort or exclude significant aspects of nature. A major thesis of this book in fact has been that the culture of modernity has a truncated repertory of images and symbols as well as a heavy dualistic construction of reality, both of which result in an inadequate language and metaphysics, which, in turn, leads to a defective physics and psychology.

As an orientation to Section Three below, we would point out here that there is one comprehensive and radical metaphysical system worked out explicitly to deal with shortcomings in the various cosmologies that give meaning to our contemporary lives. This is the process theory developed initially by Whitehead and Hartshorne. Whitehead's position is that the common sense modern (19th-century) view of the actual world contains a number of serious errors. First, it places inordinate stress on the most obvious and public things around us as the underlying or core definition of our natural world—in Barfield's terms, we begin our conception of knowing at a second level, with figuration, *after* the unconscious micro process of participation has already taken place. Second, Whitehead argues that the subject-acting-on-object structure of our perceptual and linguistic experience may work as a convenient abstraction for manipulating aspects of our macro world but certainly does not provide an adequate feeling for or understanding of the micro world such as Barfield describes in his notion of "participation." Whitehead maintains, rather, that the subject–object relationship is relative: reality is made up of dynamic "occasions" in which object or datum provokes subject but is subsequently subsumed and transformed by the subject, which has its own aims and purposes, its own "subjective forms". Third, it is erroneous to construe the world, in any basic sense, as static. A rock, for example, is not a stable material 'thing'; rather it consists of millions of micro events constantly in the process of creating and recreating themselves. Finally, human experience is intrinsically in and part of the physical reality of the natural world. We do not process information coming from 'out there' with a disembodied mind that exists independent of nature.

Within the process framework it is, therefore, perfectly plausible to interpret instances of preliterate or spiritually oriented people's seemingly 'bizarre' engagement with nature as genuine participation, and to assume that vibrations or micro occasions literally flow from trees and animals and water and are physically transformed and interpreted at a pre-senuous level within the human nervous system. As Barfield says, this experience is presumably premythic and prelinguistic. Whitehead suggests that it requires feeling with the whole body—he uses the term "non-sensuous perception." It is evident," he says, "that this definition is wider than the narrow definition based upon sense perception, sense, and the bodily organs."[9] To illustrate the fact that this deeper and more comprehensive capacity for perception is available, he observes that we apprehend at each microsecond a great deal more than our physiological or cultural resources allow us to bring to consciousness.

> Roughly speaking, it is that portion of our past lying between a tenth of a second and a half a second ago. It is gone, and yet it is here. It is our indubitable self, the foundation of our present existence. Yet the present occasion while claiming self-identity, while sharing the very nature of the bygone occasion in all its living activities, nevertheless, is engaged in modifying it, in adjusting it to other *purposes.* The present moment is constituted by the influx of *the other* into the self-identity which is the continued life of the immediate past within the immediacy of the present. (p. 181)

"It is gone and yet it is here" means, paradoxically, that we apprehend, although we may not consciously experience, a fullness in the multiplicity of micro occasions interacting within and between us and nature—all in a split second; yet what we can actually reconstruct through our gross sensibilities and later in our memory and language is only a sliver of that totality.

Conclusion

It is clear to us that moving beyond modernity toward a more coherent and authentic cosmology will require substantial risk-taking and uncharted action. However, prior to such action it may be wise and useful to work toward the imaginative study of the various possibilities that emerge from the long record of ways humans have attempted to construe the cosmos of our universe. Here we return to the search not only for metaphors, symbols, and images but also for plausible visions. For us the process thought that has emerged in philosophy, theoretical physics, and religion over the past fifty years and is currently emerging in transpersonal psychology and education—with its central image of organic creativity, balance, and the internal relatedness of all being—provides us with a vision of considerable hope for moving beyond the limitations of sensate, fragmented modernity. The rest of this book is an effort to share some of this vision with the reader, especially as it relates to possible ways we might think about curriculum and teaching.

PART THREE:

Process Cosmology

Introduction and Overview

In Part Two we presented and evaluated a number of subject matter areas which would seem, initially, to offer a broad and integrated conception of knowledge. We found that while there may be holistic fields of academic study, they are increasingly burdened with the weight of overspecialization. We concluded that the category which most closely fits our conception of deep and comprehensive knowing is denoted by the somewhat ambiguous term *cosmology*.

We then described a type of thinking and subject matter—call it a curriculum theory—that might characterize the process of comparing and contrasting various aspects of differing cosmologies. We argued that within such a curriculum students should be encouraged to raise not only the broadest of philosophical and scientific concerns but also more specific questions which could presumably be referred back to the framework of whole cosmologies wherein one might test the significance, relevance, or power of both the question and the cosmology. (One might explore in considerable factual detail, for example, the question of whether or not a Hopi world view, which posits a vivid 'physical' connection between an unseen world of thought and imagination and the public material world, is more or less adaptive for either the survival or simple comfort of a human society than is the modern cosmology, where we sharply separate fact from fiction, thought from substance.)

Once having accepted a cosmologically oriented curriculum, a more difficult issue presented itself: How does one learn to think beyond the confines of one's immediate cosmology (or its related neighbors) when such thinking would seem to require that we make radical shifts in how we actually perceive the world and structure the language used to describe that world? This issue emerged from our suggestion that we need not only to study the more commonplace cosmologies that implicitly rattle around in our heads but also to engage ourselves imaginatively with bold new cosmologies that might deviate sharply from the metaphysical and cultural assumptions of modernity.

At this point in the book it is important to alert the reader to the fact that we are here making a substantial new claim—beyond simply assuming the desirability of developing and using a broadly based curriculum presenting and critiquing alternative cosmologies. We are now arguing that there is on the scene a metaphysical cosmology that deserves special consideration as a basis from which to evaluate the strengths and deficiencies of modernity and the historical cultures out of which it was formed. That cosmology is perhaps most approriately called *process.*[1]

We should emphasize at the outset that process has been developed largely as an abstract metaphysical cosmology and is only now beginning to generate the specific cultural underpinnings that would be required to give such a meaning system flesh and blood. (We do know that there have been fully developed living cultures, such as the Hopi, which show striking process characteristics.) The implications of this are that we construe process, initially at least, not as a necessarily separate *cultural* cosmology. Perhaps its most useful function is as a metaphysical system to provide us with a range of metaphors, queries, and strategies by which to evaluate the contemporary cultural choices that daily appear before us.

So our explication and advocacy of process cosmology should not mislead the reader to conclude that we support the abandoning of existing cosmologies (even assuming that were possible) and the building of some totally new alternative or counter culture. Our understanding is that there are qualities of process in all cosmologies, especially given the broad range of interpretation within any particular meaning system. (One may think of Judeo-Christianity, for example, and its complex history of ambiguous and contradictory interpretation.) Obviously the issue is not simply one of constructing a postmodern process world to replace the more limited or inadequate culture currently consisting of some admixture of nativism, Platonism, Judeo-Christianity, and/or modernity. That would be naive in the extreme. The problem, rather, is to select an approach toward being and knowing that will engage modernity in a profound and constructive dialogue with other meaning systems that may ameliorate or remedy its shortcomings. For cultural cosmologies do not simply die and waste away; they are rather transformed by historical circumstances into variations of the old and eventually into new ones. Such transformations require a capacity to understand the old cosmologies as well as a vision of the transformative connections between the old and some new or renewed cosmology. The most imaginative and creative cosmologists, we think, are those who are attempting to work out these transformative connections.

At this point we see connections between a modern and post-modern world being built along three possible lines:

1. *First is the effort to restate concepts of the perennial religions and philosophies* (Buddhism, Sufism, Judeo-Christianity, Hinduism, and so on) *to make them more compatible with our notions of modern science.* Notable in this effort, for example, is the work of Ralph Wendell Burhoe, who states:

> When thus properly translated or interpreted, not only our traditional Western religious species but all the great religions can again become more effective in enculturating in the "brain pool" of the "natural" or commonsense self of the body, a new being that integrates intimately with the species and with the intimate reality system called "nature," the "natural system", or "the way things are" in the sciences and called God or the Kingdom of God in Christian theology.[2]

Thus Burhoe maintains that reconstruing the Christian conception of "God" or the "Kingdom of God" to encompass the naturalistic drama of biological evolution, including such non-theological insights as mutation, sexual variation, and individual and species extinction, helps move our thinking toward this kind of compatibility.

2. *Second, there is the attempt to unveil or emphasize the more mystical or poetic qualities in science and technology; to make them strike a more personal chord and resonate with our theological sensibilities.* We would note, for example, the TV series *Cosmos*, written and narrated by Carl Sagan, whose singsongy voice often intoned more in the style of a priest or cantor than a scientist. Included within this genre are works already mentioned—Capra's *Tao of Physics* and Zukav's *The Dancing WuLi Masters*—which attempt to show that theoretical physics has moved beyond the limits of materialistic positivism and now describes nature in ways strikingly similar to the Eastern perennial traditions.

3. The third strategy for transforming modernity is through what Whitehead calls *speculative philosophy*—that is, the systematic construction of imaginative new cosmologies and explicit statements of their underlying metaphysical assumptions, as well as their application to our common sense experience in science, morality, art, and religion.

Which of these strategies (or combinations thereof) will be most effective in transforming modernity is problematic. Those who choose one of the first two options—reconceiving either perennial religions and philosophies or modern science within some broader context so as to include the other—at least have the advantage of building on rich and longstanding cultural bases. Religions have an established theology, sacred text, ritual, martyred heroes, and a full range of artistic icons. The sciences have disciplined research methodology, classic experiments, the discovery of predictable events and universal constants, elegant theory, and Nobel laureates. The disadvantage, of course, is that these two traditions have now gone their separate ways for some four hundred years and each bears the distortions of living with the separation.

The strength of the bolder adventure called *speculative philosophy* or explicit cosmology-building is precisely that it can begin with the universe still in one piece. Metaphysical constructs such as nature/God/culture and body/spirit/mind are still together. We need not rationalize in some especially persuasive way, for example, how to fit God, the unmoved mover, into an all-inclusive conception of universe or nature, unless our logic or creative intuition pushes us toward such a necessity. (We need only note Burhoe's strained effort to equate science's "natural system" with Christianity's "Kingdom of God" to anticipate the difficulty of working from the core statements of existing cosmologies.) But there are certainly questions to be asked of this approach. How do we compose powerful imagery, poetry, drama, and liturgy to transcend the meanings and structures of language associated with prior cosmologies? How do we move beyond the complex hyperintellectual/conceptual language still used by an elitist group of academic process philosophers? Where do we find new vivid metaphors?

Despite these problems, our sympathies are very much with the speculative approach. In the next three chapters we shall introduce the reader to our particular variation of process thought based mainly on a Whiteheadian theme, although we clearly see both process and its educational implications in broader terms. Chapter Six, "From Scientific Modernity Toward a Process Universe", describes some of the assumptions of a nineteenth-century materialistic cosmology and then shows how transitional thinkers in the fields of biological evolution (Lorenz, Thomas, Koestler, Bateson) and physics (Fraser, Von Weizsacker) have struggled to move beyond the contradictions and limitations of this earlier conception of nature. In Chapter Seven, we summarize as briefly and coherently as possible the central concepts of Whitehead's speculative philosophy. The freshness and power of the approach is, we think, its ability to relate a naturalistic conception of becoming and being, an ontology, to human perception and experience, so as to avoid the fundamental dualisms of the earlier 'scientific' world view. Statements describing aspects of process presented in Chapter Five provide something of an introduction to these ideas, since here we confront a strange new Whiteheadian language.

In Chapter Eight, "The Moral Basis of Process Education: Intimacy, Intensity, and Balance," we speculate on how the connection in process thought between ontology and epistemology, between the nature of becoming and being on the one hand and the nature of experience and symbolization on the other, clarifies important difficulties inherent in the heavy reliance placed by contemporary democratic theory on the presumed power of cognition, conceptualization, and linguistic reasoning as bases for understanding and resolving current problems of modernity.

Chapter Six

From Scientific Modernity
Toward a Process Universe

Modern people see the world within a single natural universe; however, hidden behind this unity are several domains of reality. There is the domain of natural objects "out there" (or the world of energy and micro particles objectified on stained microscope slides or revealed as waves on the oscilloscope). There is the world of the perceiving subject, the senses of touch or smell or the picture registered on the retina. There is the domain of ideas, abstractions, facts, stories, and myths which give significance to the world of objects and the senses. Scientiists study the world of nature and describe the elaborate procedures and instrumentation required to gather data but rarely talk explicitly about the perceiving meaning-making person as one of the instruments. This leads to considerable confusion, since the perceiving–conceiving apparatus of the observer is itself part of the objective reality and both together provide the matter and energy for what we call experience.

What humans "know": The biological evolutionary perspective

The question of how to think about the 'scientific observer' has become even more difficult and ambiguous with the discoveries of modern biology. When we come to understand the tremendous diversity with which different types of creatures apprehend and know the environment, one must ask how we, as humans, can construe our own species as the self-evident touchstone of reality for all nature; for it now seems obvious that humans register, amplify, and make sense out of only a limited part of the information available in the universe around us. Like all living organisms we have information intake, storage, and response loops, yet we know very well that various organisms differ from each other in the elements they take in, the amount they store, and in the behavior available by which to respond to

99

information. Input–storage–response capacities provide organisms with different world view potentials or what Fraser[1] calls *umwelts*, after the earlier work of Von Uexküll. Von Uexküll was concerned with the functional cycle of the animal. This cycle is an information-carrying loop. Along the loop, external signals pass and become internal signals. They are processed and evaluated in terms of the capacities of the organism and the modalities of its functions. They are passed on as commands that control, more or less, the animal's behavior. Through the consequent behavior, the external signals themselves become modified. The *umwelt* of the species can have only such characteristics as may be processed by the functional loop. In terms of modern semiotic theory, organisms do not perceive a final and absolute reality but only the signs that have been filtered and formed by their specific capacities. From these signs they construct what, for each species, is the reality of the world.

The reality of each of these self-constructed worlds is presumably internally consistent and closed: whatever is beyond the *umwelt* of the specific organism simply is not perceived. Fraser's examples illuminate:

> For instance, certain butterflies have patterns on their wings which show up in ultraviolet light. These patterns exist for other butterflies but not for the vertebrates whose eyes are not sensitive in the ultraviolet region . . . [or] consider the spider's web. . . It is a sort of polar coordinate, an extension of the spider's sense: from its vibrations the spider can tell the size and location of its prey. Flies not caught do not exist for the spider. This eight-legged relative of the insect would have little use for a Cartesian space of three dimensions; its space has only angles and distances. (p. 20.)

For others, such as sightless animals, the universe has neither angles, distances nor depths. "Tactile space" exists for these animals only to the extent that they apprehend it by touch. Out of touch, objects in tactile space cease to exist. Organisms such as the paramecium need only a two-dimensional idea of space; mammals function with three.[2] So, like other organisms, humans not only select a limited set of data from which to understand and cope in the world; they also distort and alter these data for purposes of adaptation and convenience. (How much we distort we shall, of course, never really know.) These perceptions are tied to and have evolved out of mutual relationships between the organism and the world "out there." We assume that the powers of living things to know and to cope are linked to conditions related to their survival in the broader ecosystem. In fact, the perceptions of the organism can be said to be selective and dynamic maps of the surrounding ecosystem. Even that sacred constant, time, will be construed in very different ways depending on a species' mode of input, storage and response. As mentioned earlier, if humans were to travel at speeds close to those of atomic particles, for example, they might well see Einstein's insight about the relativity of space and time as common sense.

A hallmark of modern cosmology, however, is the belief that these realities of space and time exist independently of humans themselves. Classical physics, as well as the whole world of industrial technology, has sanctified several beliefs: that natural processes are somehow separate from human consciousness; that their study is independent of historical biases; and that our uses of them are value-free. It is widely believed that humans have a comprehensive or universal capacity to discover and understand the mysteries of their physical universe, albeit with the help of instruments to extend their senses and the speed of their logical calculations.

Our process view of the natural world is somewhat different. It rests on two assumptions: first, that particular beings have different information loops available to them in their domains (allowing us, for example, to speak of the *umwelt* of an electron, a tick, or a human being); and second, that reality is a flowing set of relationships which includes all the various domains and *umwelts* within a single universe. So, from this point of view, one can move to a third premise: that all being evolves from other being; none is ever separate and independent from the natural world; various forms of life, matter, and energy are sensitive to and, on some level, 'understand' one another. The surface of the lake is sensitive to the warmth of the sun; it evaporates and forms clouds. As the air in the atmosphere is warmed to different temperatures at different levels, there are winds. Winds blow clouds. Clouds then condense and form rain, which falls to earth and sustains life. Process cosmology stresses the intrinsic and inextricable relationships among 'external' environment, our internal physiological environments, and the evolutionary history within which these relationships came into existence. Modern cosmology assumes that same history, but emphasizes the 'struggle' of individuals and species within a partly hostile and partly supportive 'external' environment. Process theory, on the other hand, stresses less the struggle for survival of individuals and sees evolution more as an interactive dance. No one can see or apprehend clearly the whole dance—only those aspects of it in which she or he feels direct participation. As the evolutionary dance changes, species die and others are created. But with the limitations of our own *umwelt*, we can have little precise or conscious technical knowledge of the broader universal scene. Humans are only vaguely aware of the microscopic world of atoms, electrons, molecules, and microorganisms. We have little or no sense of the great forces in the universe that may affect us on this planet. We know of the sun and the moon and the tides, and we have a good deal of intuitive folklore (e.g., astrology) about other stars and planets affecting us. But in the last analysis, we know very little for certain about the complex web of relationships within which we live and have our being.

While we seem encased within the *umwelt* of our particular species and individuality, the process point of view presumes a dim level of understanding and communication across the different species of being. (Folklore, for example, is filled with stories in which various species of animals and plants are able to communicate with one another.) Process cosmology assumes an underlying ground of feeling that binds all beings together. Out of this ground or body of potential communication, each species and individual amplifies and comes to apprehend a limited range of understanding according to the sense it has evolved and according to the internal structures that allow it to decode and store the sense data, create patterns, and ascribe meaning to them.

Meaning thus functions at many levels. The ground of meaning is everywhere in the universe. At a second level, organic sensibilities sharpen and amplify elements of the ground so that we can participate in the meaning. The system of deciphering allows these senses to form patterns upon which the individual can act. "Meaning," as Carini states, is therefore an experience of relatedness:

> . . . meaning is not a thing. . . rather it designates the experience of relatedness which enhances and makes more vivid each of the events and persons it joins. For meaning to arise there must be recognition. Hence, meaning addresses an *underlying unity among persons, things and the world.* (emphasis added)[3]

Communication and understanding happen because entities are in the 'ground' and share the reality of that ground. Specific kinds of understandings happen because particular entities have *umwelts* dependent upon particular sense and conceptual equipment. All entities share a common ground (Carini's underlying unity) and, to varying extents, a common apprehension of the mutuality of being. But in the long process of evolution a great variety of different beings have come about who amplify qualities of apprehension in their own unique ways. All beings are in some ways different and in some ways the same—in some ways separate but in all cases involved and embedded in the larger whole of universe.

The process reading of our evolutionary history thus maintains the unity of nature. No primordial form of being came before all others, like the unmoved mover; no forms of being break out of nature as qualitatively unique or superior entities (like humans with a divinely inherited soul). This view of reality is, of course, radically different from the Judeo–Christian cosmology, which is sharply divided into God, mind (soul). and matter, and the modern cosmology that sees human mind as separate from objective nature. This fundamental splitting of nature by both Judio–Christians and modernists carries with it a progressive view of the human condition. It assumes that throughout the history of the universe, life differentiated from matter, and consciousness from life: that the universe has passed through upwardly spiraling stages of development toward some ultimate perfection or paradise.

From such a progressive point of view, an historical evolutionary cross-section of the universe would reveal numerous strata: simpler atoms having evolved into molecules, molecules having evolved into living cells, cells having evolved into complex and differentiated organisms, organisms having evolved into sentient beings, and sentient beings have been "blessed" with consciousness and self-consciousness and ultimately, for the Judeo-Christian, consciousness of God. The modern world is thus seen as the culmination of this evolutionary process. Primitive forms are left behind, or continue to exist either as useless remnants to be exterminated or as natural resources to be exploited for human benefit.

Process cosmology, on the other hand, stresses an integrity and inter-relatedness of all being that comes from the historical/evolutionary insight. There is only one fundamental nature, one fundamental realm of being. God, soul or mind (however one construes them) are still in nature. Humans have no God-given capacity to raise themselves above other creatures or beings. There is no sharp and qualitative moral distinction between a human being and a maple tree, because the context of value is the unity of nature, not a group of exploitative beings outside of nature competing for survival.

The Hopi, for example, who are clearly process people, see all events in the world as somehow interrelated both historically and existentially and morally interdependent. The ear of corn, the kiva in the earth, the sun, the snake, and the coyote are not fundamentally separated from the human or from human destiny. Process cosmology suggests that although we are endowed with organs (eyes and ears) that provide sense data, a category and logic construction mechanism (mind), and an information storage system (memory), and although these endowments guide our response to the environment in the interest of survival and pleasure, the notion that we are uniquely separate beings in nature is merely a cultural interpretation of reality, not a universal fact. Differences among organisms and species fade as one steps back and looks at the larger pattern. For example, as humans we divide colors into discrete categories—red, yellow, green, or blue; yet this perception is only a function of the limited perspective of individual organisms and often of the individual culture.

Koestler resolves the issue with the idea of holarchy:

> We have seen that biological holons, from organisms down to organelles, are self-regulating entities which manifest both the independent properties of wholes and the dependent properties of parts. This is the first of the general characteristics of all types of holarchies to be retained; we may call it the *Janus*

principle. In social hierarchies it is self-evident: every social holon—individual, family, clan, tribe, nation, etc.—is a coherent whole relative to its constituent parts, yet at the same time part of a larger social entity. A society without holarchic structuring would be as chaotic as the random motion of gas molecules colliding and rebounding in all directions.[4]

Holarchic structuring describes more than societal organization: humans are intrinsically part of an ecological whole. We are, in Koestler's term, a holon; at one and the same time a separate individual and part of a larger organism. The larger organism may be construed as earth, solar system, universe, or flowing occasions.

In *The Lives of a Cell*, Lewis Thomas vividly illustrates the interrelatedness of all aspects of nature:

> . . . A good case can be made for our nonexistence as entities. Humans or beings are not made up of successively enriched packets of their own parts. They are shared, rented, occupied. At the interior of their cells, driving them, pervading the oxidative energy that sends them out for the improvement of each shining day, are the mitochondria, and in a strict sense they are not theirs. They turn out to be little separate creatures, the colonial posterity of migrant prokaryocytes, probably primitive bacteria that swam into ancestral precursors of our eukaryotic cells and stayed there. Ever since, they have maintained themselves and their ways, replicating in their own fashion, privately, with their own DNA and RNA quite different from ours. They are as much symbionts as the rhyzobial bacteria in the roots of beans. Without them, we would not move a muscle, drum a finger, think a thought.

> Mitochondria are stable and responsible lodgers. But what of the other little animals, similarly estabished in our cells. . . Our centrioles, basal bodies, and probably a good many other more obscure tiny beings at work inside our cells, each with its own special genome, are as foreign, and as essential, as aphids in anthills.

> I like to think that they work in my interest, that each breath they draw for me, but perhaps it is they who walk through the local park in the early morning, sensing my senses, listening to my music, thinking my thoughts.

> But green plants are in the same fix. They could not be plants, or green, without their chloroplasts, which run the photosynthetic enterprise and generate oxygen for the rest of the planet. As it turns out, chloroplasts are also separate creatures with their own genomes, speaking their own language.

> We carry stores of DNA in our nuclei that may have come in, at one time or another, from the fusion of ancestral cells and the linking of ancestral organisms in symbiosis. Our genomes are catalogues of instructions from all kinds of sources in nature, filled for all kinds of contingencies. As for me,

I am grateful for differentiation and speciation, but I cannot feel as separate an entity as I did a few years ago, before I was told these things, nor, I should think, can anyone else.

. . .The uniformity of the earth's life, more astonishing than its diversity, is accountable by the high probability that we derived, originally, from some single cell, fertilized in a bolt of lightning as the earth cooled. It is from the progeny of this parent cell that we take our looks; we still share genes around, and the resemblance of the enzymes of grasses to those of whales is a family resemblance.

The viruses, instead of being single-minded agents of disease and death, now begin to look more like mobile genes. Evolution is still an infinitely long and tedious biological game, with only the winners staying at the table, but the rules are beginning to look more flexible. We live in a dancing matrix of viruses; they dart, rather like bees, from organism to organism, from plant to insect to mammal to me and back again, and into the sea, tugging along pieces of this genome, strings of genes from that, transplanting grafts of DNA, passing around heredity as though at a great party. They may be a mechanism for keeping new, mutant kinds of DNA in the widest circulation among us. If this is true, the odd virus disease, on which we must focus so much of our attention in medicine, may be looked on as an accident, something dropped.

. . .I have been trying to think of the earth as a kind of organism, but it is no go. . . It is too big, too complex, with too many working parts lacking visible connections. The other night, driving through a hilly wooded part of southern New England, I wondered about this. If not like an organism, what is it like, what is it *most* like? Then, satisfactorily for that moment, it came to me: it is *most* like a single cell.[5]

The unity of nature suggested by looking at the earth as a "dancing matrix of viruses" might well violate our modern sense of self-importance both as individuals and as members of the human species: we believe ourselves to have a value unique in the universe. Moreover, since our own existence is fragile, transitory, and predatory we tend to see life as a struggle against other forms of life rather than as a support for them.

Yet, in a more profound sense, Thomas' vision of life on the planet seems more accurate than the Darwinian premise of life as the consequence of random adaptation. The insight of viewing the planet as a cell requires us to consider that there is a broader array of information in the cosmos than human equipment can directly perceive. Modern genetics has pieced together a picture of nature that is actually more consistent with the Hopi view than with modernity. The uniformity and interrelatedness of life is, as Koestler tells us, much more astonishing than its diversity.

Our discussion thus far has focused on the relationship between the human organism as a whole, as a sensing, acting, and reacting part of nature, and its place in the larger ecosystem or universe. We have made the case that it is more reasonable to see humans as embedded within the fabric of natural relationships (as holons) than to consider ourselves as somehow having been liberated from or lifted out of nature on to a special position 'above' nature. So we necessarily see culture as an aspect of nature. This issue can, of course, be focused more narrowly on the specific place of the human mind in nature or universe. In the common sense experience of this culture, a tree appears on the landscape, the image of the tree appears in the complex physiology of the eye, and finally the mind (brain?) interprets and perhaps remembers the image as an idea. The tree is part of the objective world; the image on the retina is matter; the brain is driven by energy. But whence the interpretation, the idea? Western culture resists the notion that this can in any sense be 'in nature.' The purposeful control and even domination of nature over the past two hundred years reinforces modernity's message that human mind stands outside nature as an observer and can, through intelligence and technology, conquer it. Yet Lorenz, Koestler, and Thomas tell us that the distinction between the 'in here' of the subjective self and the 'out there' of objective nature, is, taken literally, an illusion, a perspective of our contemporary cosmology. This distinction is what Bateson calls confusing the map with the territory.

The map, both the physiological equipment and the conscious perception, is *part* of the territory. The physiological reality 'in here' (in the human body) is inextricably connected to and part of the reality 'out there.' We are separate as individuals and as a species but we are physically and biologically in all nature. We did spring from a common cell. Somehow our maps must feel, understand and reflect this connection. When our maps are objectified as describing only the 'out there' and the perceiving organism is assumed to be only an observer, we commit serious errors in understanding our place in the cosmos.

Bateson describes these levels of reality in much the same way that Koestler talks about holons and holarchy, but explicitly introduces the concept of 'mind.' It is obvious that the biological world 'in here,' in the organism, has a receptor/storage and feedback loop, a cybernetic system which we consider 'mind.' It responds adaptively to the environment. But the question becomes: What is the unit that is adapting? What is surviving? How broadly do we construe mind? Batson responds:

> We get a picture . . . of a mind as synonymous with a cybernetic system — the relevant total information-processing, trial and error completing unit. And we know that within Mind in the widest sense there will be a hierarchy of subsystems, any one of which we can call an individual mind.
>
> But this picture is precisely the same as the picture which we arrived at in discussing the *unit of evolution* . . .

In considering units of evolution, I have agreed that you have at each step to include the completed pathways outside the protoplasmic aggregate, be it body-in-the-environment. The hierarchic structure is not new. Formerly we talked about the breeding individual or the family line or the taxon, and so on. Now each step of the hierarchy is to be thought of as a *system*, instead of a chunk cut off and visualized as *against* the surrounding matrix.

This identity between the unit of mind and the unit of evolutionary survival is of very great importance, not only theoretical, but also ethical.

It means. . .that I now localize something which I am calling "Mind" imma-nent in the larger biological system—the ecosystem. Or, if I draw the system boundaries at a different level, then mind as immanent between mental and evolutionary units is broadly right, then we face a number of shifts in our thinking.

. . .the very meaning of "survival" becomes different when we stop talking about the survival of something bounded by the skin and start to think of survival of the system of ideas in the circuit. The contents of skin are random-ized at death and the pathways within the skin are randomized. But the ideas, under further transformation, may go on in the world in books or works of art. Socrates as a bioenergetic individual is dead. But much of him still lives as a component in the contemporary ecology of ideas.

It is also clear that theology becomes changed and perhaps renewed. The Mediterranean religions for 5000 years have swung to and fro between imma-nence and transcendence. In Babylon the gods were transcendent on the tops of hills; in Egypt, there was god immanent in the Pharoah; and Christianity is a complex combination of these two beliefs.

The cybernetic epistemology which I have offered would suggest a new approach. The individual mind is immanent, but not only in the body. It is immanent also in pathways and messages outside the body; and there is a larger Mind of which the individual mind is a subsystem. This larger Mind is comparable to God and is perhaps what some people mean by "God," but it is still immanent in the total interconnected social system and planetary ecology.

Freudian psychology expanded the concept of mind inwards to include the whole communication system within the body—the autonomic, the habitual, and the vast range of unconscious process. What I am saying expands mind outwards. And both of these changes reduce the scope of the conscious self. A certain humility becomes appropriate, tempered by the dignity or joy of being part of something much bigger.[6]

These insights of Bateson paint a picture of earth and universe that stresses the historical–evolutionary unity and relatedness among all forms of life—both those which are extinct and those which exist in our contem-porary world. Our lives and the ecological network within which our lives exist are what fifteen or so billion years of history have made us. So we come to see entities in nature less as discrete organisms and more as holons in an all-encompassing pattern of relationships. We apprehend this pattern from our sense of a shared evolutionary ancestry as well as from the current discoveries in genetics and microbiology which link our humanness with other forms of life and with the circumstances which surround and support life. For example, the saline content in human cells is roughly similar to that in sea water; atoms within living organisms are similar to those originally processed in stars millions of years ago. We share a heritage that makes the world of atoms, microorganisms, plants, water, and air all part of an interacting whole. Our being, as well as that of the earth and its other residents, can no longer be seen as products of an instantaneous creation by a distant God or the fumbled work of a demiurge. We can now have a plausible authentic sense of connection between the present moment and an awesome geological natural history. We can imagine a whole universe, from the macro galaxies to the micro strands of DNA, in which our own being is again at home, in which mind as well as body are both part of nature.[7]

From Biology to Physics.

While the biological evolutionist has come to apprehend a unity and relatedness in all nature by tying together the long historical record of the universe, physicists have been struggling to reformulate the clockwork universe in an even more profound way. For if Newtonian mechanics was able to reduce the objective universe to parameters of time, space, energy, matter, and causation, we have come to realize within the past eighty years that energy and matter are not independent qualities of being and that matter itself is no longer reducible to stable elementary particples.

The most obvious interpretation of the fact that matter behaves in dramatically different ways in different contexts (e.g., the atom is really not a mini-version of the solar system, or the photon behaves both like a wave and a particle, depending on the circumstances) is to give up the building blocks assumption and imagine the universe as a set of qualitatively separate domains. Using this strategy, Fraser[8], for example differentiates the physical universe into six major levels. While maintaining that the levels are internally related, he claims that they can be seen as distinct and stable. These levels include:

1. The world of particles with zero restmass, always on the move at the speed of light.

2. The world of particles with non-zero restmass, always on the move but at speeds below that of light.

3. The world of massive, ponderable masses gathered into stars, galaxies and groups of galaxies.

4. The world of living organisms.

5. The world of humans as a species, as well as the human as a member of a species.

6. The collective institutions of human societies to the extent that they function as semiautonomous structures.

Fraser's multi-domain paradigm may give us an orderly account of the alarming discontinuity observed by the new physics, yet it still contains modern cosmology's qualitative distinction between matter and life, life and mind, mind and culture. Such schemes do not deal with the startling finding that micro-particles seem, in some sense, to know what they are about and they seem to relate to the intentions both of other particles and to those of the human observer.

In a more radical vein, von Weizsacker[9] wrestles with these new facts and attempts to find the unity in nature that Bateson describes, one in which mind becomes inseparable from the more traditional categories of time, matter, energy, and motion. He begins his search with the observation that there are alternative potential realities (not domains of reality) implicit in the virtual particles of quantum mechanics. Alternative objects, i.e., *the possibility of particles coming into being*, are essentially quanta of movement. (The words particle and object are acutely misleading, implying as they do a "small piece.") Since the final reality is a movement, it has an unpredictability; this unpredictability enables us to speak of the alternative possibilities that go before the emergence of a novel entity. The entity, which is internally free, decides how it will accept the world. It decides the amount of data it will prehend and the mode of its apprehension. Every entity is set within a realm of alternative interconnected entities.

But how does substantial matter appropriate form? Quantum physics instructs us that virtual particles (also known as force fields) emerge as probabilistic alternatives which are then transformed into substance. This transformation is the elusive link in the chain of being. We do know that both human consciousness and the movement of subatomic particles are themselves a mysterious combination of mental and physical processes. (The influence of the human observer—no matter how far removed from the scene physically—on the movement of subatomic particles is a singularly puzzling phenomenon.) We are not able to understand that realm where form and matter are interchangeable, where there is only (uncategorized) energy.

Von Weizsacker begins his explanation of the relationship between form and matter by returning to classical Greek conceptions. In the Platonic cosmology, the genesis of a differentiated material world is attributed to 'forms' which inhabit a timeless domain, dimly apprehendable by humans. All material things presumably share a common, transformative experience as they pass from undifferentiated matter to increasingly ordered and shaped matter. Von Weizsacker suggests that in this transformative process, form and matter are inseparably conjoined. He gives the well-known example:

> A cupboard, a tree are made of wood. Wood is their "matter". . . But the cupboard isn't simply wood; it is a wooden cupboard. "Cupboard" is what it is intrinsically; cupboard is its eidos, its essence, its form. But a cupboard must be made of something; a cupboard without matter is a mere thought abstracted from reality. On the contrary, this cupboard made of wood is a real whole of form and matter, a *synholon;* form and matter are "grown together" in it; it is something concrete. (p. 274–5)

Given the synholon (the form/matter construction of reality), we can speculate about how different occasions come into being. There is, in Aristotelian terms, formal cause (the form or idea behind the occasion); material cause (the substance of which it is made); final cause (the underlying purpose which explains the interaction between form and matter); and efficient cause (the particular historical circumstances that brought the occasion into being). When we understand that *all* entities share these common ontological causal characteristics, we feel a greater sense of relatedness to and unity in the cosmos.

A second ancient ontological tradition, Von Weizsacker notes, is atomism: belief in a final form of true matter, the indivisible, smallest building blocks of the universe. Of course, within the building block framework there remains the question of how the blocks come to form themselves into their various sizes and shapes. The Newtonian physics of modernity requires not only atomistic matter but a new concept, force (or energy), and its absence, inertia. According to Von Weizsacker:

> In the nineteenth century, a new term paired with matter arose—namely, energy. . . Physics is the science of the motion of matter. Motion is subject to laws. The laws prescribe how matter moves in given circumstances. But the circumstances are characterized in terms of the presence of causes of possible motion (or, in accordance with the law of inertia, causes of possible changes in motion), and these causes are termed 'forces.' Forces as individual entities were suspect in the seventeenth century as "occult qualities." One tried to reduce them to the essence of matter, to its filling out of space or —put in popular language—to pressure and collision. From this point of view, force as the cause

of motion resides in matter itself; and from these reflections the concept of "living force" or as we now say, "kinetic energy," finally developed.

We note: energy is the capacity for moving matter. This capacity is turned into substance as a result of the Law of the Conservation of Energy. Energy can be quantitatively measured, and it turns out that its quantity, just like the quantity of matter, is conserved in time. . . .

Relativity theory has, in a certain sense, taught us the identity of the two substances. In contemporary terminology, conservation of matter is called conservation of mass; and energy and mass are relativistically equivalent. (pp. 275–276)

Responding to both relativity and quantum theory von Weizsacker then suggests that underlying matter/energy is movement and *underlying movement is form*, the measurable equivalent of which is information. He puts his position within the framework of quantum particle behavior:

In general we can therefore say: Wherever a particular form is found empirically, a number of simple alternatives are being decided empirically. Formulated as the basic hypothesis of "ur-alternatives"[10] we say that all forms "consist of" combinations of "final" simple alternatives. . .[11]

Matter is form. Today we understand matter in terms of elementary particles. These are to be constructed in terms of elementary ur-alternatives. Ur-alternatives are the final elements of possible forms; decided ur-alternatives are the final elements of actual forms. The simplest example of form is spatial structure. The theory must therefore deduce the possibility of spatial structure, and does this by reducing space to the quantum mechanical state of the isolated simple alternative. (p. 291)

Yet at the same time the "ur-object is the simplest form" it is the quantum of movement:

It is form because it is form (through interaction) for something else, it is form in a universe in which it moves something else. It is itself moved as a form in the universe by which it is moved.

The universe appears in this theory as the totality of forms. In its basic conception, the theory thus carries out the radical objectification of semantics. . . .Understanding is a part of the great process of self-movement. pp. 292–293)

This definition of reality as the totality of forms is contrasted with the meaning of understanding (or thought) in the physics of modernity:

In the mechanistic world view, the idea that matter can think is an empty postulate. The explanatory power of that view depends on the explicit specification of the defining properties of matter (extension in space, impenetrability); all that could ever be derived from it is the movement of matter thus defined. In our view, however, matter is nothing but the possibility of the empirical decision of alternatives. This presupposes a subject who decides. If this subject can know itself and express this knowledge in terms of empirically decidable alternatives, one must assume that it itself is a part of the universe that is the totality of these alternatives. (pp. 293–294)

Von Weizsacker's argument pushes the assumptions underlying the facts of both the relativistic and quantum world to their logical limits, yet he seems unable to find the language of scientific or philosophic exposition to conclude the argument, at least in a coherent or comprehensive way.[12] His conclusion, in fact, shifts explicitly and radically from science to theology:

For all these questions, however, the conceptions of our approach no longer suffice. Objectifiable forms are static, they can be repeated; the concepts of probability and information are of this kind. In its historical development, knowledge transcends this static quality. The cybernetics of truth would have to describe the process of objectification; and in the objectifying delineation of the possibility of its own method, it would then come up against the limits of that method, which are the limits of objectification itself. From the point of view of transcendental philosophy, the idea of the objectification of a final subject confuses the empirical with the transcendental. It is of the nature of meditation not to objectify. God is not the totality of forms, but their ground. (p. 294)

Von Weizsacker's strategy for achieving a sense of unity in nature seems to be the reduction of ontological categories (space, time, energy, matter, causation, form, motion, alternatives) to the smallest possible number, much like the physicist's fascination with the reduction of various forms of energy or force—gravity, atomic, electromagnetic—to a single type. Thus, the climax of his argument states that "the conceptions of our approach no longer suffice" for "the cybernetics of truth would have to describe the process of objectification" and "would then come up against the limits of that method, which are the limits of objectification itself". By this we assume he means that when mind, "the cybernetics of truth", must both describe the process of objectification *and* become part of this process, we have come against the limits of the mind–body dualism and require some new methodology. For it is separation of mind or consciousness from material reality that allows for objectification—indeed, for the conversation that von Weizsacker is having with the reader—and the sense of rigor implicit in that conversation. Suddenly the rigor evaporates in the statement that we are simply confusing the empirical with the transcendental. We thus end with the sense that mind somehow becomes folded into material reality or material reality is formed in mind, and however this process is to be described, it does not fit into the language of modern science.

Our hunch is that we require, at this point, new metaphors and new conceptions of knowing to carry us beyond the dualistic or tripartite universe, i.e., mind (idea), sensate being, and object. A more adequate cosmology can be generated, perhaps, if we begin not with the machine metaphor but that of an organism.[13] This is, in fact, where Whitehead begins.

Whitehead was one of the first to make philosophical use of the new quantum physics, citing its influence on the development of his organic philosophy:

> . . .organic [process] theory represents directly what [postmodern] physics actually does assume respecting its ultimate entities. We also notice the complete futility of these entities if they are conceived as fully concrete individuals. So far as physics is concerned they are wholly occupied in moving each other about and they have no reality outside this function.[14]

The core unit of reality then shifts from substantive objects or individuals to what Whitehead calls "actual occasions" or "actual entities." The name itself implies a movement, a happening, a transformation. The actual occasion is a dynamic process, an ever-changing pattern of relationships, not an item of mindless material; every final real thing is in the process of becoming something. It is perhaps more appropriate to say that the occasion is a unit of becoming new. Hocking supplies the analogy:

> The actual entity (or occasion) is not a term of description in the direct sense. It is a hypothesis. It cannot be kept in place by pointing to its presence as a datum; it can only hold its own if it proves to be a valuable conceptual tool. It shares this character with the electron. But the electron is upheld by precise verification and precise prediction whereas the nature of the case "the occasion" cannot secure such support. It can have, at best, the general support derived from consideration that if the world were a world of "occasion" concrete nature would be a scene of qualitative change, and it is such a scene.[15]

If the final realities are events that are constantly transformed, then we should see nothing static in the universe. And that is just what we do see.

When a new occasion is formed, the components do not maintain their separate identities, even in the common everyday occurrence of a subject manipulating an object. We say, for example, John drinks the water. We are accustomed to considering John and the water as distinct from each other. Their separate identities remain intact. However, looked on as an occasion, the participation of these two entities involves a fundamental change for both. As objects in the environment in a given moment, they come together to form an event. The event does not stand outside the participants: the drinking of the water is not external to John, nor external to the water. In the process of synthesizing many data (i.e., John, his physiological processes, his cognitive decision to drink the water, the water itself, the respective histories of John the person and that particular water up to that time, and so forth) in the evolving moment, modifications do enter. John, as well as the water, is fulfilled, and they come to a novel reality (however modest). John becomes the water and the water becomes John. Seen from the perspective of either participating entity, a new occasion evolves. And like the physicist who might train his electron microscope at the place where his hand meets the bark of the tree, we cannot tell where the subject leaves off and the object begins. We can only say that in the conjoining of their two realities the occasions together formed a new one.

For Whiteheadians, the essence of being is neither information nor mind nor material world but the transformative process wherein being moves from fragment and purpose to satisfaction and completion and finally to perishing and the recreation of new being. The organic metaphor suggests this transformative process by bringing to the force two central principles the clockwork universe ignores: self-transformation and novelty. Living things come out of the stuff and the form of that which has perished; yet they come forth as unique and novel entities. They are not 'created' by others; they create, in some mysterious way, themselves. The organic metaphor thus begins with the novelty and creativity in nature rather than with the static regularities or scientific laws that describe the operation of the machine.

Describing a process universe is as much story and poetry as it is disciplined science and philosophy—it is one expression of what Whitehead calls "speculative philosophy." The rest of this book is really an attempt to persuade the reader to move toward such imaginative speculation as we sketch out a postmodern process paradigm and its implications for curriculum and teaching.

Chapter Seven

Whitehead's Process Cosmology

Introduction

The cosmology developed by Alfred North Whitehead considers the material world we know with our senses as only one transitory phase of that process which is existence in the universe. Process cosmology sees all creation as a flow, the dissolution of one occasion in the becoming of another. In the final explanation of how things come into being, process theory abandons the simple notion of cause and effect: that a solid set of objects (atoms, molecules, people, stars, winds) impinge on other objects to make them move or change. In process there is no external cause; the universe—and everything—makes itself. Nor is there a precise fitting together of old parts and new parts such that old parts create new parts. A living organism is constantly making, reproducing, growing, aging, constantly changing. Some of the changes are more or less predictable—what we call natural laws. Other changes are novel, as in the creation of offspring.

In a complex occasion such as in the conception of an embryo, millions of sperm seek to fertilize one egg; only one completes the fertilization. Out of the potential of millions of alternatives comes only one specific occasion. In another less dramatic example, a person may sit and contemplate a course of action such as choosing a meal from a menu; out of a world of potential comes a decision and a consequent action. But the final reality is that dynamic process by which an occasion comes into being. The process includes the imagining, the selection, and the ordering. Reality is more than the consequence of an action. Reality is more than the decision and the action. Reality includes the imaginative potential for a variety of decisions. It is all one interrelated process.

What follows below is a more detailed and technical description of the cosmology of Alfred North Whitehead. A full description of this prodigious work is limited by considerations of space and our own experience as Whitehead apologists.

The ultimate creature of the universe is what Whitehead calls the actual occasion. This final reality defies subdivision because it is not a thing but an act, a movement into a new unity of data. The act of engaging new data and synthesizing them into a compatible whole is called prehending. All types of actual occasions (or entities), from sub-atomic particles to people, societies, and planets, are prehending other entities.[1]

Nor is an actual occasion simply the physical prehension of data into novel circumstance; an actual occasion also includes what Whitehead calls "eternal objects." An eternal object is an ideal, a pure potential, a universal. Since its existence in the universe is independent of any moment in time, it resembles the Platonic form, but for Whitehead there is a difference: the eternal object loses its value apart from the necessary reference to the world of passing fact. Eternal objects are the only entities which do not require other entities in order to exist; they become actual by being prehended by an actual entity, by becoming part of its constitution. They are the characteristics of an event, e.g., its color or shape. Because they are universals they can and do recur. Their existence transcends their occurrence; how they occur in another actual occasion depends on that entity's subjective aim or intent. If the subjective aims of an entity are sphericity and color, then roundness and redness, let us say, occur to the extent needed by that entity for its own purposes. The entity determines the quality of the eternal object.

An actual occasion *is* engaging in relationships. It is a process, and that process is the becoming of an actual occasion. Whitehead says its being is constituted by its becoming. How that occasion *becomes* constitutes what it is. There are, we could say, no dancers; there is only the dance. In a manner of speaking there are no actual entities either, there are only their prehensions.

The prehension is the *sine qua non* of the actual entity's existence; an entity does not exist on its own, apart and insensitive to its surroundings. There is no such thing as an entity with no relations with others. The entity and its prehensions possess something of an ontological fluidity: the entity is a becoming; the prehension is a relating. Whitehead borrows a term from mathematics, 'vector,' to describe the prehension's function. A vector is a carrier, an organism that transmits. A prehension carries the object that is being felt or prehended into the makeup of the subject. The subject is the actual entity in the process of becoming something new. The entity grasps, or has a feeling for, the new item or datum. The threads of process between the actual entity doing the feeling and the datum being felt is the prehension; the prehension feels what is there and carries it to here.

A *feeling* is a positive prehension and has five factors in its makeup: 1. the subject that feels, i.e., the actual entity; 2. the initial data that are to be felt; 3. the elimination of other data by virtue of negative prehensions (what the entity decides not to use or be); 4. the objective datum that is felt; and 5. the subjective form, which is how that subject feels that objective datum.

Feeling is also the operation of passing from the objectivity of the datum to the subjectivity of the actual entity. This is not what we ordinarily mean when we say we feel something. We say, for example, that we feel anxious that the car will not start because it is thirty degrees below zero outside. *We* do the feeling; the car is the object of our anxiety. In the world as we understand it, the car does not have a single feeling for us. But for Whitehead a feeling is the act of cause-creating-its-effect. Since it is an act, a feeling is not merely a cause or merely an effect; it is the transition between both. Thus, "...subject and object are relative terms. An occasion is a subject in respect to its provocation concerning an object; and anything is an object in respect to its provocation of some special activity within a subject."[2] The entire activity of feeling anxious about the car is a togetherness of many occasions which is immanent (or within) the subject occasion.

How does a new occasion come into existence? The act of coming into being (called by Whitehead *concrescence*) is the result of several occasions prehending each other in such a way that a new occasion results. Concrescense means having become something novel as a result of a unifying of diverse elements. Concrescence is not managed from without, it is impelled from within; coming from within, it has its own motive, its ideal of itself: its subjective aim. Concrescence is the process of self-creation. The entire operation is dependent on that Whitehead category of "feeling." Concrescence is a useful notion of many influences acquiring a complete reality.

The unifying process that results in a togetherness of prehensions is the reason why 'becoming' eludes the categories of cause and effect. Ordinarily, we speak of a separation of mind and material, of subject and object. Human mental actions have 'final' causes—i.e., purposes and aims outside the material world. Other forces and powers have "efficient" causes,—e.g., attraction or repulsion,—which apply only to physical bodies. The two types of entities are commonly considered to be separate. But for process philosophy, every occasion is a consequence of both final and efficient cause; mind and matter influence each other. In the becoming of experience (the definition of process), both final and efficient causes share credit. This is because while the occasions of the past giving rise to some new occasion cause some effect (they are a force which has a result), the result is also conditioned by the aim or ideal entertained by the actual occasion coming into being. For example, something must be hoped, feared, or imagined as a possibility. Concrescence involves not only the objects given rise to its becoming, but final cause as well. In classical physics, anything is describable in isolation; any effect can be extricated from its cause and vice versa. In process philosophy this separation is inconceivable. No concrete thing has simply one cause; it is a unity of many causes. Whitehead sees himself as exemplifying this unity:

> I find myself as essentially a unity of emotions, enjoyments, hopes, fears, regrets, valuations of alternatives, decisions—all of them subjective reactions to the environment as active in my nature. My unity—which is Descartes' 'I am'—is my process of shaping this welter of material into a consistent pattern of feelings.[3]

This welter of feelings is analogous to a feedback loop: it reacts to efficient causes but is conditioned by the final aim (the final cause) of the person doing the experiencing. The mingling of efficient and final causes gives rise to a new occasion. This occasion is composed of an occasion from the past bringing on the reaction *and* a reaction that itself is dependent on some ideal entertained: the enjoyments, hopes, fears, regrets, valuations of alternatives, and so on, that make up the process Whitehead calls his "I am." It is impossible to consider the object without its context in the (emerging) actual occasion.

Whitehead's theory of occasion applies to all aspects of the universal process, whether we speak of electrons, atoms, crystals, amoebae, plants, or humans. The specious present of human experience and the quantum events of physics are two examples of occasions. The specious present refers to your experience at a given moment, arising from an integration of nerve impulses and of conscious and subconscious emotions and attitudes. Only with great concentration can we begin to consider a very immediate experience as overlapping another moment which has all its own environmental, emotional and physical components. Perhaps you have searched for a lost toddler in a crowded department store for several minutes before suddenly spotting her. You then experience a flood of relief, a feeling which contrasted quite exquisitely with the feeling of panic that had built up. When relief replaced panic you could have recognized the specious present—i.e., that integration of nerve impulses, emotions and attitudes that caused you to behave in certain way up to that moment. The specious present is like the actual occasion because at the moment you attempt to consider it, it has perished, defying 'chronologization' as much as it defies subdivision.

Quantum theory says that subatomic particles are not isolated grains of matter but are actually probability patterns, interconnections that include the human observer and his or her consciousness. To be an actual occasion, the leap of the electron fits all the criteria: its movement is self-impelled and unpredictable, and out of a disunity of many, competing alternatives, it chooses one unifying, real direction for itself.

Whitehead's theory of prehension by which (in a generally unconscious way) one bit of life responds to another is an unusual approach to subject-object relations. It introduces the idea that although sensa provide the material for the interpretation, we do the interpreting with 'no thanks for the feat' due to the material. The nature of the material discloses nothing to us of its past or future; it stands there starkly:

> But the mind in apprehending also experiences sensations which, properly speaking, are qualities of the mind alone. These sensations are perfected by the mind so as to clothe appropriate bodies in Nature. Thus the bodies are perceived as with external qualities which in fact are purely the offspring of the mind. Thus Nature gets credit which should in truth be reserved for ourselves: the rose for its scent, the nightingale for its song, and the sun for its radiance. The poets are entirely mistaken. They should address their lyrics to themselves and should turn them into odes of self-congratulation on the excellency of the human mind. Nature is a dull affair, soundless, scentless, colorless; merely the hurrying of material endlessly, meaninglessly.[4]

But Nature's impact on our lives is hardly meaningless; and Whitehead, a realist, knows that, however dull, Nature is real. He does not say that we live in a world of sights, sounds, and smells that are imaginary. ("It is nonsense to ask if the color red is real. The color red is an ingredient in the process of realization."[5]) He does mean that the process of realization, called prehension, is a perception which, more often than not, is *not cognitive*. It is a perception ". . .here in this place, of things which have reference to other places."[6] We might say that what is realized when we see the color red is a gathering of things into a unity of prehension; and that what is thereby realized is the prehension, not the color red. Consider, for example, members of the Hanonuo tribe in the Philippines, who report only two colors, red and green.[7] Shown blue, yellow, purple, or orange, the Hanonuo will categorize them as either red or green. Whitehead would affirm that the prehensive unification between the color red and the Hanonuo person on the one hand and the prehensive unification between the color blue and the anthropologist on the other are qualitatively different, based as they are on a different "gathering of things," a different togetherness of prehensions, into their respective moments of perception. The gathering of things refers to the fact that the sense data are indeed received from the external world but only in the form of "innumerable faint pulses of emotion."[8] The actual occasions in the animal body, the eyes of the Hanonuo person, for example, gather these impulses together and from them experience sizable feelings; these feelings—say, the enjoyment of a color—are transmitted by the brain into an expression of an eternal object. In this process the original physical feelings, called by Whitehead "causal efficacy," are subsumed (not eliminated) by an inrush of conceptual feelings, such that the causal world of the very immediate past seems to be presented to us as a passive display of qualities *in* the data. This second stage is called perception in the mode of *presentational immediacy.* Lowe explains:

> The higher animals have learned to interpret these sense-qualities, thus perceived, as symbols of the actualities in the external world—actualities which are themselves perceived only by vague feelings of their causal agent. The epistemology of sense perception is the theory of this "symbolic reference." The recognition of these two levels of perception distinguishes Whitehead's epistemology from other realistic ones.[9]

What goes on between the two levels of perception—between causal efficacy and presentational immediacy—is symbolic reference. Barfield calls this work of construction "figuration."[10] Sense organs give rise to sensations; the mere sensations are combined and reconstructed by the percipient mind into nameable objects. Whitehead rejoices in this transaction:

> The lesson of the transmutation of causal efficacy into presentational immediacy is that great ends are reached by life in the present; life novel and immediate, but deriving its richness by its full inheritance from the rightly organized animal body. It is by reason of the body, with its miracle of order, that the treasures of the past environment are poured into the living occasion. The final percipient route of occasions is perhaps some thread of happenings wandering in "empty"space amid interstices of the brain. It toils not, neither does it spin. It receives from the past; it lives in the present. It is shaken by its interstices of private feeling, adversion, or aversion. In its turn, this culmination of bodily life transmits itself as an element of novelty throughout the avenues of the body. Its sole use to the body is its vivid originality: it is the organ of novelty.[11]

The "final percipient route of occasions" is always novel because no one crosses the same river twice, even in the rivers of one's own mind. Every fusion of non-sensuous perception and sense perception (and we know now that the two are inseparably conjoined) is new. Still our language and culture make the interpretations of 'barren sensa" commonsensical and habitual, so that for example when we speak of a something being red, white and blue, the listener, if he is not Hanonuo, will immediately have several (non-sensuous) perceptions which we could discuss intelligibly.

In our everyday experience the most compelling example of non-sensuous perception is our knowledge of our immediate past: the past constituted by the occasion or group of occasions which "enters into experience devoid of any perceptible medium intervening between it and the present immediate fact. Roughly speaking, it is that portion of our past lying "between a tenth of a second and a half a second ago."[12] What is continuous from past occasion to present occasion is what Whitehead calls the "subjective feeling": that unique affective tone with which a subject experiences an object. A subjective feeling is the way in which a datum is welcomed by a subject. Remember that the characteristics of the data available to our senses is their *emotional* significance for the person experiencing them. A subjective form gives the dominant tone to the entity. The tone may be anything from rage to ennui, from adversions to aversions; cumulatively it gives the entity its purpose, value, intention. Lowe gives an example of a subjective form: ". . .the unconscious annoyance with which you experienced this page when you turned to it and saw another solid mass of print."[13] Just any variety of subjective form cannot appear at any place or at any time in the universe, because the brute facts of the universe will determine in part what subjective forms are possible in that instance. All the components of our previous experience as well as of the environment make a contribution to the tone of our experience, not simply its content.

Whitehead's Cosmology: A Discussion

It is important to understand that there is no ultimate hard stuff of matter. There is substance—an objective world for humans—but this is merely one phase of the process by which occasions, events, things come into being, reach objectification, and pass away to become part of the new occasion. Universe-wide emergence into novelty, called creativity, is Whitehead's central metaphysical principle. Creativity is not an entity,nor is it an eternal object. It is the reason for the existence of both. It is the name of the fact of 'process' applying to both; it is the name of the phenomenon by which actual entities become, and then themselves enter into the act of becoming of other occasions. As Whitehead states:

> . . .creativity is not separable from its creatures. Thus the creatures remain with the creativity. Accordingly, the creativity for a creature becomes the creativity with the creature, and thereby passes into another phase of itself. It is now the creativity for a new creature. Thus there is a transition of the creative action and this transition exhibits itself in the physical world in the guise of routes of temporal succession.

> This protean character of creativity forbids us from conceiving it as an actual entity. For its character lacks determinedness. It equally prevents us from considering the temporal world as a definite actual creature. For *the temporal world is an essential incompleteness* [emphasis added]. It has not the character of definite matter-of-fact, such as attached to an event in past history viewed from a present standpoint.[14]

Since it does not have the character of a definite matter-of-fact, we cannot point to it the way materialists can point to substance for their proof. We can only claim that if we accurately describe the world as, ultimately, a movement into novelty, then we would see a world of continual change. The world of fact consists of a parade of actual entities, becoming and perishing. The 'force' behind this pulse of life is creativity; it is inherent in every form of existence.

A creativity which is self-effected is a mysterious notion. It implies a creator who is not transcendent (beyond the world) but immanent (within the world). It fact, the word creator is not aptly applied to Whitehead's deity. God exists in the world; and as an actual entity, it also is in the continual process of becoming. (The idea of an incomplete God is antithetical to many religious traditions, needless to say.)

God can be construed as having an extremely important function in relation to the actual entity. The entity comes into being by prehending two types of data: physical data supplied by the environment in which it finds itself and mental data supplied by the realm of eternal objects. Since God *is* the realm in which eternal objects stand in contrast to each other, and since the urge toward novelty depends, in every concrescence, on prehending an eternal object, we see that God is in the world as the lure for the subjective aim. God is here to sustain the entity's aim at vivid experience. God is that lure by virtue of the fact that it is God who offers the possibilities for value. God is "the conceptual feeling at the base of things."[15] Simply put, the past does not supply all the necessary components for the present; the urge towards novelty presumably comes from somewhere. God, as the source of order, supplies that urge. God is that actual entity which supplies the initial aim from which self-causation (for the concrescing entity) begins. All subjective aims originate in God but it is the combination of the subjective aim from the divine realm *and* the actual world which jointly initiate the new entity. In a radical theological departure, Whitehead tells us that God and the world require each other for existence:

> Neither God nor the world reaches static completion. Both are in the grip of the ultimate metaphysical ground, the creative advance into novelty. Either of them, God and the world, is the instrument of novelty for the other.[16]

As instrument for the novelty at which we aim, God is also the entity that sets the limits on what is possible. Innocent spontaneity is not nearly enough to maintain any sophisticated form of life. Unlimited creativity, like a river over its banks, is unaesthetic if not destructive. The control supplied by the divine river bank, so to speak, acts as the counterpoint to the spontaneity of a flowing creativity. The entity, which is internally free, determines how it will accept the world. It decides, for example, the amount of data it will prehend and it decides its mode of prehension. We recall that the mode of appropriating data is directly dependent on the subjective aim of the actual entity. The mode or pattern is the way in which a certain eternal object contrasts with another eternal object. This contrasting 'action' occurs in the realm ascribed to God where an eternal object is determinate—that is, where "each eternal object has its status in this general systematic complex of mutual relatedness."[17] And it occurs in the actual world where an entity prehends the eternal object. In the worldly realm the eternal object is indeterminate—that is, it depends on the entity's subjective aim guiding that entity's concrescence (although the unique contribution of the eternal object is always the same).

In sum, there is the fact that two eternal objects do contrast. And there is the manner in which they contrast, their pattern. By confining our attention to eternal objects, we can see the most obvious example of contrast. "The contrast between red and blue cannot be repeated as that contrast between any other pair of colors, or any pair of sounds or any color and sound."[18] In a painting the pattern of the colors is the manner of their relation to each other. More blue is not simply a case of the addition of the eternal object, the color blue; it is also the alteration of the arrangement of sense data in the painting known as its pattern.

Change occurs not when an eternal object changes, because its essence never changes, and not when an actual entity changes because an entity is what it is: a prehensive center of relationships to all other entities. Change occurs when eternal objects have a variety of ingressions in actual entities. Each actual entity and each eternal object is what it is, but change occurs *over the series* of their ingressions. To Whitehead change is "the adventure of eternal objects in the evolving universe of actual things."[19]

These adventures vary widely from one group of entities to another. Brumbaugh[20] describes three different *patterns* of change. The first is a *pattern of dissipation*, in which a pattern loses stability and cannot regroup. An example of this is atomic fission. A second type is *repetition*. This pattern is stable and repetitive. An example of this is an enduring object. An enduring object is a type of nexus (a togetherness of entities) called a society, that is, it has an order and a history and a defining form:

> A nexus enjoys social order when (1) there is a common element of form illustrated in the definiteness of each of its included actual entities and (2) this common element of form arises in each member of the nexus by reason of the conditions imposed upon it by its prehensions of some other members of the nexus. . . [21]

If the nexus forms a single line of inheritance of its defining characteristic, it is an enduring object. Enduring objects exhibit this massive inheritance and, having few perhensions at the mental pole, remain essentially what they are.

For Whitehead ". . .endurance is the property of finding its pattern reproduced in the temporal parts of the total event."[22] The notion that endurance is really change is a difficult one for the materialistically minded. We would be caused no small amount of anxiety if we continuously considered that the chairs we are sitting on are made up of billions of moving particles. We want our chairs to be enduring objects, at least for the time we are putting them to their intended use. But in Whitehead's scheme of things the chairs are nexus, a series of repetitious and stable patterns.

The third type of pattern is called *reiteration,* in which a pattern is reconstituted but modified. This last is where we can observe process. Animal evolution over time is one example of reiteration. The use of the word 'time' may mislead here if it is seen to imply a time that passes steadily amid the material world. The theory of relativity showed that the clockwork universe was an illusion: there was no absolute simultaneity of time suffusing, as it were, a conglomeration of irreducible brute matter. Time as we ordinarily consider it is the sequence of events which have a causal connection. In process cosmology, the most significant sense of time is that which is relative to the occasion in question. The time for the shifting of a mountain range has little relation to the time it takes for a wave to break on the shore. What mountains and waves do have in common is that, like all of the material world, they do not exist apart from transition. It is useless to consider nature to be a static fact, even for an instant. It is the *passage* of nature which is the actuality, a passage which is the creative force of its own existence.

A nexus (plural nexūs) is Whitehead's term for the set of actual entities "in the unity of the relatedness constituted by their prehensions of each other, or. . .constituted by their objectifications of each other.[23]" In fact,there is no such thing as an actual entity existing on its own by itself. We have seen that an actual entity is by definition in the process of becoming and that that very process is dependent on its being in a relationship of feeling with other entities. When a set of entities mutually prehend, constitute, and are objectified in each other, we have something that is (finally) recognizable to us: an object, a living organism, a person. But Whitehead is not content to leave it there: nexus that have some kind of history are called by him "societies." Societies come in one of six types of occurrence in nature: human existence, animal life, vegetable life, single living cells, large scale inorganic aggregated, and the infinitesimal happenings disclosed by modern physics.[24] What these categories have in common is that they all—to varying degrees—require each other for existence; their physical boundaries are indeterminate; and they are all made up of actual entities.

A human being (a complex 'society') has the most activity at the mental pole of any nexus and is therefore most capable of modification of pattern. The human being endures, but has a dramatic capability for effecting and experiencing novelty. In fact, its capability for creativity has accounted for its endurance.

Each episode of construction of a new pattern consists of Whitehead's three stages of concrescence. There is first an encounter with some new datum. This is followed by an adaptation of the original entity to the new information—anything from genetic material to more of the color blue on the canvas. Lastly, there is the emergence of a new stabilization of the parts. The recaptured pattern is done. It becomes data for those who come after it. So not only is the entity or occasion the subject doing the feeling, it is also the superject—i.e., it survives as data for those who come after it. As Lowe says, "The past has had its chance at becoming; it transfers the opportunity to the next runner. The past is there to be apprehended, but not to grow and change."[25] The entity—once it has embraced the entities available to it—perishes, becoming in itself a datum for all entities to come after it. In this way it achieves "objective immortality."

The three-step pattern of change is one we can apply to organic or inorganic societies. Although Whitehead divides nature into six types of occurrence, he thinks the division between our mentality and nature is groundless: "We find ourselves living within nature . . . we should conceive mental operations as among the factors which make up the constitution of nature";[26] consequently, his boundaries between types of existence are purposefully vague.[27] The boundaries do serve to distinguish one classification of nature from another in terms of Whitehead's concept of importance, sometimes called by him "interest." Whitehead knew that all forms of existence, organic and inorganic, support and require each other. But that conceptualization of the universe is not adequate to consider that vast difference between (to use one of Whitehead's favorite examples of an enduring object) Cleopatra's Needle on the Thames and a human being. We recall that the entity enjoyed its concrescence of other entities at the physical pole and the mental pole. The eternal objects are the entities at the mental pole. The more prehension takes place at the mental pole, the more importance/interest that entity has in the scheme of the universe. Thus, for a large-scale, inorganic aggregate, its structure survives but most of its individuality is obliterated by the sheer weight of its physical existence. Most of the aggregate's existence is dedicated to a forthright expression of itself. It does not need the ingression of anything but the simplest of eternal objects, a certain shape and color, to endure.

As we move into the other classifications, such as vegetable life, animal life, and human life, the idea of a mental pole becomes more important.

According to Dunkel, "Importance emphasizes the contribution of the infinite cosmos beyond and behind the occasion whence it rose and out of which it is constituted."[28] As we move through the complexity of types, mentality (or activity at the mental pole) becomes increased and effective. In human beings we find it possible for knowledge to be entertained, categories to be structured and ideals to be consciously considered.

Yet Whitehead would remind us that the human's perspective of the universe does not in itself deserve special consideration:

> The terms "morality," "logic," "religion," "art," have each of them been claimed as exhausting the whole meaning of importance. Each of them denotes a subordinate species. But the genus stretches beyond any finite group of species. There are perspectives of the universe to which logic is irrelevant, to which religion is irrelevant, to which art is irrelevant... the generic aim of process is the attainment of importance, in that species and to that extent which in that instance is possible.[29]

The concrescence of any entity is a process and that process is the attainment of importance. This wide-ranging definition seems less than helpful: if anything is important simply by virtue of its self-creation, how do we distinguish between Event A which is good and Event B which is evil without slipping into an indefensible relativism? Whitehead does not ascribe a worthiness to importance, as we do in ordinary discourse; in fact, he disparages the "extreme trivialization" of its meaning in our speech: "In common use... [it is] a silly little pomposity."[30] The fact that a concrescence occurs at all gives it its importance. It occurred because it acted in its own self-interest, to the fullest extent possible: "The generic aim of process is the attainment of importance, in that species and to that extent which in that instance is possible."[31] A close synonym would be "interest," meaning to guard one's purpose closely.

> An actual individual of such high grade (i.e., possessing consciousness) has truck with the totality of things by reason of its sheer actuality but *it has attained its individual depth of being by a selective emphasis limited to its own purposes.* The selectiveness of individual experience is moral so far as it conforms to the balance of importance disclosed in rational vision, and conversely the conversion of intellectual insight into an emotional force corrects the sensitive experience in the direction of morality... *Morality of outlook is inseparably conjoined with generality of outlook.* The antithesis between the general good and the individual interest can be abolished only when the individual is such that its interest is the general good, thus exemplifying the loss of minor intensities in order to find them again with finer composition in a wider sweep of interest.[32] (emphasis added)

An individual with consciousness not only acts in its self-interest as every entity must, it has the potential to select its experiences and its emphases to conform with the general good. We account for this morality (or that logic or that beauty) by considering the entity's participation in a universal harmony. If it is in your self-interest to become 'good' at anything, you will maximize your interest in that endeavor to the extent to which you approach the ideal. This aim at vivid experience Whitehead calls "intensity." Furthermore, to the extent that you choose to conform your interest with a generality of outlook, as a result of which a general (not simply your individual) benefit obtains, then that result is a moral one.

Harmony is essentially an aesthetic concept, and we would do well to keep in mind that for Whitehead beauty is a much wider concept than goodness, truth or any virtue. The concept of harmony brings us again to the discussion of patterns and their emergence.

The difference between any two processes is a matter of their participation in a pattern. The larger or more universal the pattern, the more moral the instance of its exemplification. ("Morality of outlook is inseparably conjoined with generality of outlook."[33])

We saw that in the actual world there are three types of pattern. Or we could say that there are three types of participation in the universe. The first is a dissipation without regrouping; the second is an endurance with repetition. Only in the third do we see an advance, which implies discrimination among the eternal objects available. At the level of conscious beings this discrimination involves choice among eternal objects that conflict as well as contrast. For a vegetable to express itself, it has only to exhibit a "democracy of purposeful influences issuing from its parts."[34] The vegetable's expressiveness has a "large average character."[35] In a human life the average character is replaced by varieties of importance. "Thus morals and religion arise as aspects of . . . human impetus toward the best in each occasion."[36] And morals and religion are no more than subsidiaries to a broader pattern of the harmony of the universe. The individual who chooses between the sometimes conflicting ideals of responsible parenting and effective writing is choosing between participating in that pattern which will contribute more to an overall harmony—universal if not familial.

> The notion of the importance of pattern is as old as civilization itself. Every art is founded on the study of pattern. Also the cohesion of social systems depends on the maintenance of patterns of behavior; and advances in civilizations depend on the fortunate modification of such behavior patterns. Thus the infusion of pattern into natural occurrences and the stability of such patterns and the modifications of such patterns is the necessary condition for the realization of the Good.[37]

We see that in typical Whitehead fashion there is more than one definition for the term pattern. *Pattern* is the arrangement of the components in all the arts—painting, music, poetry, mathematics, and symbolic logic—in fact, of all components of human civilization. The study of pattern becomes the study of value, the sharing of criteria.

Pattern also refers to the fundamental 'good' in the universe which provides the model for the instances in the actual world. Good *patterning in* the world refers to the depth of experience of the entity involved. The more profound its harmony, the more the entity approximates the ultimate source of harmony which is divine.

In one of his last two lectures, Whitehead confesses that his first love is symbolic logic because it is purely the study of pattern in abstraction from particulars. As such, symbolic logic holds more promise than any other subject for being the vehicle to apprehend the ultimate concepts:

> ...in the distant future... Symbolic Logic, that is to say, the symbolic examination of pattern, with the use of real variables, will become the foundation of aesthetic. From that stage it will proceed to conquer ethics and theology.[38]

Harmony as expressed through the aesthetic is more central to our sense of the good than logic, religion, art and ethics because the production of beauty is the teleological force in the universe. The endurance of the universe can be explained (at least in part) in terms which refer to its coordinated creative pattern, its harmony.

Whereas inorganic nature is characterized by considerable acceptance of matter of fact, human nature is characterized by a more ambivalent response, in that it seeks both the stability of fact and a continual challenge to the *status quo*. God's immanence in the world (for the realm of eternal objects, as we have seen, does not exist without reference to the world) provides us with the novel possibilities of contrast toward the end of achieving an intensity of feeling and a more vivid experience.

The aim at experiencing a higher intensity of feeling is an irresistible motivator. We cannot and do not meet (apparent) chaos indifferently. Benedetti says that we are creative when we are impelled to "re-pattern the known world into meaningful new configurations."[39] Taking the opposite point of view, Fraser says that creativity is "re-patterning the unpredictable."[40] Whether we agree with Benedetti that creativity is taking the old and making of it something new or with Fraser that creativity is taking the new and making a pattern of *it*, the commonality of these two definitions is that creativity involves the *absence of preconceived outcome*. This "Unforeseen Theory of Creativity" is viewed by some as intolerably paradoxical because it does not include instances of work we deem to be creative but which the artist admits were preconceived. Nor does it explain the notion of control essential to the intelligibility of an artistic work. We are not uncomfortable with the unpredictability-plus-control paradox. Naturally all creative work needs some control: an actor cannot go onstage and say whatever comes into his head, nor does an abstract artist apply paint to a canvas indiscriminately. However, every single performance is different in its own way, just as every single painting is different from every other. This is because the artist who accomplishes the work is different in every confrontation with his or her material. Certainly there is some preconception of end result, but preconception does not mean prediction. The Whitehead definition of creativity is repatterning the known world, within the realm of the unpredictable. It is a unity which results from a disunity. It is a seeking of new configurations, reconciling the past with the 'chaotic'/unforeseen/unpredictable future.

A very Whiteheadian-sounding definition of creativity is given by Rollo May:

> Creativity comes from that struggle—out of the rebellion the creative art is born. Creativity is not merely the innocent spontaneity of our growth and childhood; it must also be married to the passion of the adult human being which is the passion *to live beyond.*[41]

Compare the need to "live beyond" with Whitehead's "creative synthesis":

> The ultimate metaphysical principle is the advance from disjunction to conjunction, *creating a novel entity* [emphasis added] other than the entities given in disjunction. The novel entity is at once the togetherness of the entities which it finds and also it is one among the disjunctive many which it leaves . . . the many become one and are increased by one.[42]

May and Whitehead disagree on one major point: May bemoans the fact that, although talent is plentiful, passion (the progenitor of creativity) is sorely lacking today. Whitehead would say the opposite: creativity as a natural urge within the human spirit is plentiful but requires a form for its expression. That form is expressed as a talent when persons observing it themselves have an aesthetic experience. We believe with Whitehead that creativity is everywhere present. And we are not at all sure that talent is drastically scarce; it only seems that educational institutions do not adequately provide for its expression. We take heart, however, from the words of Henry W. Holmes: ". . .Whitehead's influence on education will have to come about in part by indirection—through interpretation of his general theory."[42]

Chapter Eight

The Moral Basis of Process Education: Intimacy, Intensity, and Balance

Introduction

The process thought of Whitehead is unsettling initially in that it requires a breadth of perspective—from quantum particles to rocks and planets; from the democratic nature of a carrot to the more hierarchical centralized nature of a mammal—as well as the capacity to envision the world as pattern, as a myriad of interconnecting relationships rather than as carefully defined linear chains of local causes and effects. This latter characteristic (pattern versus linear causes) creates, perhaps, the most difficult confusions when applied to moral judgments or questions relating to the social and ethical concerns of a human society. For as modern people living within a plurality of cultures, we have developed a moral/legal strategy which relies heavily on the manipulation of precise and explicit language in resolving and justifying controversial positions—positions on what is true, right, beautiful, and so forth.

This strategy[1] and the assumptions behind it run something as follows. When humans lived within the confines of a single culture, their behavior was determined by reflexive unreflected custom. One did not think in terms of moral alternatives; one's life was mapped out by traditional solutions to life's problems. What is one to do for a living; whom is one to marry; what rights of passage must one pass through to gain the status of adulthood; how does one establish guilt for hurting the community? When human groups, tribes, or societies began moving around the planet and especially when they began to come together in cosmopolitan urban centers, they eventually realized that there was not a single tradition for all of humanity. We then evolved the distinction between custom and law. Custom is the appropriate behavior for a particular group of people, based on their particular tradition. Broader than custom, however, is the notion that there are general conditions required for decent and appropriate behavior for all humans. The notion of law lifts custom to a level of universality. So we search for the basis for such an elevation. We learn in our high school ancient history class that one such justification resides in the notion of a single universal God—in the case of Western peoples it is initially the God of the Jews who gave the ten commandments to Moses. The idea of universal laws, rights, or principles is later embodied in such honored or quasi-sacred documents within Anglo-American thought as the Magna Carta, the Declaration of Independence, and the Bill of Rights. After world War II it is embodied as law on a worldwide basis in the Universal Declaration of Human Rights of the United Nations Charter.

In the nineteenth century, the theory of universal or natural law (which in the American instance presumably filtered from Locke through Jefferson into the United States Constitution) foundered mainly over the issue of whether or not such laws were absolute. It became increasingly clear that higher law was to be conceived not as an absolute to be upheld at all costs but rather as a principle to be applied pragamatically[2] within the framework of particular circumstances. Thus, for example, in the early part of the twentieth century the notion of property rights, which is explicitly spelled out in the United States Constitution, was modified in light of the fact that corporate entities used the concept as a justification for abusing employees who had sought redress through government.

The process of moral deliberation which sees principles as guides but not as absolutes in the resolution of moral conflict is, of course, as old as the Talmud and the English Common Law, which employ a similar intellectual–verbal apparatus. The essential strategy of the process involves separating the idea of higher law or natural law from the notion of moral, ethical, aesthetic, or epistemological principles. The former is then no longer considered obvious and easily accessible to human consciousness, but rather resides in the dim background informing us of the importance of non-absolute evolving principles. But the sharpest separation comes when we distinguish between both the deliberative process itself—along with the intellectual or linguistic apparatus used within the process (controlled rational arguments)—and the notion of action or facticity in the world. Liberal or modern moral theory now sees principles, values, and purposes as somehow separate from entities or events that happen in the world. This leads to the separation of justification from the natural history of becoming. It is the separation of the *what or the becoming of the what from the why or what for.* A man kills his wife. This is a factual circumstance in the substantial world. We then ask: Was the man justified in his actions? We now appeal to values, principles of ethics, law, and logic to find out whether or not the action was justified. We then develop principles of justifiable homicide (e.g., did he kill her in self-defense?). If she was old, suffering from a long terminal and painful illness, we have no immediate available legal principles, so we search for new ones.

This model, of course, applies not only to moral and legal issues but to empirical and aesthetic ones as well. We search for principles of beauty, e.g., balance, form, contrast, harmony, surprise. We search for principles of fact—e.g., reproducibility, coherence, theoretical elegance, consistency of observer reports. Within all of these domains—law, morality, fact, aesthetics—the unit to be judged is some discrete existential substantial being: a person, a painting, an action, a garage, a superhighway. The being is seen as having a reality that is isolatable, separable from the broader pattern of events within which it occurred, as well as independent from the human consciousness that makes the judgment and employs the abstract principles of justification available to that consciousness. Facts are seen as essentially external and neutral.

Education is, of course, construed by modern people within this moral/factual framework. When we ask: "What is the purpose of schooling?" we are searching for principles of justification which would allow us to change in some systematic way discrete beings: children, teachers, parents, curricula. We then employ principles of value justification to support our moral judgments, principles of empirical justification to support our aesthetic claims. Within this tradition, Bloom,[3] for example, divides the world of educational objectives into the cognitive, the affective, and the psychomotor, and then each of these qualities of experience is ordered hierarchically according to their level of complexity. In Bloom's scheme the intellectual process of "comprehension"—simply understanding in one's own terms what another person has said or written—is seen as less complex than applying that knowledge to a new situation (called "application") or applying external standards of verification or significance to what is understood (called "evaluation"). The point, however, is that in the modern universe there is a domain of substantial being (actions, people, relationships) and then there is a domain of intellectual understanding. In the world of understanding, the more general or universal and abstract the understanding, the more valued it is educationally. This harks back to the Platonic cosmology which posits that universal form and principle are divine; that the immediate facts or occasions which surround us are imperfect instances or representations of these more universal forms; and that the true search for knowledge involves transcending the immediate instance so that one can frame it in somewhat perfected abstract terms. This style of knowing, which has passed from ancient Greek thought down through Judeo-Christian institutions and finally into European and Anglo-American social and political styles of justification, is so general and deeply imbedded in our language and consciousness that it has come to seem natural. The 'why' question immediately seems to us intuitively more important or profound than the 'what' question. Moreover, when we construe the 'what' question as simple fact and the 'why' question as leading to a moral justification or scientific explanation, we assume that we have somehow moved closer to the essence of human meaning and intelligence. When we say, for example, that the old man killed his wife because his heart was filled with compassion for her endless suffering, we immediately transcend the specifics of this case and appeal to the cogency and consistency of more general principles of action—for which we invent names, e.g., mercy killing—that may enter into the lexicon of higher moral purposes. We then ask general moral questions—such as, when is mercy killing justified—which are seen as separate from many of the questions associated with this specific instance.[4]

Process cosmology rather sees knowing as integrated with and inseparable from the world of fact, the concrescing occasions[5] emerging into the substantial realm that modern people call 'reality.' The world of value, from the process point of view, has its essence in the capacity for realization in the world of action. The worlds of action and potential, of action and value are inextricably bound together in *specific occasions.* Permanent value always enters into the creation of temporal fact. There is no fact without value; no value without fact, imagined or real. Thus each domain is by itself futile, except in the function of embodying the other. There is only one mode of existence; every entity or occasion is to be understood ultimately in terms of the way in which it is interwoven with the whole universe. When we enjoy realized value, we enjoy aspects of an inseparable world. Truth, beauty, goodness, justice have meaning only insofar as they connect with an actual occasion, with what modern people call 'fact.' Within this process conception, thought or intention or imagination, rather than standing outside fact as a way to judge or manipulate the 'real' world, are construed as prehensions contributing to the making of occasion as it moves toward satisfaction. We understand that occasion has both physical and conceptual prehensions, but we do not see the conceptual as 'higher' or determinative. It would be somewhat alien to process, for example, to assume that we determine objectives for a curriculum conceptually, 'make them real' by bringing them into the physical everyday world, and finally evaluate our substantial actions again conceptually. Rather, conceptions and intentions move with occasion every step of the way. The notion of formative evaluation in educational research is useful here. When a group of teachers is planning a curriculum, there are substantial things happening as much as when the curriculum is being taught to children. The implications of process thought are that one becomes involved in the creation of occasions in careful and incremental ways with tremendous sensitivity toward the totality of the occasion. Within this framework of social intervention, whether it involves curriculum-making or urban development (i.e., building whole neighborhoods or cities), the critical concern would be the capacity for all the prehending participants to share in the imagining and creative development of the mature occasion. With this in mind, we find it difficult to imagine education-making without the involvement of the whole community, including parents, teachers, children, trees and buildings, the existing culture, and beyond.

The modern consequences of separating a world of abstraction from what is often referred to as the 'real' world are, of course, radical. The world of abstractions is presumably inhabited by statements, hypotheses, principles, values, qualities of beauty. The world of 'fact' is inhabited by dead neutral objects. So we can say that "beauty is in the eye of the beholder." Amidst the ugliness of the Vietnam War, for example, as we saw the destruction of village people's lives and homes and communities daily on television, we were assured that this was done for higher principles, for democracy, for freedom. Many of us now suspect how limited was this kind of judgment.

Within process the emergence of knowing and the emergence of being happen simultaneously. The becoming and being of occasions have qualities of truth, goodness, and beauty, but there is the sense that these are not really separate and separable, even as abstractions. It is difficult to imagine, for example, that within the ugliness of the mass violence of modern warfare there is a higher good or a great beauty. Nor does the highest quality of knowing necessarily seem to reside in abstract knowledge. The fullness of knowing goes right along with the fullness of being.

Process Cosmology and the Plurality of Knowing.

Process cosmology suggests there is a primary mode of perception inherent in the very process of becoming—whether one is becoming an electron, a snow crystal, or a living creature. This is the perception of the *inheritance of feeling* from past data. Living organisms are in constant transition. New cells are being created; new consciousness is evolving. Through the process of meditation and the stilling of the 'noise' from our common-sense experience, we may come to feel ourselves participating in Whitehead's 'causal efficacy' or primary perception. When we do, we come to share in the experience of becoming, undergone by all occasions. We feel what Whitehead calls the "hand of the settled past in the formation of the present"[6]

A second level of perception is what we call our senses. Through our senses we come to have a clear and distinct extension into the world. We have subtle senses, like white cells observing microbes. Our eyes reach out to other beings and objects, as does our touch, or we have our "self-consciousness" sense—hearing.

Primary perception is the mode of our understanding in which we can feel inheritance from the past, as well as the transmission into the present of data with massive (though vague and inarticulate) emotional power. Our senses, on the other hand, (Whitehead's "presentational immediacy") transmit data that are sharp, precise, and spatially located but also isolated, cut off, and temporarily self-contained. They have no power of continuity, for they are simply an awareness of those extensive relationships that make up the contemporary world in this organism's *umwelt*.

Everyday consciousness is the mode of perception of the fully alert human. It is an integration of the most basic mode we have called causal efficacy and the more focused information brought to us by our senses. The experience earlier called grounded or ontological consciousness assumes that we apprehend both primary perception, which connects us to the process of being in the broader universe, and our sense of immediate occasion in our own lives. We strive especially toward grounded consciousness in sacred moments, such as prayer or meditation.

It is possible for cultures to create occasions in places of holiness and worship during which the experience of grounded consciousness is more likely to happen. The ability to speak in universal tongues, to communicate with plants and animals, to feel the forces of the stars are all evidence of grounded consciousness. Modern people often discredit or deny the possibility of such events, seeing it as superstition, animism, or blind mysticism. They stress the ability to understand precisely and clearly, to predict, and to control the substantial world, and maintain that this is all of reality. They deny, or shroud in sentimental mystery, the becoming and perishing which process sees as intrinsic to the definition of reality. Modern cosmology maintains that as we gain scientific knowledge, we will be able to build more sophisticated technology, and control more of nature. Process cosmology sees this vision as dangerously inflated. Instead, it stresses the creative and novel element in the continuous process through which occasions, events, 'things' happen. The creative element occurs both because material reality dissolves and reformulates itself in different ways and because eternal objects in the domain of pure information combine with substantial prehension in novel ways as new occasions. Nor are eternal objects or pure information part of some "other" domain of spirit. They are immanent; they are in the here and now; they constantly participate in the process of creation of new occasions. When an embryo develops or an ice crystal forms, there is developing actuality, out of nothing as it were. Where is the information that guides this creation? We can often find such information coded in the material world, as in DNA, but we do not know from where that information first came, either for the species or for the individual.

Thus, entities or actual occasions are mediated within a process which combines that which is substantial or temporal with that which is timeless potential. This potential can be called 'eternal objects,' pure information, or elementary form. Modern cosmology denies its existence. It is renamed 'variables' by the abstract scientific mind. However, religiously oriented cosmologies, as well as process, postulate it as an essential ingredient for understanding the universe around us.

Being and the Nature of God.

Before we move on to elaborate the essential relationship between morality and the process conception of being and knowing, we should discuss possible conceptions of God, since this notion has played such a long and central part in the ethical sensibilities of Western people. Whitehead stresses creative potentiality and the yearning toward fulfillment as a central aspect of God. Yet it is not difficult to imagine the gods in various human cultures as any of a number of the aspects of the process conception of becoming and being.

For example, there is the god of void—not suggesting nothingness, but rather the quality of pure information, eternal objects, form. This god does not inhabit a special domain off in the heavens, but is rather here in the split second in which each concrescing occasion begins. There is the god of ground, related perhaps to what Bohm refers to as the "implicate order."[7] Here pure form expresses itself as a limited range of potentialities, as candidates for complex substance. Ground is as a shadow world of partially formed realities, only some of which will be expressed in the here and now of everyday life. The implicate order of ground emerges into what the human *umwelt* calls real substance. In terms of energy, these are force fields and electronic events. In terms of material things they are the patterns of atoms, molecules, and more complex forms we associate with the visible, audible, touchable world around us. Substance takes the form of the most elementary sense of motion associated with energy and force (e.g., gravity) to the massive objects in the heavens, the sun and planets. This is the god of any materialistic cosmology.

From our conception of a process universe, we know that nothing lasts. This god emerges from data, from the data of void and from the data of perishing occasions. It has pattern and potential in the domain of ground. It emerges into the world of possibility expressed in energy and motion associated with the world of particle events in the quantum world. The entity then proceeds into a world or individual mind and consciousness. It becomes a subject as well as an object.

So in process one can imagine a universe of being with a void, a ground, and a domain of objectification. But none of these domains is the essence of reality, like the Judeo–Christian's heaven and hell and earth. The essence of reality is the transformative process by which being happens. The essence of reality is the flow of events and/or the relationships among events.[8] Void or form or information is not reality. Implicate order or ground or potential events are not reality. The objects around us and ourselves are not reality. The essence of reality is transformative process and the relationships within it, which include all the aforementioned.

To 'find God' means that we experience ourselves as connected with both the universality of the process and the particular concrescing events that characterize our own individuated person as being at some point in the process, for the occasion or entity that characterizes us.

In process cosmology, God is not a person in the sense of having human shape and form. God is not the void from which the implicate order is formed (the unmoved mover); God is not the ground or implicate order from which the objective world is formed (the Holy Spirit); God is not the perishing and dissolution which reconstructs itself in ground and void (the Resurrected One). If one uses the term at all, God would perhaps best be thought of as the creative process of becoming and being whose essence enters each act of transformation. God is the lure for the movement to complete itself.

Here there is a sharp distinction between Judeo–Christian and modern cosmologies on the one hand and process cosmology on the other. According to the former, there are domains of existence with different qualities of being in the different domains. There is heaven and earth. Earth was created by God, who may still participate in the creative aspects of earth and in human history. Humans and the earth have an historical destiny determined by His will. Modernity recognizes two domains: material nature and human mind. Nature is assumed to be governed by a complex set of laws. Human mind can come to know these laws and, through this knowledge, to control and manage nature for the benefit of humans and nature alike. Process, on the other hand, sees human mind as in the universe, in nature, in the world. Moreover, unlike modern cosmology and possibly Judeo–Christian cosmology, which see the universe as grounded in fixed natural laws, process sees nature as essentially incomplete. There is no final setting or resolution of a world or universe, either now or at some distant time toward which we are moving. Nature is always passing beyond itself in a rhythm that swings between novelty and unity. So the value of each momentary fact is not determined by its contribution toward some ultimate goal—e.g., to conquer nature or to conquer space or to carry out appropriate actions to gain admittance to heaven. Rather every throb or pulse of existence has some value for itself, for its own importance, whether it be photon, a snowflake, a leech, or a human being.

It should be noted that this conception of God in process has obvious moral implications. One might guess that it is required in the nature of things to respect others, not only human beings, but all beings, all occasions, precisely because they are all individuals in an endlessly reconceived natural world. Moreover, from this point of view, there is no thing in the universe that is dead, mere material which we may treat as the object of human gratification or the subject of scientific study or the sludge of mistaken creation. However, vegetarianism and kindness to bacteria do not automatically follow from a process philosophy; what does follow is the knowledge that all deliberate destruction or meanness requires caution and special consideration. What follows is a generosity of heart and generality of concern as we enter into and participate within occasion.

*Holarchy and Relationship vs. Discrete Entities and
the Hierarchy of Modernity.*

Modernity builds a morality based on the human capacity to construct and understand principles, theories, values, ideals for 'higher' knowing which inform the neutral facts of 'lower' knowing. As important as this sense of higher principled versus lower factual knowing is to the modern conception of moral reflection, there is a second and equally important consideration: the nature and ordering of the entities themselves. Both modernity and Judeo–Christianity grant the human entity a special place in the universe at the top of a hierarchy. The ultimate reason Judeo–Christians make that judgment is "man's" unique relationship to 'the' deity: man is created by God in the image of God; Jesus is the Christ–God incarnate come to save Man from his self-inflicted imperfections. No other entity or occasion is so favored, and much of the meaning of the universe follows from this fact. Modern cosmology stresses human intelligence and the capacity of humans to discover and use the laws of nature as a basis for humanity's special place in the universe. What follows from this central place of human being and personality is a hierarchy of the relative importance of the diverse and various entities on the planet. (See Figure 8.1 below.)

GOD	Highest possible intelligence and power. Pure spirit or value or principle, uncontaminated by earthly qualities of substance, morality. Not present for some modern secular people.
CULTURED HUMANS	"Saved" humans with some of power and enlightenment associated with God, Includes scientists and philosophers who have power associated with technical and conceptual understanding of the universe.

CIVILIZED HUMANS	Humans who can be trained, managed and directed by cultured or enlightened humans.
UNCIVILIZED PRIMITIVE HUMANS	Humans who lack intelligence or training to do systematic science, to build complex technology, or even literacy to do history and record-keeping.
DOMESTICATED FRIENDLY ANIMALS	Animals useful to humans, which offer no threat or challenge to human domination of planet: cows, dogs, honey bees. Protected by SPCA.
DOMESTICATED FRIENDLY USEFUL PLANTS	(Similar to domesticated friendly animals.)
UNDOMESTICATED OR "WILD" ANIMALS	Animals not under the control of humans, although some, like rats and pigeons and cockroaches, may live with humans.
UNDOMESTICATED UNCULTIVATED PLANTS	(Similar to "wild" animals.)
USEFUL LIFELESS "BEINGS" IN NATURE	Rivers, minerals, the atmosphere, etc.
USELESS LIFELESS OR UNTAMABLE"BEINGS" IN NATURE	Swamps, jungles, mountains, deserts, glaciers, etc.

Figure 8.1
Hierachy of Valued Beings in Modern and Judeo–Christian Cosmologies.

The spirit of modernity presses us to construe the world as discrete and separate wholes and to treat these wholes as individuated units of concern within the hierarchy of being that places humans at or near the top of the pyramid.

Process, on the other hand, sees morality as a search for the fullness of fact or occasion as well as a search for balance, harmony, and direction toward which occasion moves. Instead of looking for the appropriate abstraction or principle constructed from human consciousness (or discovered in some domain of natural law) by which to judge the value, beauty, or truth of a specific occasion, in process one searches for the appropriate range and intensity of experience to give one an adequate context from which to know (feel, apprehend, consciously describe) an interconnected and balanced world. The spirit of process, moreover, moves one to see occasions not on a hierarchy of relative importance and value but rather as intriniscally *both part and whole,* and to stress as a primary reality the interdependence and interrelatedness among occasions. This paradoxical state of always being both part and whole is elaboratored by Koestler:

> What do we mean by the familiar words "part" and "whole?" "Part" conveys the meaning of something fragmentary and incomplete, which by itself has no claim to autonomous existence. On the other hand a "whole" is considered something complete in itself which needs no further explanation. However, contrary to these deeply engrained habits of thought and their reflection in some philosophical schools, "parts" and "wholes" in an absolute sense do not exist anywhere, either in the domain of living organisms, or in social organizations, or in the universe at large.
>
> A living organism is not an aggregation of elementary parts, and its activities cannot be reduced to elementary "atoms of behavior" forming a chain or conditioned responses. In its bodily aspects, the organism is a whole consisting of "subwholes", such as the circulatory system, digestive system, etc., which in turn branch into sub-wholes of a lower order, such as organs and tissues—and so down to individual cells, and to organelles inside the cells. In other words, the structure and behavior of an organism cannot be explained by, or "reduced to," elementary physico-chemical processes; it is a multi-leveled, stratified hierarchy of the sub-wholes, which can be conveniently diagrammed as a pyramid or an inverted tree, where the subwholes form the nodes, and the branching lines symbolized channels of communication....
>
> The point first to be emphasized is that each member of this hierarchy, on whatever level, is a sub-whole or *"holon"* in its own right—a stable, integrated structure, equipped with self-regulatory devices and enjoying a considerable degree of *autonomy* or self-government.
>
> Cells, muscles, nerves, organs, all have their intrinsic rhythms and patterns of activity, often manifested spontaneously without external stimulation; they are subordinated as parts to the higher centers in the hierarchy, but at the same time function as quasi-autonomous wholes. They are Janus-faced. The face turned upward, toward higher levels, is that of a dependent part; the fact turned downward, toward its own constituents, is that of a whole of remarkable self-sufficiency.
>
> The heart, for instance, has its own pacemakers—actually several pacemakers, capable of taking over from each other when the need arises... And as we descend the steps of the hierarchy to the lowest level observable through the electron microscope, we come upon sub-cellular structures—organelles—which are neither "simple" nor "elementary," but systems of staggering complexity. Each of these minuscule parts of a cell functions as a self-governing whole in its own right, each apparently obeying a built-in *code of rules.* One type, or tribe of organelles looks after the cell's growth, others after its energy supply, reproduction, communication, and so on. The mitochondria, for

instance, are power plants which extract energy from nutrients by a chain of chemical reactions involving some fifty steps; and a single cell may have up to five thousand such power plants. The activities of a mitochondrion can be switched on or off by controls on higher levels; but once triggered into action it will follow its own code of rules. It cooperates with other organelles in keeping the cell happy, but at the same time each mitochondrion is a law unto itself, an autonomous unit which will assert its individuality even if the cell around it is dying.[9]

So we understand that in nature each holon (to use Koestler's term) or entity is an occasion in its own right, and that its meaning or significance is always relative to its relationships to a broader pattern, to the multiplicity of relationships that extend to and from its being. The core of any contrast between the morality of process and that of modernity or Judeo–Christianity settles upon two issues: our conception of the interconnectedness versus the separateness of individual 'things' and the extent to which we construe humans as separate 'things,' with a divine or qualitatively special link between heaven and earth, or, in scientific terms, as the only intelligent or 'mindful' being currently known in the universe.

In process, humans have no obvious ultimate value as personalities and objects qualitatively separate from the rest of nature and are defined rather by their multiplicity of relationships within nature; all the way from the mitochondria in our bodies to the love and meanness expressed among friends and relatives to our awe and involvement with the wind, the skies, and the planets. We understand that even the substantial thing we call our physical body is in constant transformation relating to the ecosystem around us, as, of course, are our more subtle and less easily defined mental, emotional, or spiritual states. From this point of view, the great and special gift of the human entity is our capacity to imagine ourselves within this broader and deeper arena of nature—to imagine ourselves as a virus, or a horse, or a carrot. With this intensity and breadth of experience and imagination, it is difficult to make sharp distinctions among entities or events which happen in or across various regions of nature—in the micro world of protons and electrons; in the common-sense world (to humans) of animals, vegetables, and minerals. Thus it is difficult to justify the deliberate aborting or destroying of one occasion in the interests of another on the basis of our own self-serving assumption that some occasions are simply qualitatively 'better' or more worthy than others. For it is apparent that all occasions evolve and 'live off' the perishing occasions that have come before. At some point all occasions in nature come into being, all perish, and humans appear not to be exempt from this fate. (We note here the Judeo–Christian's dissent.) In a sense all novel occasions come into being 'at the expense of' other entities or occasions, by stealing[10] from occasions which have come before. So we must always ask whether or not in any specific instance such thievery is justified. We humans intuitively consider the plant's 'stealing' of light (photons) and carbon dioxide less robbery than when humans deliberately slaughter large animals—cattle, pigs, sheep. Breathing seems less predatory than eating vegetables, which seems less so than eating meat. But this is surely a rather local, human judgment.

The issue of predation and exploitation becomes more acute when we move to the problem of parasitism. Worms invade the intestines of animals and live off the labor of the larger animal as it attempts to obtain nutrition for itself. Richer and more powerful humans live lives of independence and leisure by exploiting other humans who do the work that often makes such leisure and independence possible. As suggested earlier, such issues seem less easily resolved in terms of abstract principles—equality, fraternity, liberty, and so forth—and more approachable in terms of process, searching existentially for the fullness of knowing. Within this latter framework, the ultimate principle becomes the range and intensity with which one feels the occasions in which one is participating. The great moral danger is to *lose* one's sense of direct participation. So to benefit from 'participating' in the poverty of others with whom one never shares a common life is a great moral danger. To participate in poisoning the air and the water for other creatures, including humans, so that one can be wealthier or more comfortable, and yet live away from the toxic environment, is a moral danger. To enjoy using inexpensive products when someone else must do drudgerous work to create them, and yet never to see the work done or know the person doing it, is a moral danger.

The effort of liberal thought to create universalistic categories, such as that of 'citizens' with basic rights and privileges and the responsibility of 'participation,' is, in fact, an effort to maintain some kind of connection among all humans within a single political context. We then create special settings where the participation is expressed—legislatures, bureaucracies, courts, police departments. However, as process people, we are suspicious of relatively impersonal settings adjudicating the harmony and balance of the occasions of our lives with abstract principles and verbal-intellectual arguments. The fullness and intensity of occasion must be felt, in some degree, as the fullness and intensity of knowing. And that knowing requires an intimacy of context with the occasions themselves. This is the moral rock of process.

Process Knowing within Authentic Culture.

Process thus assumes a range and depth of knowing occasions within limits available to the human *umwelt*. We are informed about whether or not to care for a hungry neighbor or cut down a forest not simply as a matter of utilitarian calculus (the gains in pleasures and losses in pain for the human sensory system) but by apprehending in the fullness of our own being the occasions that may be aborted, or reach satisfaction and the connections that may be maintained by such actions. In our own involvement in nature, for example, the destruction of the forest means the loss of potentiality for significant occasions in our own being (not simply our physical human self, but the broader ecosystem). This capacity for an intense and significant understanding requires that we live within a culture which provides us with a range of experience and the specific symbols, habits, and language by which that experience is transformed into what we call knowledge. Such a culture must have at least two major qualities. First it must be within an environment which involves us in grounded or primary experience. (If one sits in a forty-story building in an urban center planning a shopping mall to be built on a salt marsh, the culture may well be deficient in the primary experience it could provide from which to take enlightened moral action.) Second, and equally important, the culture must contain a sufficiently rich semiotic code for the interpretation of the plurality of experience, the plurality of modes of knowing of which humans are capable. The code must explicate or 'reveal' the manifest and material aspects of our existence, as well as the hidden or implied aspects—i.e., those that stand behind obvious reality. In short, culture must amplify the fullness of the transformative cycle: the process by which information is transformed into images and patterns; the process by which patterns are amplified and become energy; the process by which pattern-made-manifest dissolves into data and is reborn in new pattern. Process cosmology thus can express itself only in those cultures which manifest this broader construction of knowledge.[11] Maintaining this full sense of the meaning of occasions, with an appropriate range and depth of grounded feeling, reflection, action–commitment, which moves rythmically through cycles of process and transformation, is that bounty few cultures seem to have been given. As Sorokin suggests, humans are prone to construct reality as either all substance or all mind (consciousness, reason, spirit, intelligence, and so forth.) As modern people we want to see reality as substance, approaching it in a practical, technical way. On the other hand we are haunted by the sense of a reality into which substance disappears and out of which new being emerges. Cultures tend to make spirit into substance with cathedrals and shrines; they tend to make substance into spirit with ritual, sacrament, and meditation. Sorokin points out that the Judeo–Christian culture of Medieval Europe, for example, represented a one-sided ideational cosmology: God and spirit were the essence of reality. Compared with heaven, the stuff of the earth was debased and chaotic, impermanent and less real. Jesus Christ demonstrated that humans could transcend the debased material world and ascend to the spiritual. The truest knowledge was spiritual knowledge, through God's word in the scriptures or through direct mystical experience, revelation, or divine intelligence. The various cultures of modernity (most fully developed in Western Europe and North America) have moved into a one-sided *sensate* cosmology. Modern people see reality only as substance (energy, force, matter) and are puzzled that it should constantly be transformed. They invent 'scientific' laws of conservation to persuade themselves that substance is permanently with us. This strong drive of modernity toward a consistency of meaning even in the face of the obvious facts of nature that do not conform to such meaning is, of course, one of its major cosmological deficiencies. Modernity wants to conserve stable building blocks of matter even when experimental physics demonstrates that the quantum world loses and recaptures particles in mysterious and unexplained transformations. It wants the photon to be all wave or particle. Such a culture, which embraces only the more superficial aspects of knowing—using only our senses and rational logic—and which denies any experiential connection to a more fundamental ground leads us to the arrogance of assuming that vagueness or ambiguity or contradiction simply reveal flaws in the logical construction of our theories rather than mysteries that transcend or lie beneath this simplistic quality of knowing.

Thus, authentic culture requires not only a cosmology that can be expressed in general abstract logical terms but one in which a fuller range of metaphysical concepts (time, space, being, relatedness, becoming) can be linked to the language, mores, folkways, and rituals that give texture and feeling to their meaning. Although we know little about how such cosmological understanding is given life, depth, and sustained meaning, we assume (as we suggested in Chapter Two) that a central mediating resource comes from the constellation of myths, core constructs, and metaphors available through the language and drama expressed within culture. We assume that metaphors are an important quality or potentiality of the human *umwelt* and are embedded implicitly in culture and explicitly in cosmology. They endow us with a richness of image which joins the deep underlying ground of occasion with our more abstract sense of knowing. Jesus on the cross, for example, becomes the image in an organic metaphor that describes the agony living things experience over the apprehension of dying and the potential release from this suffering by a compassionate father.

We must admit that when we move into the field of myth, metaphor, and the archetypes or unconscious symbols which somehow inform human consciousness from a deeper region of natural connectedness, we are on highly speculative ground. Anthropologists such as Levi-Straus and Mary Douglas have ploughed this field, as have many other scholars: Mircea Eleade and Joseph Campbell, as well as the earlier work of Freud, Casirer,

Jung, and Stephen Pepper. Yet at this point we would like to make a hypothetical case for the importance of a broadened range of metaphor (which we began in Chapter Two), as well as some comments on how they may be related to each other.

Pepper suggests a finite list of metaphors or "world hypotheses":

mysticism
animism
organism
machine
form
context

We might elaborate the common-sense connotations of these ideas. Mysticism suggests a larger unity which somehow connects all occasions or being in nature. It is in some loose way related to the idea of universal spirit or God, or to Bateson's notion of Mind. Animism suggests that out of the oneness or universality of a mystical unity come plurality, individuality, and uniqueness, yet the connectedness to the one means that each occasion has a quality of intention, of individual mind, is alive. Animism means that nature is indeed alive in all its particles and parts. Both Judeo–Christianity and modernity deny this premise, assuming that only God or a human being has divine spirit and all else has a lower station. Modernity assumes, generally, that everything in nature except humans is really object, matter.

Organism suggests that there is an aspect of some beings which has the quality of self-generation, not requiring external cause for its existence. Machine suggests subject and object; a living subject which creates an inert object; that the whole is the sum of the parts; that the parts are known; that the purpose of the machine is known not to the machine but to the maker of the machine. One can conceive of culture, generally, as emanating from the machine metaphor. Humans and, in fact, other living beings create ideas, habits, and artifacts, in a self-conscious and deliberate way, to improve their quality of life. Beavers build dams to create a more hospitable and secure life in the midst of the harsh cold of winter. The dams, the mounds, the stored-up bark from twigs are technology; they require intenton, technique. Humans, of course, build much more complex culture, which includes language and patterns of kinship. But, again, these are presumably techniques constructed for the comfort and convenience of the individual or group. They are technological extensions of the simpler reflexive or instinctual self. They are machine.

Form suggests the capacity to differentiate the world into ideas, hypothetical structures, realms of existence, and so forth. Our penchant for rules, lists, taxonomies, dictionaries, and the like emanates from the form metaphor. Context takes us out of our place in the universality of nature and places us in the specifics of history. One has an ontological context, the specifics of one's own concrescence. One has the broader context of the history of one's community, society, species.

Within this repertory of metaphors one can make comparisons among various cosmologies, among Judeo–Christianity, modernity, and process. Modernity, for example, tends to deny myths or metaphors associated with the idea of mysticism or mystery. (Pepper himself maintained that mysticism and animism were 'defective' metaphors.) The broader idea of 'mystery' is seen rather as a playful and trivial aspect of reality, useful merely for one's dramatic amusement. For the modern person there is a sharp distinction between true or authentic stories and statements and those which are only the products of one's imagination. It is, in fact, assumed that scientific and technological discoveries will continuously uncover mystery and that all will eventually be known. The idea of a permanent sense of mystery associated with the novelty inherent in the continuing process of a world of becoming is avoided, if not denied.

If mystery or mysticism are fundamental metaphors for the human *umwelt*, its denial by a culture can lead to cultural distortions or mistakes in how we understand the world. Modern scientists often wonder at the stronghold that Judeo–Christian mystical practices have on seemingly educated or non-superstitious people. Millions of apparently rational and sensible people commonly "take communion," which presumably allows them to experience a mystical union with the blood and flesh of Christ/God, with the sense of death and rebirth, with the connectedness of all being. Process cosmology assumes that this experience is a cultural instance or interpretation of the ontological facts that characterize all occasions. All share a common process of becoming, of satisfaction, of perishing, of rebirth in new being; all share participation in a universal and interconnected nature so that none and nothing is separate and cut apart. The exhilaration that sometimes comes from the communion experience is presumably based on the sense of 'giving up' the burden of one's individuality and the responsibility of nurturing the objective aspects of separate being. One 'gives in' to the apprehension of being part of all and all being part of one. Whether one calls this God, or Love, or Spirit is less important than that a specific culture has a mediating rite or metaphor through which mystical unity can be understood and experienced.

Contradiction and Complementarity of Meaning.

We are saying, in short, that the cosmology expressed within more authentic cultures should have a sufficient repertory of basic metaphors through which deep meaning can be experienced and understood. Moreover, there is a second important criterion one can apply to the adequacy of metaphorical experience, beyond its range and content—and that is the way in which the cultural meaning system handles the problem of contradiction. As categories relate to each other at the level of simple literal meaning, they often appear contradictory or in opposition. The idea of form (the differentiation of the world into various categories), for example, may well seem contradictory to the idea of mystical unity (implicate connectedness). One stresses plurality; the other stresses unity. In other more obvious examples, we may see male as opposite from female, machine as opposite from living organism. In Western thought there is a history of difficulty, even unresolvability, with opposed aspects of reality. We commonly employ two intellectual and practical techniques in our effort to deal with such contradiction. One is domination or destruction: we either attempt to dominate one pole of the antimony—e.g., males over females—or we attempt to destroy one pole—e.g., we construe the whole world as a machine which can dominate and destroy the self-organizing and uncontrolled quality of 'alien' living organisms. The second strategy for dealing with contradiction is the dialectic: the effort to transform both poles of a contradictory set of metaphors into some new and higher state of understanding. Hegel and Marx are, of course, prime exponents of this device in Western thought. Both also embody a commitment to progress and a departure from primitive dualities in favor of new dualities that eventually lead to 'highest' unity— the perfect society or God.

Process searches for an understanding of knowing and being at a deeper ontological level, where it sees the emerging (concrescing) being as unitary occasion; so that what may appear as opposites comes to be understood as complementary sets[12] within a single entity. There is maleness within femaleness and vice versa; males and females also comprise an organic unity; in essence all being is both mystical unity (or "in" a unity) as well as differentiated form. Nor is this distinction between a complementary versus a contradictory understanding of metaphor some fine metaphysical point. It has profound consequences for the way humans respond to, or in, nature. The modern person who inhabits a world filled with a multiplicity of antagonistic opposites sees domination and destruction as the necessary and normal condition of life. We make war on our opposites: as peace lovers we must destroy our enemies; we are a higher form of life and we must dominate other species in the animal kingdom; we are the affluent so we must make war on poverty, or perhaps simply on poor people. We even make war on the rules and restraints in our own culture so that we can be liberated into a new and more emancipated culture—i.e., we make war on the old in search of the new.

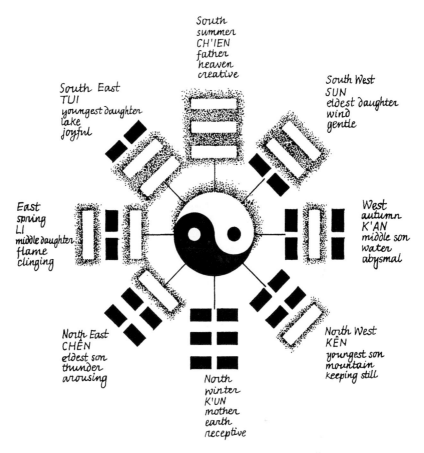

Figure 8.2 I Ching Symbol System Expressing
Complementary Nature of Diversity

Figure 8.2 represents the complementary rather than contradictory nature of diverse elements in the cosmos as presented in the 4000 year old *Book of Changes* or *I Ching* from ancient China. The cosmology represented in the diagram is based on the dynamic unity of the dark (yin—represented by the broken line) and the light (yang—represented by the solid line) principles. We would note the balanced statement of abstractions (the trigrams) in relationship to the grounded concrete aspects of nature (e.g., lakes, mountains) as well as the facts of human community (kin and temperament designations). The world is thus presented as a unity of related plurality, rather than as a series of adversarial fragments which compete with each other for domination or privilege. We are thus not forced to ask, which is superior, the abstract or the concrete? Nature or humans? Earth or heaven? The son or the daughter? Plurality/diversity complements unit.

Within the framework of process, the more authentic culture is one which generates or participates in images and celebrations that link or connect seemingly opposite categories and metaphors so that we have an intuitive grasp of them as complementary sets. We might look at the contrasting way process and modern cosmologies see organism/nature/life in relationship to (or as an opposite of) culture/machine/technique. Modernity places culture over nature in a hierarchical relationship. Nature is portrayed as unfinished, blemished, in need of repair if not domination. The wilderness must be cut down and changed into farms and cities. (One is reminded of Theodore Roosevelt's phrase "the winning of the West"). Children are, as primitive peoples, to be educated and cultivated. 'Wild' rivers are to be straightened and dammed. 'Wild' animals, like primitive peoples, are to be tamed or put onto reservations where they can be observed as curiosities of the past. We should note, of course, that this view of nature as somehow debased and in need of correction has deep springs flowing from both Platonic and Judeo–Christian cosmology.

From the point of view of process, culture is an aspect of nature; it emanates from it but is always within it. The bird's nest requires technique, represents culture, but is in no sense unnatural. (The sharp distinction modern people make between the technique of presumably mindless, instinct-driven lower animals and the actions of purposeful intelligent humans seems to us more a matter of degree than kind.) Humans, like many other animals, build shelters which are evidence of culture, but they too are within nature. As Heidegger points out, the common linguistic basis of the idea of *being* within nature and of *building* so as to dwell within nature is now lost from our own language.

> When we speak of dwelling we usually think of an activity that man performs alongside many other activities. We work here and dwell there. We do not merely dwell—that would be virtual inactivity—we practice a profession, we do business, we travel and lodge on the way, now here, now there. *Bauen* originally means to dwell. Where the word *bauen* still speaks in its original sense it also says *how far* the nature of dwelling reaches. That is, *bauen, buan, bhu, beo* are forms of our word *bin* . . . : *ich bin*, I am, *du bist*, you are, the imperative form *bis*, be. What then does *Ich Bin* mean? The old word *bauen*, to which *bin* belongs, I dwell , you dwell. The way in which you are and I am, the manner in which we humans *are* on earth, is *Baun*, dwelling. To be a human being means to be on the earth as a mortal. It means to dwell. The old word *bauen* which says that man *is* insofar as he *dwells*, this word *bauen* however *also* means at the same time to cherish and protect, to preserve and care for, specifically to till the soil, to cultivate the vine. Such building only takes care—it tends the growth that ripens into its fruit of its own accord. Building in the sense of preserving and nurturing is not making anything.

Shipbuilding and temple-building on the other hand, do in a certain way make their own works. . . Building as dwelling, that is, as being on the earth, however, remains for man's everyday experience that which is from the outset "habitual"—we inhabit it, as our language says so beautifully. . .

At first sight this event looks as though it were no more than a change of meaning of mere terms. In truth, however, somethig decisive is concealed in it, namely, dwelling for modern people is not experienced as man's being; dwelling is never thought of as the basic character of human being.

That language in a way retracts the real meaning of the word *bauen*, which is dwelling, is evidence of the primal nature of these meanings; for with the essential words of language, their true meaning easily falls into oblivion in favor of foreground meanings. Man has hardly yet pondered the mystery of this process. Language withdraws from man its simple and high speech. But its primary call does not thereby become incapable of speech; it merely falls silent. Man, though, fails to heed this silence.[13]

As Heidegger so clearly illustrates, 'building' or the making of human culture (cultivating) is an essential quality of being, as being is within nature rather than alien from it. The dichotomy between nature and culture thus disappears as we better understand the origins of our language and the deeper meaning that emerges from it. From the point of view of process, culture, and the education that culture requires, may come from a world in harmonic balance within such a complementary framework.

This view of complementarity as a more adequate view of nature is an extension of our general position that the morality of process comes from, is inherent in, our understanding of the facts of the world rather than from any new set of abstract moral or ethical principles or a redressing or rebalancing of the importance of existing principles (as, for example, in the case of 20th century liberalism, when it suggested that we place greater importance on human rights rather than property rights). Process makes the claim that if we seek to know the world in a more intensive and comprehensive way, with a more adequate cosmology, with a deeper sense of knowing, a new morality will follow. In this case, for example, we are suggesting that the world simply is more adequately construed within complementary sets than within the framework of contradictory forces. Once this paradigmatic shift emerges, we then find countless ways to understand and elaborate our new understanding. In the words of Jeffrey Stamps[14]:

Realizing that two polarities are complementary, equally valid and somehow connected is only the starting point for the question of how that relationship is most appropriately described. In quantum mechanics , two self-consistent but contradictory descriptions are used alternately to produce a common description which cannot be contained in either approach alone [the particle or the wave]. Other options are to choose one pole and ignore the other (e.g., body is real but mind is not), or to regard neither polarity as real in itself but to consider only the conflicting tension between the dual aspects as real (e.g., Heraclitus)...

Complementarity is easily recognized in binary relationships which are completely meaningless without the implication of an opposite. Convex/concave is one example: a concave form, like a radar dish, which focuses radiation to a point, is always accompanied by a convex form with the implied diffusion of radiation to the whole universe. Inside and outside are complementary... Janus... is a symbol of the unity underlying inside and outside, peace and war, open and shut, past and future. Left/right, on/off, yes/no, hot/cold, and up/down are complements of the same sort.

From the mundane to the sublime, complementary is a fundamental explanatory principle—yin/yang, being/becoming, self-assertion/integration, entropy/syntropy, atman/brahman.

Conclusion

Perhaps, as best we can put it, process implies a morality of intimacy, intensity, community, balance, and connection rather than a morality of principles, dialectics, personalities, and objects. We come to know how to act from our deep involvement within the occasions of which we are a part. The core of immorality comes about when we are distinced from or disconnected from thoughts, actions, and impulse of which we, in fact, are a part. Many implications for moral action now become clear. Consider these examples. The longstanding practice of trusting the care of the weak and helpless (children and the aged, for example) to those who are deeply connected with them—i.e., their kin and loved ones—is seen as moral. To trust the care and education of the weak and helpless to paid mercenaries is morally precarious. The president or leader who orders a war might do better to fight at the front lines in the midst of its killing and destruction. The person who can press the button to destroy another nation as well as his own would do better to have no bomb shelter, as the others on whose behalf he acts.

We believe hierarchy to be intrinsically morally dangerous, for it means that one person orders and manipulates the lives of others whom he or she may never see or experience. It means that having large units of human life dwelling in relative isolation from each other is morally dangerous, for all are affected by others whom they can never know and understand. It means that the diversity of nature (its resources and people) in the world on which we all now depend should be represented in the communities in which each of us lives. It is morally dangerous for some to live physically isolated in concrete cities; for others to live in a manicured green belt around the cities; for others to live isolated on large industrial farms; for others to live in isolated villages.

It is morally dangerous for some people to live in institutions for the helpless or dependent; for others to live in large, costly, and mostly empty houses; for others to live in luxury apartments; for others to live in squalid poverty in shacks at the city's edge. For under these circumstances we cannot understand the occasions in which, in a true sense, we all participate. The morality of process suggests that we all share, in some degree, the diversity of humans and the diversity of our natural environment in which we all have a common being.

PART FOUR:

Process and Education

Introduction and Overview

Our description of process comes from two different approaches toward understanding the universe: metaphysics and cosmology. The more traditional philosophical category, metaphysics, refers to the most general questions one can ask about the cosmos, questions that explore the nature of time, space, causation, substance, force, purpose, action, process, relations, and so forth. Cosmology adds another quality to metaphysics; it is the way our resolution of questions, dichotomies, contradictions, paradoxes, and the like come together within the framework of a meaningful story. The story may deal with metaphysical questions only indirectly, as in a myth or parable (e.g., the Platonic story of the cave); or it may give the appearance of directly telling some abstract universal truth, as in the literature of science and philosophy. The story may be specific and graphic, describing how the world was created from the word. Or the story may be speculative; less in the heavy-handed affirmative tone of a Genesis; more in the way geologists speculate about the history of continental drift over the life of this planet.

So there is a relationship between metaphysics and cosmology, in that the former tends to provide underlying questions or an abstract framework which provokes stories (cosmologies) about how the world and universe works. Or the reverse: stories told in a direct and unambiguous way may lead toward the metaphysical categories which give us a structure within which to question their truth or authenticity. From either direction, once we move into the cosmological–metaphysical mode of understanding, our mind does not rest with easy answers.

We would guess, moreover, that it is only when we shift from the dominant paradigm into a more speculative mode—when we are led (provoked?) to compare the conventional wisdom of modernity with other plausible cosmologies—that our thinking may become both complicated and confused. To clarify, we might return to our earlier example. When we think in conventional modern terms about thought, language, and physical objects, the relationship among them seems unproblematic. Ideas are the totally nonmaterial qualities of reality created or discovered by the human mind; language communicates the ideas; and substantial objects such as rocks and plants are the real things out there in nature. Yet when we look at the cosmologies and underlying metaphysics of various cultures, we find

156

striking differences on this issue. In the Hopi world view, for example, there is no sharp separation between the reality of unseen vibrations that characterizes thought and sensate audible speech and the palpable world of earth and water and mountains.

In Chapter Nine we use *metaphysical categories* as a point of departure to show how our notions of curriculum and teaching might be rather fundamentally altered when we begin with a process cosmology rather than the modern paradigm. We have chosen such categories as being, language and communication, knowing, power, time, and space as bases from which to select significant essays from process literature to elaborate the differences between process and modernity as they apply to our understanding of curriculum and teaching.

In the area of language and communication, for example, we summarize a classic article by Reddy on what he calls the "conduit metaphor." Reddy suggests that modern people have a rather magical notion about the way humans communicate with one another. They assume there is a conduit that carries accurate pictures / ideas / stories of the content that is in one person's head directly into another person's head. An alternative to this notion is what Reddy calls the "toolmakers metaphor." In this model of communication we understand that individual people have very different interior subjective terrains, so that the maps and symbols of our abstract language have to be reconstructed in a highly speculative way by the receiver of the message. Communication is thus seen as an activity requiring mutual craftsmanship. Each of us must apply the maps of other people's interior reality to our particular subjective world—an activity that takes considerable effort and skill to avoid serious and unintended errors. For those who believe in the conduit metaphor, communication is a dualistic process. There is mind, which understands; there is the message which carries the content of the mind. If there appears to be difficulty in communicating, we simply make the message clearer, less vague or ambiguous. From the point of view of the toolmaker, understanding is intrinsically problematic, because it must be constructed within the inner terrain of one's unique subjective reality out of what are, at best, only partial cues that come in the message from 'the outside.'

As this example illustrates, we have searched out and summarized what we consider to be significant and provocative essays dealing with important metaphysical questions that cut across the process–modern distinction and have special relevance to education. In Reddy's essay, for example, the distinction between the conduit and the toolmakers metaphor suggests that the latter is much closer to our common experience in attempting to teach people to understand one another. Likewise, it comes more out of a process paradigm, because it posits no finished external message "out there." Rather it searches for degrees of internal relatedness between subjective worlds. From a teaching point of view, it also suggests that for two people to 'understand' one another through verbal communication inevitably requires the *reconstruction* of meaning and is a good deal more complicated and difficult than we ordinarily recognize in the formal teaching of these 'skills' in school.

In a similar vein, we present Douglas Sturm's discussion of the term *power* and the way it is used both in modern political science as opposed to process theory; we draw on Evelyn Fox Keller's biography of the great geneticist, Barbara McClintock, and find striking confirmation of a process methodology in McClintock's way of coming to know nature. We present ideas from the writings of the arthitect Christopher Alexander in a discussion of *space,* as well as the work of Whitehead and Priestly in various constructions of the idea of *time.* Overall, the chapter makes two points. First, it shows that there is a body of scholarship moving out of the process paradigm that provokes one to give serious reconsideration to our modern cosmology. Second, it shows that once we make this kind of shift in our thinking, there are significant implications for curriculum and teaching, as is suggested in the example of Reddy's toolmakers paradigm.

In Chapter Ten we move out of the specific teaching context and describe more generally a variety of fields, people, and projects within the field of education which, we feel, have a sympathetic connection with the kind of educational practice described in Chapter Nine. When we identify such people and projects, we cannot help but emphasize what has been a persistent theme throughout the book: the difficulty of communicating across profoundly different paradigms. One can identify a variety of postmodern educational movements that are clearly related to what we have been describing as process. We assume that all are, in some manner, dealing with the transitional problem of moving out of the fragmentation, gross materialism, and human-centeredness which has such a strong hold on modernity. But the spectrum of such efforts stretches from those who simply dress up the egocentric practices of modernity in the words of process (e.g., 'holistic,' 'integrative,' 'non-dualistic,' 'natural') to those who are searching for a genuinely different way to experience the world. There are, for example, those who stress the need for greater expressive or artistic emphases in education as opposed to the need for the more utilitarian basics. The problem, of course, is how to emphasize the arts without seeing them as representing simply another fragment of contemporary life. From the viewpoint of process, the more fundamental issue is one of seeing aesthetic experience within a broader construction of the way we apprehend the fullness of our daily lives. It is not simply "another perspective." It is a deeper perspective which should bring together the many facets of experience into a coherent and multifaceted apprehension of the world.

In any of these transitional efforts, we would emphasize that the effort to communicate across paradigms often creates tremendous frustrations. Our livelihoods, careers, and reputations are often at stake. As process educators we want a sympathetic hearing from interested students and colleagues. So we may 'tone down' or bias our speech or writing to make it seem less alien. We then give mixed messages. Our audience does not know whether the only differences are in our abstract beliefs (in which case, they could respond ideologically) or whether we truly think that our underlying perceptions, images, metaphors and apprehensions differ. We are caught in a paradox. As we increase the focus and clarity of our verbal communications, we may betray the spirit of the central process insight—that the fuller meaning of human experience comes out of our whole diffuse bodily understanding, including its ecological grounding: movement, expressive behavior, and unconscious feelings of connection with other beings.

Our own mode of persuasion, i.e., using philosophical and analytical language to move the reader to take process seriously, is a hazardous, difficult, and perhaps even hypocritical adventure. We hope, of course, that enough transitional people will come to glimpse the vision intellectually and thus be inspired to create more powerful modes of expression— painting/poetry/drama/music/dance/liturgy—to transform our reality into what seems to us a healthier and more balanced way of thinking, teaching, knowing, and being.

Chapter Nine

Teaching and Learning Within the Occasion:[1] Notes on Process Education

The challenge in this chapter is to move from a general statement of process cosmology to more specific implications for teaching. Since it is obvious that one does not simply teach process as the content of a curriculum but rather uses it more as an orientation or posture toward the nature of reality and being, it is somewhat difficult to designate how and where to begin. Our inclination is to elaborate various philosophical and metaphysical ideas and show ways in which the process experience shifts how one thinks about teaching and learning with respect to these ideas. We shall deal with the concept of being, self, learning, language, power, knowing, space, time, and change.

Being

We begin our discussion with the notion of being. What is the unit of being? What does becoming or coming-to-be mean? In process thought, being is a constant changing, punctuated by throbs of fulfillment. The changing is accounted for by the urge toward novelty (or 'creativity') which characterizes all forms of being. Being itself has an inherent resistance to stasis. It does not encounter the present passively or indifferently. Rather, being confronts, relates to, prehends the present in terms of all its past experiences and its own intent. All being is endowed with purposes. One being does not cause another thing to be (like god being the first cause). Complex beings (nexus) consist of a holarchy of smaller being. All relationships are internal: no one stands outside and 'runs' something.

The implications of this vision for education are, first, that it is misguided to see an educational setting sharply separated into teacher, students, knowledge, curriculum, materials of instruction, and so forth. Seeing teaching as a set of different components driven predictably toward a controlled objective derives directly from the modern machine metaphor. In the modern cosmology, the *student* is a substantial being who can be caused (motivated) to learn *subject matter* by being provided with an adequate *curriculum* managed by the *teacher*. The student is the product to be developed, manufactured by machines (lessons) once they are provided with the raw materials (the curriculum). Within this cosmology, intention begins with the teacher, who constructs a (lesson) plan. This intention is communicated to the student as if it were a little packet that could move from one head to another. The teacher then shapes the student into a new product. If, in the process of student–teacher interaction, one loses sight of the objective and an unforeseen outcome results, the student must be further motivated. If the teacher cannot adequately 'motivate' the student, the teacher must be supervised by another manager who 'trains' teachers (i.e., engages in professional development) to teach properly.

Process teaching on the other hand begins by assuming that teacher, student, curriculum, materials (books, crayons, paper, etc.) are all moving into a novel occasion. We do not begin from the special position of nothing (before the class begins) to 'making something happen.' Teacher and student are constantly in the flow of occasions as they move toward fulfillment, are transformed, perish, and become part of another occasion. The major thrust of planning for the teacher is to imagine what circumstances might move an occasion from potentiality into concrescence. The teacher sees himself or herself as moving within time in the midst of a happening, in the midst of emerging pattern. The teacher has a sense or vision of what this pattern might be, of what is the intention of the occasion (not exclusively his or her occasion), but such a vision commonly involves much less detailed advanced planning and manipulation of students than is assumed in the modern model. It requires much more that the teacher be sensitive to the multiplicity of prehensions coming from student and setting. The teacher may begin to paint something for himself or herself, inviting others to share or imitate. The teacher may begin to write some mathematical language on the board and invite students to complete statements. We think about teaching (or 'the teacher') as providing the initial energy and imagination to stimulate particular reaching-out qualities (prehensions) of students into a shared happening. Such a happening would include people, things, ideas, actions. We would not think of 'shaping' a student so that she or he can do long division. We prefer to think of a happening characterized by a verb. The teacher, student, and blackboard were 'longdivisioning' or dialoguing about long division. The teacher is not 'transferring' a piece of knowledge or a skill to the student; the teacher is seeking to share a common world with the student as the student enters the world of the teacher and *vice versa*.

The great problem with constructing plans to manage a setting is that while they are to some degree required (one must have the tools and materials necessary to craft an idea or an object if it appears), they tend to prevent the teacher from using the sensitivity and imagination to move along with the student to the convergence of a shared intention. We are reminded of the time the Hopi spend in prayer and meditation so as to have good intentions, which lead to good ceremonies and hence good crops. But intentions do not 'create' ceremonies, they are part of them. In order for a broader range of imagination to focus shared intention between teacher and student, the pace and timing must be slow enough to allow for emerging reflections. We assume that every act of coming to understand, feel, and know, is novel. Each act of knowing comes out of relationships among the various prehensions of an occasion. Student and teacher learn by being part of an occasion that itself is novel, one which demands that certain aspects of the persons participate and consequently change. These prehensions consist of feelings, ideas, and actions of the people in the setting, as well as the materials, which are presumed to have intentions of their own (green paint clearly intends to make things green). They also include the historical conditions of repeated pattern that tend to narrow the potential of an occasion. If we think in terms of English sentences, for example—subjects, verbs, and objects—we are much less likely to understand process cosmology than if we think in terms of unitary verbs. The language of Western modernity would say, 'the teacher teaches science to the student.' In process terms, we would say that the teacher and student and book and blackboard and chalk are all doing science; all are part of a common occasion, sharing different aspects of it.

Process teaching takes seriously the mutuality of the intentions of the 'actors' or prehensions in the setting. The teacher does not move forward to cause something to happen; the teacher moves when there is a good feeling, when things feel right. This will seem strange for modern teachers and children who see their tasks as coming from the outside—from the requirements of a syllabus, lesson plan, or set of instructions. In the modern world we have a hierarchy with each level of the pyramid being external to the one above and below; the teacher is outside of and above the student, the principal or supervisor is outside of and above the teacher, the superintendent is outside of and above the principal, and so on.

Observing process settings and process cultures, we are struck by the sense that 'things just happen.' There seems to be a spontaneous convergence of intention—with little resistance or distraction as a group moves ahead within an occasion. In modern settings, before a task is begun (at the beginning of the day) or in transitions between tasks (e.g., between classes in a school), where the stream of mechanical time seems broken and where there is ambiguity about who is in control or what is to be done, there comes about a heightened sense of self and ego by the people in the situation, each wanting to go his or her own way; it is then that the setting often falls apart. In schools we call this a 'discipline problem' and are usually called upon to find external methods of motivation (giving tests or grades) or having the superior (teacher) act with added toughness. We make people 'shape up' or 'shut up.' We 'knock heads.' Or, in a more gentle way, we make people feel guilty about not living up to the expectations of the external authority. From a process point of view, we would prefer to have people trust in the possibility that mutual intentions of the people in the setting will converge into a significant novel occasion. Operationally, this does not mean sitting around passively waiting for something to happen,. It does mean that a teacher might wait for a student to begin a significant conversation. Or that the teacher might be prepared to begin several conversations until one 'takes hold.' This, of course, requires a culture of patience and meditation. It requires that time be slowed down so that imagination and potentiality have the opportunity to let occasions emerge from the mutual intentions of the actors. If there is no such cultural press in a setting, if the setting is permeated with impatient restlessness, waiting for the bell to ring to begin a treatment that will shape the students into educated people, process teaching has little chance of happening. In this sense, process education may require a fundamental change in culture and cosmology, in the way people feel as they come to a setting and what they expect to find there. In the culture of modernity, where life is often timed by the pace of television, punctuated by commercials, the audience sitting as passive spectators, waiting to be entertained or instructed—under these circumstances process teaching is obviously both inappropriate and futile.

Self

The paradox of ego and self is that when one is in the process of a fulfilling moment (when one is most oneself), one is least conscious that there is an ego making things happen. Yet these are the central constructs of the modern cosmology, in which 'self-actualization' is often stated as the ultimate goal of education. One does this by using the ego (as the conductor of the machine) to perfect the machine. For the 'self' in the modern cosmology, there are always two units of being: the individual mind or ego, on the one hand, and on the other objects, things, people out there which the ego uses for its fulfillment.

In process cosmology one is more concerned with the quality of emerging occasions in which aspects of oneself are a part. In child or ego-centered education, the object is to make the student imitate the teacher—i.e., do the things that the teacher does and can do. In more liberal circles, the goals are to make each separate student independent of the teacher, critical, and self-conscious of his or her own powers and potentials. In process teaching we are interested in creating significant occasions, which means that various prehensions (emanating from teacher, students, materials, physical space) may all play an essential part. We know that an occasion is significant or 'real' only fleetingly or afterward, for when it is happening, we are caught up in it, almost as if we did not even know it was going on. When a group of children is jumping rope—counting, or inventing and chanting rhymes, taking turns, making little contests, squabbling over who will turn the rope and who will jump, negotiating and resolving the squabbles—there are clearly occasions. But we rarely find that such occasions are planned, or have a formal leader who decides that it will last 33 minutes before the next game will take place.

Learning

When we relate the Whitehead metaphysics to education, another productive perspective is that of the student. The student's perspective is quite congenial if we consider him or her to be a metaphor for the actual entity; we see then that she or he is the phenomenon undergoing the experience of creating her- or himself. The entity is not only the center of the action, it is the cause of the action. And no matter what political issues come and go in education, the student is still the center of the learning experience. What is more, the student's own participation is an essential ingredient to that experience.

Like the actual entity, the student is, at once, in the experience and having the experience. When she or he makes sense of his or her experience, she or he reconstructs it in terms of symbolic reference; this way she or he can think of it, speak of it, recall it. The experience comes first; then, in a moment too fast to calculate, it is understood. It is a prehension; as such it refuses to submit to a strict chronology.

Whitehead's creativity is the principle underlying that process by which an entity enters into a relationship. We do not believe that the entity needs an experience or education or treatment to make it whole and sound; the entity has its own integrity, and has relationships because of its inherent resistance to stasis. Engaging in relationships is what defines it. Whereas others would claim that the student requires help in order to meet an educational criterion, after which she or he is improved, Whitehead's theory of metaphysical creativity suggests that the student, as entity, himself or herself experiences the novel for its own sake. It is not that the entity needs improvement but that it has movement. And this movement is naturally self-impelled.

Growth seen as an improvement process presupposes a deficiency in the student and a level of attainment to which someone else wishes she or he would aspire. Growth seen as a movement presupposes an urge on the part of the student to "advance into novelty".[2] The difference between improvement and movement has the same implications for education as the difference between the teacher's perspective and the student's perspective, between production and action, or between something which is administered and something which is sought. Such differences have tremendous impact on the components of curriculum design—for example, the definition of goals, selection of content material, the percents of lecture time, discussion time, activity time, or even the type of evaluation. The level of student participation will be the main consideration when one views educational growth as a self-impelled movement.

Knowledge, treasured as the gift of education, is really only useful as a catalyst for the active use of the student's creativity. Not used for this purpose, knowledge simply amounts to inert ideas, Whitehead's definition of the most useless thing in education. "What is wanted is activity in the presence of knowledge, novel viewpoints, knowledge applied to experience".[3] One place in the secondary schools where we are reasonably confident of seeing activity in the presence of knowledge is in the arts.

Art has two functions, as does Whitehead's subject/superject. It expresses gloriously the artist's experience, and it becomes data for the experience of others who come after its creation. Works of art always involve an imaginative transformation on the part of the observer or participant. Works of art are not problems to be solved or lessons to be learned; they invite speculations and invoke possibilities. Their subject matter becomes Dewey's "pregnant matter of new experience."[4] As such, art works are an example of the principle of organic philosophy which says that our whole experience is composed of our relationships to the rest of things.

The creative process has been defined by Beardsley as ". . .that stretch of mental and physical activity between the incept and the final touch— between the thought 'I may be on to something here'—and the thought 'it is finished'".[5] Thus seen, creativity is not something which can be managed from without. Only the individual can realize value in him or herself. Education should facilitate this natural process but it does not accomplish it. Education cannot be accomplished for a student any more than the aesthetic experience can be accomplished for the observer or concrescence for the entity. The artist and the student are prototypes of Whitehead's actualization of potential: As individuals each one apprehends, then manifests, his or her own data. As he says, "no one, no genius other than our own, can make our own life live."[6]

We should say, however, that those of us who believe with Whitehead that the natural urge of the individual is to play oneself as the instrument do not disregard the intellectual and emotional value of tradition. It is the springboard, Whitehead tells us, of all our art:

> The origin of art lies in the craving for reenaction. In some mode of repetition we need, by our personal actions or perceptions, to dramatize the past and future, so as to relive the emotional life of ourselves and our ancestors.[7]

Participating in any aspect of the curriculum goes a long way toward reliving the lives of our ancestors. Yet tradition alone is insufficient; there is a need to release our inherent creativity:

> . . .the secret of art lies in its *freedom*. The emotion, and some elements of experience itself are lived again, divorced from necessity. The strain is over, the joy of intense feeling remains. Originally, the intensity arose from some dire necessity, but in art it has outlived the compulsion that was its origin.[8]

We would suggest that the secret of learning also lies in its freedom. Learning that stops in the memorization stage does little to deserve the name. What activity there is is usually compelled by the teacher, and yet we know that true creativity is self-impelled. When students are allowed, in the presence of their intellectual heritage, to be creative—i.e., to actualize their potential—we see a situation which has the extraordinary effect of satisfying curriculum essentialists and Whiteheadians at the same time. We wonder why more of education cannot be this happy blend of conservatism and creativity. We think that as teachers we could learn some things from artists—Whiteheadian things, things which see the student as a *movement*. As teachers we could learn to allow activity in the presence of knowledge, to let students discover meanings and form novel viewpoints, to develop a sense of shared pursuit of knowledge (which involves risking failure in front of students). Above all we could learn from artists that learning, like the aesthetic experience, is something teachers can facilitate but not force.

The objections to general suggestions like these are invariably dreary: they are inefficient, there's too much unpredictability, there's too little time, there's not enough control. The objections stem from a perspective which sees education as something teachers give, like a treasure box from the attic, a perspective which overlooks the fact that in learning every student packs his own box.

Language

Language is the center of modern education. We make distinctions between knowing and thinking on the one hand and doing and feeling on the other. And we see knowing and thinking as language–based skills central to education—which is preparation, as it were, for doing. When we think of the relationship between language and education, the central problem is not simply how we might use language, but rather the *paradigm* (or metalanguage) we use when we think of language as a basis for communication. We assume, at least in English, that the whole process of "coming to know," as well as what is known, can, in the last analysis, emerge in a relatively clear and unambiguous way through the use of specific words and numbers. This means that one person can communicate what she or he means to another person through words. Language is a kind of physical package that is exchanged between selves, pesons. Freire has called this the "banking" metaphor. Reddy, in a more elaborated statement of this issue, calls it the "conduit" metaphor. As Reddy points out, we urge students to "get their thoughts across better," or to "give us an idea of what you mean." The assumption is that language physically transfers human thoughts and feelings: we "capture an idea in words," or we "pack thoughts into words;" a sentence is "filled with emotion." Reddy continues:

> The logic of the framework we are considering—a logic which will henceforth be called the *conduit* metaphor—would now lead us to the bizarre assertion that words have "insides" and "outsides." After all, if thoughts can be "inserted," there must be a space "inside" wherein the meaning can reside.[9]

Reddy then suggests that speakers of English cannot appreciate how deeply they are embedded within the conduit paradigm which construes communication as the transfer of physical substance from one speaker to another. The paradigm is consistent with the modern mechanistic model that sees all reality as composed of thought and substance. Thus we tend to think of meaning as physical messages and communication, almost as a computer program in one person's head which then connects to a printer in another person's head. When the switch is thrown, an "idea" is transferred in the form of electronically computed information from one person's mind to another person's mind.

In order to provoke the reader to take the conduit metaphor seriously, Reddy asks us to consider an alternative model of communication, which he calls the "toolmakers paradigm." We would see this, at least operationally, as much akin to a process theory of communication:

> Simply speaking, in order to engage in frame restructuring about human communication, we need first an opposing frame.
>
> To begin this other story, I should like to suggest that, in talking to one another, we are like people isolated in slightly different environments. Imagine, if you

will, for sake of the story, a huge compound, shaped like a wagon wheel (see figure below). Each pie-shaped sector of the wheel is an environment, with two spokes and part of the circumference forming the walls. The environments all have much in common with one another—water, trees, small plants, rocks, and the like—yet no two are exactly alike. They contain different kinds of trees, plants, terrain, and so on. Dwelling in each sector is one person who must survive in his own special environment. At the hub of the wheel there is some machinery which can deliver small sheets of paper from one environment to another. Let us suppose that the people in these environments have learned how to use this machinery to exchange crude sets of instructions with one another—instructions for making things helpful in surviving, such as tools, perhaps, or shelters, or foods, and the like. But there is, in this story, absolutely no way for the people to visit each other's environments, or even to exchange samples of the things they construct. This is crucial. The people can only exchange these crude sets of instructions—odd looking blueprints scratched on special sheets of paper that appear from a slot in the hub and can be deposited in another slot—and nothing more. Indeed, since there is no way to shout across the walls of the sectors, the people only know of one another's existence indirectly, by a cumulative series of inferences. This part of the story, the no visiting and no exchange of indigenous materials rules, we shall call the postulate of "radical subjectivity."

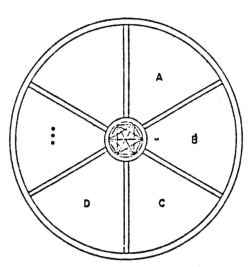

Figure 9.1 The toolmakers paradigm.

In the analogy, the contents of each environment, the "indigenous materials," represent a person's repertoire. They stand for the internal thoughts, feelings, and perceptions which cannot themselves be sent to anyone by any means that we know of. These are the unique material with which each person must work if he is to survive. The blueprints represent the signals of human communication, the marks and sounds that we can actually send to one another. We shall have to ignore the question of how the system of instructions became established, even though this is an interesting part of the story. We shall simply assume that it has reached some sort of steady state, and shall watch how it functions.

Suppose that person A has discovered an implement that is very useful to him. Say he has learned to build a rake and finds he can use it to clear dead leaves and other debris without damaging the living plants. One day person A goes to the hub and draws as best he can three identical sets of instructions for fashioning this rake and drops these sets in the slots for persons B, C, and D. As a result, three people struggling along in slightly different environments now receive these curious sheets of paper, and each one goes to work to try to construct what he can from them. Person A's environment has a lot of wood in it, which is probably why he has leaves to rake in the first place. Sector B, on the other hand, runs more to rock, and person B uses a lot of rock in his constructions. He finds a piece of wood for the handle, but begins to make the head of the rake out of stone. A's original rake head was wood. But since it never occurred to him that anything but wood would be available or appropriate, he did not try to specify wood for the head in his instructions. When B is about halfway finished with the stone rake head, he connects it experimentally to the handle and realizes with a jolt that this thing, whatever it is, is certainly going to be heavy and unwieldly. He ponders its possible uses for a time, and then decides that it must be a tool for digging up small rocks when you clear a field for planting. He marvels at how large and strong person A must be, and also at what small rocks A has to deal with. B then decides that two large prongs will make the rake both lighter and better suited to unearthing large rocks.

Quite happy with both his double-bladed rock-pick and his new ideas about what this fellow A must be like, person B makes three identical sets of instructions himself, for his rock-pick, and inserts them in the slots for A, C, and D. Person A, of course, now assembles a rock-pick following B's instructions, except that he makes it entirely of wood and has to change the design a little if a wooden, two-pronged head is to be strong enough. Still, in his largely rockless environment, he cannot see much use for the thing, and worries that person B has misunderstood his rake. So he draws a second set of more detailed instructions for the rake head, and sends them out to everyone. Meanwhile, over in another sector, person C, who is particularly interested in clearing out a certain swamp, has created, on the basis of these multiple sets of instructions—the hoe. After all, when you are dealing with swamp grass and muck, you need something that will slice cleanly through the roots. And person D, from the same sets of instructions, has come up with a gaff. He has a small lake and fishes quite a bit.

Although it would be interesting to get to know C and D, the primary heroes of this story are persons A and B. We return now to them for the climax of the great rake conversation, in which, to everyone's surprise, some real communication takes place. A and B, who have had profitable interchanges in the past, and thus do not mind working quite hard at their communications, have been caught up in ths rake problem for some time now. Their instructions simply will not agree. B has even had to abandon his original hypothesis that A is a huge man who has only small rocks to deal with. It just does not fit the instructions he is getting. A, on his side, is getting so frustrated that he is ready to quit. He sits down near the hub and, in a kind of absentminded display of anger, grinds two pebbles together. Suddenly he stops. He holds these rocks up in front of his eyes and seems to be thinking furiously. Then he runs to the hub and starts scribbling new instructions as fast as he can, this time using clever iconic symbols for rock and wood, which he hopes B will understand. Soon A and B are both ecstatic. All sorts of previous sets of instructions, not just about rakes, but about other things as well, now make perfect sense. They have raised themselves to a new plateau of inference about each other and each other's environments.

For purposes of comparison, let us now view this same situation once again, as the conduit metaphor would see it. In terms of the radical subjectivist paradigm for human communication, what the conduit metaphor does is permit the exchange of materials from the environments, including the actual constructs themselves. In our story, we would have to imagine a marvelous technological duplicating machine located in the hub. Person A puts his rake in a special chamber, pushes a button, and instantly precise replicas of the rake appear in similar chambers for B, C, and D to make use of. B, C, and D do not have to construct anything or guess about anything. Should person B want to communicate with C and D about A's rake, there is no excuse for him sending anything except an exact replica of that rake to these people. There will still be differences in environments, but learning about these is now a trivial matter. Everything B has ever sent to A has been constructed largely of rock, and A is thus perfectly aware of his neighbor's predicament. Even if the marvelous machine should falter now and again, so that artifacts arrive damaged, still, damaged objects look like damaged objects. A damaged rake does not become a hoe. One can simply send the damaged object back, and wait for the other person to send another replica. It should be clear that the overwhelming tendency of the system, as viewed by the conduit metaphor, will always be: success without effort. At the same time, it should be similarly obvious that, in terms of the toolmakers paradigm, and the postulate of radical subjectivity, we come to just the opposite conclusion. Human communication will almost always go astray unless real energy is expended.

This comparison, then, brings to light a basic conflict between the conduit metaphor and the toolmakers paradigm. Both models offer an explanation of the phenomenon of communication. But they come to totally different conclusions about what, in that phenomenon, are more natural states of affairs, and what are less natural, or constrained, states. In terms of the conduit metaphor, what requires explanation is failure to communicate. Success appears to be automatic. But if we think in terms of the toolmakers paradigm, our expectation is precisely the opposite. Partial miscommunication, or divergence of readings from a single text, are not aberrations. They are tendencies inherent in the system, which can only be counteracted by continuous effort and by large amounts of verbal interaction. In this view, things will naturally be scattered, unless we expend the energy to gather them. They are not, as the conduit metaphor would have it, naturally gathered, with a frightening population of wrong-headed fools working to scatter them.[10]

Like all occasions, an understanding comes into being as it goes through a process of self-creation, of concrescence. By contrast, in the mechanistic (conduit) metaphor we assume that all 'things' are constructed by an agent from simpler parts and pieces of physical stuff. The toolmakers paradigm assumes that words, pictures, and diagrams are a partial basis from which new meaning occasions are constructed. The stuff itself is not the meaning; they are only the physical prehensions which (along with conceptual prehensions) will be made into a new meaning. While Reddy uses the idea of "radical subjectivity" to characterize the toolmaker's paradigm, we must assume a shared intention between the various aspects (prehensions) of the meaning-making occasion. The person who makes the diagram, the person who re-constructs the tools from the diagram, the constructed artifacts, and the landscapes all contribute to the new meaning. If the toolmakers use a piece of wire for a rake tooth instead of a stick, the meaning is different. So the wire as well as the toolmaker and the mapmaker all share an intention; all are prehensions.

Process cosmology assumes that there are two types of prehensions as bases for new meanings—conceptual and physical. There is some mutual organizational or patterning process involving both concepts (eternal objects) and physical stuff in order for there to be a novel occasion. Communication is seen as an active process in which both the symbol/craft-maker and the symbol craft-receiver actively participate. Suppose we think of teaching someone to ride a bicycle. It cannot be done simply by diagram and explanation. For the initiate, the experienced rider's balance is as mysterious as the other person's terrain which surrounds Reddy's hypothetical characters; moving does not seem possible without falling. Communication is essentially an act of shared imagination, an act involving the whole body, an act involving trust, encouragement, and a certain commitment to intelligibility.

Once the difficulties of the conduit metaphor as an adequate explanation for communication (or better, miscommunication) are raised, the question remains: Why the illusion? As Reddy confesses, the illusion is built into the English language. Our own explanation would add that the illusion is woven within the fabric of the modern cosmology, and is related to the way we construe being and becoming. Newtonian things 'happen' because one substantial mass with power and force attracts or collides with another. Communication is the transfer of power within the framework of power relationships. Masses are moved by power. Words are the physical objects that flow through conduits which communicate that power. Because students do, in fact, respond to orders and instructions and often try to follow the intentions of teachers, we assume that orders are being faithfully communicated. When people do not understand the instructions, we see it not as the breakdown of an occasion (an aborted occasion) but as a deficiency on the part of the sender or the receiver of a message. At this point the stability of power relationships is threatened, and the response requires the reframing of how power is to be used as well as the reframing of the message.

Reddy develops other social implications of the conduit metaphor which are spelled out with considerable elegance:

> This model of communication objectifies meaning in a misleading and dehumanizing fashion. It influences us to talk and think about thoughts as if they had the same kind of external, intersubjective reality as lamps and tables. Then, when this presumption proves dramatically false in operation, there seems to be nothing to blame except our own stupidity or malice. It is as if we owned a very large, very complex computer—but had been given the wrong instruction manual for it. We believe the wrong things about it, and teach our children the wrong things about it, and simply cannot get full or even moderate usage out of the system.

> Another point from the story worth emphasizing is that, to the extent that the conduit metaphor does see communication as requiring some slight expenditure of energy, it localizes this expenditure almost totally in the speaker or writer. The function of the reader or listener is trivialized. The radical subjectivist [toolmakers] paradigm, on the other hand, makes it clear that readers and listeners face a difficult and highly creative task of reconstruction and hypothesis testing. Doing this work well probably requires considerably more energy than the conduit metaphor would lead us to expect.

> But we are still a long way from government policy in these effects. Let us turn, then, to the second example of the impact of the conduit metaphor, which will help us to close this gap. [Take the expression] "You'll *find* better *ideas* in the *library*." [It] is derived from the conduit metaphor by a chain of metonymies. That is, we think of the ideas as existing in the words, which are clearly there on the pages. So the ideas are "there on the pages" by metonymy. Now the pages are in the books—and again, by metonymy, so are the ideas. But the books are in the libraries, with the final result that the ideas, too, are "in the libraries." The effect of this, and the many other. . .core

expressions is to suggest that the libraries, with their books, and tapes, and films, and photographs, are the real repositories of our culture. And if this is true, then naturally we of the modern period are preserving our cultural heritage better than any other age, because we have more books, films, tapes, and so on, stored in more and bigger libraries.

Suppose now that we drop the conduit metaphor and think of this same situation in terms of the toolmakers paradigm. From this point of view, there are of course no ideas in the words, and therefore none in any books, nor on any tapes or records. There are no ideas whatsoever in any libraries. All that is stored in any of these places are odd little patterns of marks or bumps or magnetized particles capable of creating odd patterns of noise. Now, if a human being comes along who is capable of using these marks or sounds as instructions, then this human being may assemble within his head some patterns of thought or feeling or perception which resemble those of intelligent humans no longer living. But this is a difficult task, for these ones no longer living saw a different world from ours, and used slightly different language instructions. Thus, if this human who enters the library has not been schooled in the art of language, so that he is deft and precise and thorough in applying instructions, and if he does not have a rather full and flexible repertoire of thoughts and feelings to draw from, then it is not likely that he will reconstruct in his head anything that deserves to be called "his cultural heritage."

Quite obviously, the toolmakers paradigm makes it plain that there is no culture in books or libraries, that, indeed, there is no culture at all unless it is reconstructed carefully and painstakingly in the living brains of each new generation. All that is preserved in libraries is the mere opportunity to perform this reconstruction. But if the language skills and the habits of engaging in reconstruction are not similarly preserved, then there will be no culture, no matter how large and complete the libraries may become. We do not preserve ideas by building libraries and recording voices. The only way to preserve culture is to train people to rebuild it, to "regrow" it, as the word "culture" itself suggests, in the only place it can grow—within themselves.

The difference of viewpoint here between the conduit metaphor and the toolmakers paradigm is serious, if not profound. Humanists appear to be dying these days, and administrators and governments seem to feel few compunctions about letting this occur. We have the greatest, most sophisticated system for mass communication of any society that we know about, yet somehow mass communication becomes more and more synonymous with less communication.[11] Why is this? One reason, at least, may be that we are following our instruction manual for use of the language system quite carefully—and it is the wrong manual. We have the mistaken, conduit-metaphor influenced view that the more signals we can create, and the more signals we can preserve, the more ideas we "transfer" and "store." We neglect the crucial human ability to reconstruct thought patterns on the basis of signals and this ability founders. After all, "extraction" is a trivial process, which does not require teaching past the most rudimentary level. We have therefore, in fact, less culture—or certainly no more culture—than other, less mechanically inclined, ages have had. Humanists, those traditionally charged with reconstructing culture and teaching others to reconstruct it, are not necessary in the scheme of the conduit metaphor. All the ideas are "there in the library," and anyone can go in and "get them."

Perhaps the most significant line in Reddy's critique of the conduit metaphor is the statement: "After all, 'extraction' is a trivial process, which does not require teaching past the most rudimentary level." By "extraction" we assume that Reddy means the learning of abstractions that have been lifted from the total experience of an occasion. Or in Whitehead's terms:

> The doctrine which I am maintaining is that the whole concept of materialism only applies to very abstract entities, the products of logical discernment. The concrete enduring entities are organisms [occasions], so that the plan of the *whole* influences the very characters of the various subordinate organisms which enter into it. In the case of an animal, the mental states enter into the plan of the total organism and thus modify the plans of the successive subordinate organisms until the ultimate smallest organisms, such as electrons, are reached. Thus an electron within a living body is different from an electron outside it, by reason of the plan of the body.[12]

The doctrine which maintains that the essence of knowing rests in abstractions or the products of logical discernment, is, for Whitehead, misguided. Abstractions have meaning in large degree within the framework of a particular organism or a particular occasion. When we say that we teach mostly facts in school, we rather mean to say that we teach mostly abstractions. To say, for example, that the American Civil War ended in 1865 is an abstraction of the highest order. We might ask for whom, where, when, how, and realize that the seeming 'fact' is an abstraction that encompasses an infinity of facts (occasions).

The implications of Reddy's two models of communication for process education are obvious. If one sees teaching as transferring physical packages of information, as in conduit thinking, then the major problem is simply one of making the information as clear and unambiguous as possible, and of finding a reasonably efficient setting in which to make the transfer. Freire's banking metaphor applies. The teacher makes out clear deposit slips, and the students accumulate learning in their bank books.

Such a view of communication makes outrageous assumptions about the relative ease with which communication takes place. The toolmakers metaphor, on the other hand, assumes that every communication is a challenging and highly creative task of constructing new meaning. From a process point of view, every time meaning is constructed, there is a novel occasion. One of the greatest difficulties with conduit schooling may well be that both teachers and students see learning as a relatively simple and routine (albeit long and tedious) activity, precisely because the quality of knowing thus conceived is so superficial. Deep knowing is creative knowing. Deep knowing requires difficult meaning-building. It requires time from the learner, as well as a certain receptivity to what is being seen and heard. Moreover, it requires commitment, an effort to build new knowledge. Deep knowing requires that the learner advance to novelty and confront it. This movement (which Whitehead calls creativity) is actually more like performing the physical work of craft-making such as ceramics than passively receiving a transfer of information. It is striking how the toolmaker's metaphor works so appropriately in interpreting the way small children learn to speak their native tongue (or even a second language), and how well the conduit metaphor works to describe the way high school students learn in literature or social studies courses. Which knowing is more likely to become a permanent part of the learner is obvious.

Reddy's next point—that by using the conduit metaphor we falsely assume that libraries, with their books, tapes, films, and photographs, are the real repositories of kowledge—is consistent with the view of modernity which contends that palpable physical things (nouns) are 'real' while the more transient prehensions, such as actions or feelings, are unreal. Process cosmology sees reality as a verb: doing, participating. It is more consistent with the toolmakers paradigm, which assumes that culture is not stored in books or libraries but rather constructed out of new occasions. Culture is the novel (if patterned) reconstruction of past ideas and behaviors, in the actions of each new generation. What is preserved in libraries are some provocative prehensions, which may combine with the actions of living people who create and live out culture. Cultural occasions combine the intentions of people, books, and the like in novel interpretations, which explains why culture is always changing and moving.

The implications for educational evaluation of these two contrasting conceptions of communication and knowing are profound. The notion that a major goal of teaching is to push students toward one understanding would seem strange indeed. In process, the importance of improvisation, rather than standardized repetition, becomes central. Process recognizes uniqueness rather than uniformity of outcome in craft, dialogue, and learning. In craft, we seek the familiarity of culture but the uniqueness of individuality—in the way we weave, paint, sculpt, wear our clothes, make our food, perform plays, take part in religious rituals. In dialogue, we enjoy improvising a conversation; we surely do not value having the same conversation twice, with precisely the same words, inflections and gestures. We invent conversation on the spot. Even though it carries the conventions of our society and language, every conversation is novel. Whitehead reminds us that the world never reaches a static completion. Education, which acts as though it has, which stresses uniformity of outcome through a repetition of similar events for all students, would seem almost a perversion of the great law of nature, which provides some balance between predictability and novelty.

Power

In the spirit of stressing the importance of cosmological frameworks, or what he calls "orienting concepts," a noted process writer states:

> ...orienting concepts do not merely delimit fields. In a sense they constitute reality, or one may say they elevate some dimensions of reality subordinate others, and may distort or totally obscure forces that remain nonetheless vital in the field of action. As such, orienting concepts make a difference in the way institutions are formed and lives are lived. Definitions of law, for instance, held implicitly or explicitly, are not without significance in shaping the professional life of the lawyer. Just so, specifications of the political are of practical import in the manner that citizen and statesman approach political life. More broadly, concept construction is a function of cosmological understanding. That is, the basic mentality of a people, its view of the world, is influential if not determinative in setting the limits and forming the character of its fundamental notions, including those of the political.[13]

Sturm then goes on to discuss the political cosmology of Thomas Hobbes, which he calls characteristically "modern":

> reality, most simply put, is matter in motion. In Hobbes' words, The world...is corporeal—that is to say, body—and has the dimensions of magnitude, namely, length, breadth and depth...

> From Hobbes' perspective, the analytic method is central to understanding. The analytic method requires the dissection of objects into their simplest components. In politics, *the simplest part is the isolated individual* acting in accordance with the passions, all of which are reduced to two forms, aversion and adversion.[14]

Modern education constructs the classroom in Hobbesian terms. The classroom is composed of objects in motion—the teacher and the students. The teacher controls information (in the form of small packages—books, tapes, films) which has the 'force' to influence and move the students. Educators have developed schema by which to describe the 'interacts' between teacher and student. In such a model we have solid objects (people), force and motion (the act and interact), and assume causal relationships between the motion of the objects and the power of the acts. Effective teaching occurs when the student object is affected (influenced) by the teacher object. We see these settings occurring in physical time counted on clocks and have expressions which embody this idea, such as 'time on task.' Within this model, we see what is "learned" as repeatable acts (such as doing items on a test, or reading a passage from a book). So the concept of power within the framework of Hobbesian politics is force driven by one unit of mass (a person or teacher) over another. The purpose is to control the nature of the force over another mass (a student) so that one can produce predictable and controlled behavior on the part of the object being influenced.

Hobbes' cosmology is then contrasted with what Sturm calls a postmodern cosmology, a Whiteheadian view of self and power:

> To Whitehead, of course, the human self is thoroughly social. It is, in itself, a dynamic interconnection of nexus ruled over at any one moment by a presiding occasion whose character endures through time. But the self is social in a more extensive sense. The irreducible individuality that characterizes each self is not an isolated or merely private individuality. It is intrinsically public in its dependency and in its implication. On the one hand, the possibilities of the self are heavily dependent on its forms of social inheritance. In turn, the determinations of the self constitute a legacy to the social future. The self's identity cannot be comprehended apart from its past or its future, its given environment or its creative formation.[15]

The "creative formation" is a dynamic occasion within which social aspects of persons participate, both with each other and with the variety of other aspects of the setting. An occasion has its own intention and moves forward to actualize that intention. The teacher's conscious intention of what she or he is teaching may be a prehension of the occasion, but is only one aspect of what happens. Individual human beings are not the only units of the occasion, nor is the occasion defined simply in individual human terms (as people). Ideas, actions, intentions of humans are prehensions or feelings which move together to create a pattern of relationship that constitutes the "occasion." However, the occasion is also, of course, defined in terms of the physical characteristics of the setting, the history of the setting, and aspects of other participants (e.g., plants, animals, sunlight, jet noise).

These ideas, in considerable degree, contradict our liberal notions about the sanctity of each human individual as the unit of being and the sacrosanct conception that each person has the right to life, liberty, happiness, and so forth. In liberal terms, education is a commitment to the fulfillment of these individual personal rights. Such a construction of (and the rights derived from) individuals then reduces to a series of logical distinctions. Are children persons? Do they belong to parents? to teachers? to the state? to God? Does the teacher have rights associated with conscience in what she or he teaches, associated with professional standards and other beliefs? When do teachers 'abuse' children? While these distinctions make interesting briefs in legal cases, in the day-to-day functioning of education the notion of the sacredness of the individual is a less than useful construct. As Whitehead says:

> The whole concept of absolute individuals with absolute rights, and with a contractual power of forming fully defined external relations, has broken down. The human being is inseparable from its environment in each occasion of its existence. The environment which the occasion inherits is immanent in it, and conversely it is immanent in the environment which it helps to transmit. The favorite doctrine of the shift from a customary basis for society to a contractual basis, is founded on shallow sociology. There is no escape from customary status. This status is merely another name for the inheritance immanent in each occaion. Inevitably inheritance is there, an inescapable condition. On the other hand, the inherited status is never a full determination. There is always freedom for the determination of individual emphasis.[16]

Here we have, now, three very different constructions of the basis of power in the politics of teaching. Power can reside in the individual units in the classroom (the people); power can be modified by contracts negotiated between individuals in a social setting (the Lockean compromise with Hobbes); power can be inherent in the occasion as it consists of aspects of both individuals in the setting, as well as some sense of patterned continuity which Whitehead calls 'custom' and we call culture. Culture is a kind of transpersonal pattern, established over time within a community of people (no one quite knows how) which influences members of a community to behave in similar ways. The *modern* model of culture-building and maintenance is one of individual teaching—actors exercising force (power) over other actors through messages, rewards, and punishments. The *process* or organic model of culture (or patterned relationships among people that we describe as personal/social occasions) would assume that the unit of the occasion was essentially social (not separate individuals influencing individuals). Patterns emerge in response to some inner desire for the fulfillment of both individuals and community. People-in-community participate in the making of occasions within which individuals, as elements (or prehensions), participate.

Within this latter framework, teaching begins with the question "How might we share a novel and fulfilling occasion?" rather than "How can I use my power and competence to transfer efficiently a message in my head into that of the student?" We believe teaching originates in imagination and passion, with the desire to participate in an occasion that has particular richness for those who contribute to its fulfillment. One of the first challenges for this pedagogy is to lose the sense of the teacher's deliberate manipulating of student and to gain a sense of teacher's and student's sharing a common relationship. How can the teacher enter the student's world and at the same time have the student enter the teacher's world? We do not think of the teacher as motivating students (in the sense of moving them); we think instead of aspects of selves (prehensions) sharing a common intention as aspects of the self move into a concrescing occasion,. Power is intrinsic to the occasion and is related to the desire of the occasion to complete itself. If children are learning a dramatic song and movement, in process terms the teacher does not impart information necessary to do the song, but rather sets the stage for the movement of prehensions along a common path. This may be done with a conversation about the song—drama or with the teacher and children acting out possibilities. The basic source of the occasion is neither exclusively the directions of the teacher (motivating the students), nor the creative acts of individual students. Rather it is shared intention moving into a novel occasion.

This kind of thinking may well be considered utopian and idealistic. Yet as we consider how children learn an oral language or how humans in general learn the most subtle aspects of social and practical skill, this approach does not seem at all out of the ordinary.

Knowing

In modern education, the predominant approach to knowing is expository and utilitarian. The student learns the instrumental knowledge necessary to present and understand clearly the requirements for achieving those ends chosen either by empowered groups in society (school boards, College Boards) or the individual herself or himself. We first learn 'tool' or 'skill' subjects—e.g., reading, writing, calculation, spelling—which place little emphasis on entities in the world and are concerned mainly with abstract communication. We then learn about more comprehensive bodies of knowledge, discovered and codified by others, presumably directed toward some personally or socially useful end—e.g., chemistry to do medicine; electronics to run a ham radio; the driving manual to get a driver's license; American history to pass a civil service exam, or perhaps to vote.

From a process perspective, the defect in this conception of knowing relates to the quality, that is to say the depth and coherence, of meaning associated with the culture of modernity, whose major conception of 'being' is acquiring that power necessary to manipulate the substantial world for human comfort and convenience. Construing the curriculum simply as personally or socially useful things to be learned about so that one can do business in a cultural marketplace consisting of people, products, and services ignores a basic human intention—to feel involved in nature and the universe as a participant in the continuous creative process which characterizes it. This kind of speculative assumption is based on the premise that the quality of culture is measured not simply in terms of the achievement of utilitarian goals: that which will achieve personal comfort, material affluence, and the variety of choices available to members, even their health and longevity. Quality of life is also importantly related to the depth with which we understand and feel our involvement in the most basic of ontological processes: coming into being, the sense of fulfillment of intention, the sense of perishing and transformation. This latter quality is seen not only as one's personal connection with natural processes but as connection also with cultural processes, which have their own continuous sense of coming into being. We might call this quality of knowing the *sense of integrity* within nature and consequently within culture. The problem is, of course, that our sense of connectedness with nature is always in some degree filtered through the range of experience possible within culture. In a culture such as the Hopi, which celebrates the inner connectedness of all aspects of nature, including human societies, one feels in an almost palpable way the world coming into being. One is not outside making things happen; one is inside participating in the happening. Superficial expository and logical knowing is then connected to knowing in the deeper religious and aesthetic sense. As Laura Thompson notes, "Hopi culture manifests an internal dynamic unity which is not merely organic and functional in type but also logical and aesthetic."[17]

Certainly this sense of connectedness between individual and culture and culture and nature (all are experienced as one) leads to the notion that there are "layers" of knowing. These layers might extend, for example, from simple vague feelings of comfort and discomfort to intuition; to the imaginative translation of feelings and intuition into images, stories, objects, dance, and the framing of stories with theories and a sense of history; and then to the critical analysis of stories, theory, and history through philosophy and metaphysics.

Much of Whitehead's work is an elaboration of this continuum of experience, which provides depth as an important dimension for both knowing and being.

> The primitive form of physical experience is emotional... In the language appropriate to higher stages of experience, the primitive element is *sympathy*, that is, feeling the feeling *in* another and feeling conformally *with* another. We are so used to considering the high abstraction, "the stone is green," that we have difficulty in eliciting into consciousness the notion of "green" as a qualifying character of an emotion. Yet aesthetic feelings, whereby there is pictorial arts, are nothing else than products of the contrasts which are made

> possible by their patterned relevance to each other. The separation of the emotional experience from the presentational intuition is a high abstraction of thought. Thus the primitive experience is emotional feeling, felt in its relevance to a world beyond.[18]

Whitehead's view of experience and reality is not unlike the distinction Northrop makes between the "undifferentiated aesthetic continuum" (i.e., the more direct intuitive apprehension of meaning in experience which he associated with Eastern cultures, as opposed to the highly differentiated conceptual–theoretical apparatus we associate with contemporary Western scientific models or theories). One does, however, occasionally find Western scientists speaking about their knowing in deeper ways. An example of this is in the research of Barbara McClintock, a Nobel laureate, which involved years of being close to, growing, and observing maize. Evelyn Fox Keller describes in strikingly process terms the intimate relationship between McClintock and her kernals of corn:

> For all of us, our concepts of the world build on what we see, as what we see builds on what we think. Where we know more, we see more. But for McClintock this reciprocity between cognitive and visual seems always to have been more intimate than it is for most. As if without distinguishing between the two, she knew by seeing, and saw by knowing. Especially illustrative is the story she tells of how she came to see the Neurospora chromosomes. Unwilling to accept her failure to see these minute objects under the microscope—to pick them out as individuals with continuity—she retreated to sit, and meditate, beneath the eucalyptus trees. There she "worked on herself." When she felt she was ready, she returned to the microscope, and the chromosomes were now to be seen, not only by her, but, thereafter, by others as well.

> If this were a story of insight arrived at by reflection, it would be more familiar. Its real force is as a story of eyesight, and of the continuity between mind and eye that made McClintock's work so distinctive and, at the same time, so difficult to communicate in ordinary language.

> Through years of intense and systematic observation and interpretation (she called it 'integrating what you saw'), McClintock had built a theoretical vision, a highly articulated image of the world within the cell. As she watches the corn plants grow, examined the patterns on the leaves and chromosomal structure, she saw directly into that ordered world. The 'Book of Nature' was to be read *simultaneously* by the eyes of the body and those of the mind. The spots McClintock saw on the kernels of corn were ciphers in a text that, because of her understanding of their genetic meaning, she could read directly. For her, the eyes of the body *were* the eyes of the mind. Ordinary language could not begin to convey the full structure of the reading that emerged.

Now that a number of biologists have become motivated to understand McClintock's work, one can get a glimmer of what the difficulties have been and what it takes to overcome them. Over and over again, these scientists locate their 'breakthrough' in the experience of 'seeing the patterns' on the actual kernels of corn; finding, in one biologist's words, 'a single color photograph more illuminating than all her papers put together.'

Evelyn Witkin's description of how her own understanding had developed, by looking over McClintock's shoulder, is further illustrative. Looking at the material, guided by McClintock's running narrative, she, too, learned to 'actually see the genes turning on and off.'

Witkin can be said to have learned a special kind of language—a language in which words and visual forms are woven together into a coherent structure of meaning. Once knowing the 'language,' Witkin could say that the arguments McClintock presented were as convincing and the proof as rigorous as any she knew. But to others with whom McClintock had not interacted as extensively, they were 'incomprehensible.'

In order to 'see' what McClintock 'saw,' Witkin had to learn more than a new 'language;' she needed to share in McClintock's internal vision. In that sense, 'seeing' in science is not unlike 'seeing' in art. Based on vision, our most public and our most private sense, it gives rise to a kind of knowledge that requires more than a shared practice to be communicable: it requires a shared subjectivity.[19]

The implications of Keller's observations of McClintock's work for curriculum and teaching suggest how difficult it would be for a McClintock-type teacher or student to survive in a modern school without considerable efforts at remediation. Science certainly is not construed as creating an intimate relationship with various aspects of nature. It is rather seen as learning objective methods of observation and experimentation that keep the observer quite removed from his or her objects of study or the data that describe them. The particular kind of consciousness or experiential quality of knowledge science encourages is explicit, clear, and superficial. It also lends itself smoothly to division into curriculum units. The frog we cut apart in the school biology laboratory, for example, is not introduced as a significant and intimate neighbor in our universe or on our planet. It is not even 'alive'. It merely provides useful data to illustrate such technical concepts as 'circulatory system' or 'the anatomy of amphibians.'

Or consider the following first grade assignment given out in a local suburban school. The major purpose of the exercise is to teach the child to order temporal events. The child most likely has never participated in these events (planting pumpkins, watching the flowers turn into pumpkins). The child is not encouraged to hold a pumpkin, to feel a pumpkin, to feel

Name _____

Read the story.

Last June I planted my seeds. A long green vine grew. Orange flowers grew on the vine. Each flower will become a pumpkin. I can give pumpkins to my friends.

Read the sentences below. Cut them out and paste them in the right order.

1	Then orange flowers grew.	3
2	A long green vine grew.	2
3	The flowers will be pumpkins.	4
4	I planted some seeds.	1
5	I will give pumpkins away.	5

Cut.

Figure 9.2 Assignment for first-grade class.

like a pumpkin. There is no effort to present the mystery of birth and life and death and rebirth involved in the five-line story. The story could be a drama; it could be visual; it could have smell and taste. It could be a dance. The kinds of participation in 'pumpkinhood' are even more plausible given its association with feasting (Thanksgiving) and the mystery of the spirit world (Halloween). Yet here it is used in a very isolated way to teach children how to order five events in an abstract series. The consequence of understanding this order has little to do with eating or celebrating. It has only to do with how a student tests on something called verbal comprehension, a 'skill' which will presumably allow him or her to interpret technical information and cope in a highly verbal abstract culture.

In a process curriculum, children might see the germination of seeds or the growing of plants as a significant occasion. This could be science in the traditional curriculum. The children would plant seeds. The children might see time-lapse pictures of plants moving. Philosophical questions might arise: "Do plants move in the same sense as animals?," "What is movement, anyway?" "Is movement [as Weisäcker argued] the essential basis of an event?"

The germination of a seed might be translated into a dramatic–musical piece. The seed swells and expands; roots emerge and grow down; a small primary leaf emerges and grows upward toward the light. The tiny plant might be threatened by 'bugs' or someone walking overhead. The musical play would deal with the experience of being a germinating seed. After this kind of experience, there are a host of both scientific and metaphysical questions that might be asked in discussion.

- The roots grow downward into the dark earth and the leaves grow upward; how do we as humans feel about the dark underground and the sunlight as places to be? Does the plant feel the same way we do?

- Are humans 'rooted' in any way similar to plants? Are humans 'freer' than plants?

- Can plants communicate? The plant responds to sunlight and moisture—is this communication? Does the plant feel loved when it is taken care of?—as does a human baby, for example?

The children might be told stories about how other cultures view plants and the relationships they have with plants. The Hopi, for example, participate in the growing of corn by thinking, singing, and dancing. Western scientific experiments suggest that talking to plants and encouraging them to grow makes a difference in their lives. Would talking to plants also make a difference for the people doing the talking—in the way they felt about the plants; in the way the plant tasted when eaten? The children might come to talk to or sing to their seedlings.

The distinction between these two educational approaches (the scientific, knowledge-as-separate object approach vs. the process, knowledge-as-intimate relationship approach) can also be illustrated further by the way we usually teach music. Rhythms and sounds are certainly primal experiences. The fetus experiences the rhythm of the heartbeat and the breathing of the mother before it is born. It experiences its own sound at the moment of birth. Children are remarkable for the rhythm, dance, and music spontaneously generated in their own play. Yet when we teach music, often it is as though a whole repertory of these musical activities and experiences never occurred. As David Keane states:

> When we begin music instruction we assume that "music" is a body of knowledge which exists independent of people and that the acquisition of musical knowledge may be carried on only with the assistance of a person who possesses a great deal of musical knowledge. Such assumptions are unfortunate because the most important aspect of the art is the direct experience of the art object. Secondary information is more often misleading than it is helpful unless the perceiver already has a thorough experience of the art object itself.
>
> We come to "know" an object through our direct interaction with it. If we pick up a stone, squeeze it, rub it, weigh it, etc., our understanding of the stone is the record of these operations . . .
>
> If this is the process by which we also learn music—and there is considerable evidence to support this idea—the rigidity of traditional music instruction with its complete disregard for personal exploration and its dogmatic clinging to a skill-development basis for musical comprehension actually impedes the development of some kinds of experiential musical knowledge.[20]

In short, modern teaching begins the process of "coming to know" from the outside. Skills, concepts, and subjects are objects, so to speak, outside the group, possessed by the teacher and given to the students. What is transferred is not shared participation in the common event; it is an object, word, product, or theory that can be written, diagrammed, and tested. This theory of learning reminds us of Whitehead's assessment of Newton's physics. It was, he said, easy to understand and hard to believe. In fact, if learning were as easy and as straightforward as transferring information we would have far more success in this enterprise than we have at present. Success eludes us because we choose not to consider learning in its most difficult essence: that moment when the separate participants (teacher, student, material) "collapse in an interaction,"[21] a process phrase for what happens when a photon of light and a green leaf participate in photosynthesis. Process teaching assumes the centrality of the teacher's and students' "collapse," their sharing aspects of themselves (prehensions) in a set of relationships with a common intent. The educational moment itself has intent; the happening has its own subjectivity and, finally, what Whitehead calls *objective immortality*: long-term aspects of teacher and students change as a consequence of the occasion's satisfaction.

Since process defines the individual as a complex set of active relationships, we suggest that the important consideration in education becomes the quality of those relationships as they overlap in the shared occasion. When in the classroom all the internal forces of the various participants resolve themselves in a harmonious pattern such that no one construct of reality is insisted upon as correct, when there is implicit recognition that the emergent occasion will define its own time, and above all when the participants feel the movement of the occasion as they themselves relate to and change within it—when all this obtains, we see an education of integrity.

Space

In modern cosmology, space and time (or more accurately, space–time) are the parameters by which we plot and describe the movement and behavior of solid events or objects. This leads to a kind of metaphorical ambiguity in which we confuse space and place. We create an airport as a space for something to happen—airplanes land and take off. We create a school building for something to happen—children enter and are taught. As modern people we have the deep sense of space as an empty place where something, presumably planned and controlled, is going to happen. Space is place and thus defines where something happens. Implicit in modernity is the notion that space is the empty stage on which life and movement occur. So we tend to build spaces with this thought in mind. We think of such monuments to modernity as skyscrapers and superhighways as quasi-permanent definitions for important happenings; they are not an intrinsic part of the happening itself. Our language reflects our consciousness: we shop 'at a mall;' we do not 'mall.' We eat 'at a restaurant;' we do not 'restaurant.'

Process thought presents an alternative vision. Space and time do not stand outside of reality to define it; they are defined by occasions and are intrinsic to them. It is not space that contains or holds occasions or objects. Process thought focuses on the whole set of interrelationships that happen in the continuous advance of occasions. One cannot separate the stage from the play, as Wallack elaborates:

> ...there is no break in reality "where" and "when" nothing is, and no empty and absolute spacetime which real things occupy. We do not lift up a book and find nothing in its place; we do not throw a stone and leave nothing in its wake; we do not sit in a chair and thereby occupy an empty space. Each new occasion assembles aspects of others from its antecedent voids of nothingness. What was behind or before another has created something else; there are no holes in the timespace continuum.[22]

Process reality is not actors defined by time and the spacial background grid of the stage; reality is the relationship of all these to each other as happenings. a central underlying metaphor is life. Nature is seen as the constant flow of concrescent being, perishing and reformulation of relationships. All being is thus alive, not *in* space or environment but *including* space and environment.

One architect who talks about space in these process terms is Christopher Alexander. Alexander assumes there are underlying patterns, organic archetypes, which participate in the organization of the existential world and which allow for positive life-enhancing occasions.

> The specific patterns out of which a building or town is made may be alive or dead. To the extent that they are alive, they let our inner forces loose, and set us free; but when they are dead they keep us locked in inner conflict.[23]

Alexander suggests that people live within a balance of forces that arise from both internal (subjective) and external (objective) conditions, forces that are not controllable by some inner will. He maintains it is foolish to hold that we are responsible within ourselves for our own problems. The state of a person's harmony depends importantly upon the spacial harmony with one's surroundings. For Alexander place and a sense of place are very significant prehensions in the creation of occasion. "Some kinds of physical and social circumstances help a person come to life. Others make it difficult."[24] He then gives a variety of examples.

The first circumstance he discusses is allowing people to be in greater harmony with their surroundings in the mingling of family, work, education, play and recreation.

> For instance, in some towns, the pattern of relationships between workplaces and families help us to come to life.
>
> Workshops mix with houses, children run around the places where work is going on, the members of the family help in the work, the family may possibly eat lunch together, or eat lunch together with the people who are working there.
>
> The fact that family and play are part of one continuous stream helps nourish everyone. Children see how work happens, they learn what it is that makes the adult world function, they get an overall coherent view of things; men are able to connect the possibility of play and laughter, and attention to children, without having to separate them sharply in their minds, from work. Men and women are able to work, and to pay attention to their families more or less equally, as they wish to; love and work are connected, able to be one, understood and felt as coherent by the people who are living there.[25]

Alexander then discusses the tensions brought about for people when the workplace is separated from homes and schools and those living in communities. A man, for example, might feel the greatest emotional pressure from the family when he is tired out from the stresses of work and commuting. Usually a woman must choose whether to be home with her children or travel to another place so that she can be part of the business and commerce of the work world. Children are isolated from the worldly, often exciting affairs of work, sheltered—in preparation for entering that world—for literally years.

In a more limited example of the importance of "living spaces," Alexander addresses the necessity of a "window place."

> Everyone knows how beautiful a room is when it has a bay window in it, or a window seat, or a special ledge next to the window, or a small alcove which is entirely glassed. The feeling that rooms with these kinds of places in them are especially beautiful is not merely whimsy. It has a fundamental organic reason behind it.
>
> When you are in a living room for any length of time, two of the many forces acting on you are...the tendency to go toward light...and [the desire] to sit down, and make yourself comfortable.
>
> In a room which has at least one window that is a "place"—a window seat, a bay window, a window with a wide low windowsill that invites you to pull your favorite chair over to it because you can see out so easily, a special ledge next to the window, or a small alcove which is entirely glassed-in this room you can give in to both forces; you can resolve the conflict for yourself.
>
> In short, you can be comfortable.
>
> But a room which has no window place, in which the windows are just "holes," sets up a hopeless inner conflict in me which I can't resolve...
>
> The instinctive knowledge that a room is beautiful when it has a window place in it, is thus not an aesthetic whim. It is an instinctive expression of the fact that a room with a window place is filled with actual, palpable organic tension, and is, from a simple organic point of view, a better place to live.[26]

Both of these examples of spatial patterns which release life, reduce blind tension, and move in the direction of harmony, intimacy, and balance have great relevance to our conception of modern versus process education. Modern schools are created as segregated environments, away from the hustle and bustle of commerce and work, away from the familiarity of home. In fact, the great move toward consolidated schools in the past thirty-five years has tended to segregate children from community. Neighborhood schools have often been demolished; high schools have often been moved from the center of town to more rustic areas on the fringes of the community. Even with the declining school populations which gave schools empty rooms, no one saw fit to make schools into a more complex and mixed environment, perhaps including stores, offices, and craft shops within school buildings. It seemed preferable to close down the whole school, make them into condominiums or offices, and transport children even farther away from their homes. As Alexander points out, the multiplicity and diversity of spatial patterns tends to increase the intensity of liveliness:

> The more living patterns there are in a thing—a room, a building, or a town— the more it comes to life as an entirety, the more it glows, the more it has this self-maintaining fire.[27]

We can only speculate about why modern cosmology tends to enclose or restrict one function for every complex of buildings. It may well emanate from the notion that specialization increases efficiency, which harks back to the basic machine metaphor and its exemplification in the grand assembly line, where each worker installs one set of parts at his or her particular station. Schools are the segregated, specialized, spacialized developmental factories where students are 'prepared' for life.

Likewise the concept of the 'window place' is striking when one thinks of educational architecture. Educational spaces are not built like living rooms, or even workshops; they are constructed more like factories. Desks are lined up in rows, or chairs are placed around small tables. Windows (if there are any) are simply holes in the wall placed along one side of the room. There may be bookcases or storage space beneath the windows, but the student is not drawn to work near them. One's attention is drawn either toward the front of the room to the blackboard and the teacher's desk, or to the corner of the room where the teacher sits.

With little effort we can recall the tensions of this arrangement. We are naturally drawn toward the light, as Alexander suggests, for light is life, expansiveness, and associated with new occasion. Yet as students we cannot move toward the light, or even look toward the windows. We are drawn toward our friends, for humans are extremely convivial social creatures, but we must not stray too far from our individual desk or chair. When we tire of the activities associated with this room (a large rectangle with holes for windows), we want to move into another space, perhaps a more private space or an outdoor space. But this kind of movement in relationship to space is highly structured and restricted.

The great insight of Alexander, the one that parallels process thought so closely, is that space, context, the physical aspects of buildings are as much the basis of prehension in creating significant occasions as are the human actors. When we move toward a window seat to read or play a board game with a friend, the prehensions include the glass, the sunlight, the seat, the sense of enclosure, the game, the relationships of the players to each other. It is significantly different to play chess on a window seat in the corner of a library than to play on a card table in the middle of a gymnasium.

Nor are these fanciful and implausible ideas. We are reminded of an architect and teacher at MIT who took the initiative to tear out the floor of one part of a building, which then opened up a tremendous area of high-ceilinged space. His students were then given the opportunity to bring in building materials (mostly secondhand lumber) and construct their own studios. The result was that students created a great maze of ingeniously constructed work places.

Another example with which we are familiar is the construction of yurts, in the form of round shed-like buildings by the teachers and students in a newly formed private school. One of the teachers had designed the yurt so that it could be constructed relatively simply by students with local building materials.

In both of these examples, there is not only the possibility of creating more harmonious and balanced places to work and study—places that are more hospitable and alive than large brick and concrete rooms with windows cut out of one wall; there is the creation of living context, wherein space is allowed the flexibility to be included in a learning occasion. Space is no longer seen as the static background.

But whether context is alive, part of a living entity, or dead is more difficult to determine than whether or not the people have some degree of control over space, as in the two examples above. A major consideraton is whether or not the pattern has the capacity to create and recreate itself, as a living thing: whether there is some underlying stability of pattern in the midst of existential change. In discussing this issue, Alexander analogizes first from ripples in a path of wind-blown sand (the ridge pattern is maintained even though individual grains of sand are constantly in motion), and finally to two more complex examples: a living ecosystem and a pattern of street life in two cities. In the ecosystem example he says:

> Consider, for example, a corner of an orchard, where the sun warms the ground, the marrows grow, the bees pollinate the apple blossoms, the worms bring air to the soil . . . This pattern repeats itself hundreds of times, in a thousand different gardens, and is always a source of life.

> But the life of the pattern does not depend on the fact that it does something for "us"—but simply on the self-sustaining harmony, in which each process helps sustain the other processes, and in which the whole system of forces and processes keeps itself going, over and over again, without creating extra forces that will tear it down.[28]

Alexander maintains that there is an intrinsic self-generating stability within living patterns, which does not depend on the sense of external motivation and purpose. He gives the example of two contrasting sociocultural contexts:

> Consider two human patterns. On the one hand, consider the fact that certain Greek village streets have a band of whitewash, four or five feet wide,

outside every house, so that people can pull their chairs into the street, into a realm which is half theirs, half street, and so contribute to the life around them.

And on the other hand, consider the fact that cafes in Los Angeles are indoors, away from the sidewalk, in order to prevent the food from being contaminated.

Both of these patterns have a purpose. One has the purpose of allowing the people to contribute to the street life and to be part of it—to the extent they desire—by marking a domain which makes it possible. The other has the purpose of keeping people healthy, by making sure that they will not eat food that has dust particles on it. Yet one is alive; the other dead.

One, like the ripples in the sand, sustains itself and heals itself because it is in harmony with its own forces. The other can only be maintained by force of law.

The whitewashed band is so congruent with the forces in people's lives and with their feelings that it sustains itself—when the whitewash gets dirty or worn people take care of it themselves because the pattern is deeply connected to their own experience. From the outside it seems as though the whitewash maintains itself almost as if by magic.

The indoor cafe in Los Angeles is almost opposite: it has no such congruence with people's inner forces. It has to be maintained by force, by force of law—because under the impact of its own forces it would gradually deteriorate, and disappear. People want to be outdoors on a spring day, want to drink their beer or coffee in the open, to watch the world go by, but they are imprisoned in the cafe by the laws of public health. The situation is self-destroying, not only because it will change as soon as the law which upholds it disappears, but also in the more subtle sense that it is continuously creating just those inner conflicts, just as those reservoirs of stress I spoke of earlier which will, unsatisfied, soon well up like a gigantic boil and leak out in some other form of destruction or refusal to cooperate with the situation.

In short, a pattern lives when it allows its own internal forces to resolve themselves.

And a pattern dies when it fails to provide a framework in which forces can resolve themselves, so that instead, the action of the forces, unresolved, works to destroy the pattern.[29]

Alexander is maintaining that within a social or cultural setting there are a variety of potential patterns to be realized. To the extent that we do not coerce or force people to maintain one pattern or another, they will move in directions that will allow destructive tensions to resolve themselves. Within this framework we wonder about the degree of concern modern schools have over issues of attendance, 'cutting,' discipline, and the maintenance of patterns of occasion that are presumed good for children and young people. Perhaps the most fundamental constraints in teaching have to do with space and time. Once one creates spatial patterns that are inhospitable to human life and creativity in the form of long lines of rooms encasing corridors and lockers, the space itself jealously guards its own intentions.

Alexander's view of architecture and spatial planning stands in sharp contrast to the way modern educators see these issues. Modernity begins with narrow human objectives for an educational system. The highest priority is given space where students can be efficiently taught algebra, English, shop, physical education. Teaching is a managed function in which the various ingredients are to be orchestrated to 'create' a planned and predictable outcome. Metaphorically, modern educators make a sharp distinction between the garden and the wilderness, and opt for the garden where they cultivate fruit and vegetables with known and controllable characteristics.[30] Modern farming is construed as a mechanical assembly line. Process construes education as a village in the wilderness. The culture of the village shows us the regularity of patterned human behavior, but we are surrounded by the unpredictability of the wilderness from which we obtain the resources to maintain our village. We see our homes as occasions in which trees and mud and rocks participated. Alexander tells us (as did Whitehead) that all life participates in its own meaning. This applies urgently in education. When we lose the sense that we are creating our own moment—either spatially, by attending large brick and concrete schools, or in communication, by assuming that all meaning is in dictionaries, libraries, and tapes and does not have to be constructed by us—when we lose this sense of deep participation in our own becoming, we must surely lose the desire to be educated at all.

Time

Perhaps the most fundamental aspect of any cosmology is its assumption about the nature of time. Judeo-Christians have a linear sacred history and a final salvation built into their sense of time. Modern people have a linear universal history based on a single time frame, but a somewhat muffled sense of salvation, which they call 'progress.' In both the Judeo-Christian and the modern cosmology, reified linear time is associated with work and struggle as sacrifice. There is always a battle mounted between the 'forces of nature,' which stand outside 'man,' and the works of 'man,' which will presumably overcome these forces and liberate humans from the constraints of time. For time not only allows for salvation and progress; it brings death and decay. The second law of thermodynamics, entropy— i.e., a tendency of nature toward breakdown-disorder—is the haunting spectre against which humans struggle. The arrow of time is awesome and seemingly inevitable.

The paradox is that the absolute linear sense of time is both a central quality of modern science, an essential requirement of its achievements, and the enemy which it must somehow overcome to successfully separate humans from the vicissitudes, the pains, and eventually the natural disorder and death wrought by entropy. Apart from disparaging modernity's obsessive effort to conquer time by controlling nature, we would emphasize that, taken as a limited construct, Newtonian or absolute time is a perfectly sensible abstraction. The error of modern cosmology's conception of time, as with Newtonian thinking generally, is not in its view that aspects of nature are understandable, predictable, or controllable; it is not the assumption that we live our lives within absolute units of time and space and hence can define the world in terms of size, density, motion, substance, and the like. The error is in *limiting* our construction of reality to this one particular set of abstractions. We do, in fact, achieve wondrous acts within this framework: the bounty of the machine model has proved generous. But we limit ourselves, both in the meaning and potentiality of our being, when we cannot move beyond the machine–mind duality.

Process cosmology moves to a deeper and more adequate construction of being, which posits both time and human substantiality as abstractions rather than as essential qualities of reality in nature. In process terms, all being involves potentiality, concrescence, satisfaction, and perishing, not of substantial hunks of things (like humans or planets) in absolute time, but of occasions or patterned relationships within their own framework of being. There is no absolute time standing outside of occasion by which we define occasions. To compare the unit of time during which two lovers are mutually infatuated to the units of time of decaying cesium molecules or with the regularities of planetary motion in absolute hours, minutes, and seconds is silly. All these events have an intention which is fulfilled "in their own good time." What does it really mean to say, "I was in love for two weeks?" Better, perhaps to say, "I was in love for the time I was in love."

So in discussing time, we are not attempting to dismiss absolute Newtonian time, but rather to see it as a useful but limited and limiting abstraction within a more fundamental framework. This is not an easy task, for, as Wallack points out, time as an absolute thing 'out there' is deeply embedded in our Western consciousness:

> The conception of time has been with us since time immemorial, so to speak. Clocks, by their mathematical regularity, lend themselves to the reification of time. In fact, the perfect running of a great cosmic clock has been imagined as the veritable cause of absolute time. The idea of a great cosmic clock of

clocks, time-keeper of all the universe, was entertained, for example, by Plato, whose master clock actually turns the heavens and the earth . . .

Plato's cosmic clock has been dismantled only in this century. Relativity physics has shown time to be the sequential relations between causally connected events only; it means that there can be no absolute simultaneity wherein all present events of the universe are actual at the same time. Quantum mechanics followed upon relativity, showing that quanta of energy do not develop or move continuously through a continuous absolute spacetime. Plato's cosmic clock [has been] unsprung by the advances of physics. . . .[31]

A central assumption in process is that time is intrinsic to occasion; that it is not a separate fact about occasion. Also important is the process assumption that duration embraces both potentiality and actualization. Presumably as an occasion comes into being it participates in the selection of a variety of potentialities until an intention is clarified and it moves toward satisfaction. While this sounds like somewhat obtuse metaphysical language, it coincides with a good deal of common–sense speculation on the different qualities of time that relate to different qualities of human consciousness. Priestly, for example, has developed a theory of "three times."

I cannot escape the feeling that Time, itself so blurred and vague and elusive, divides itself into three to match . . . different modes of consciousness. We are at least entitled to say that it is *as if* there are three kinds of time. (And this is hardly an impudent claim when Time itself, on close examination, can be turned into an *as if*, even though we have in this age transformed it into a ball-and-chain to keep the spirit a prisoner).

. . . I propose to call these three times—time One, time Two and time Three.

As visible creatures of earth we are ruled by time One. We are born into it, grow up and grow old in it, and die in it. Our brains have developed through eons into marvelous instruments of time One attention . . .

Our relation through the brain with time One tends to be practical and economic, good for our matter-of-fact handling of business, which helps to explain why we are now great time One people and mostly try not to believe in anything else.[32]

Time Two for Priestly is the time of dreaming and is used to explain experiences of precognition in dreams. He documents many instances in which humans dream an event that occurs after the dream, or of possible tragedies that are prevented because of the warning provided by such dreams. He sees time Two as a poorly understood variation of time Three that in some ways connects potential with actual. He links it with imagination and sets forth the following thesis:

Because imagination appears to be free of the limitations we know in time One, we think of it as being outside Time. It is there, however, that the nothings begin. We might do better if we thought of it as belonging to a different Time order, to another time. . .imaginative creation seems to imply not a second time order, contemplative and detached from action, but a third, in which purpose and action are joined together and there seems to be an almost magical release in creative power.

If there is a part of the mind or a state of consciousness that is outside the dominion of time One and time Two but governed by a time Three, then that is where the creative imagination has its home and does its work. And it may be that there imagination is not somethig escaping from reality but *is itself reality*, while the world we construct from our time One experience is regarded there as something artificial, thin, and hollow. (italics author's)[33]

The process interpretation of Priestly suggests that imagination is a name for the human capacity to apprehend potentiality, possibility; that imagined possibility is intrinsic to the creation of being, the concrescense of occasion; that Newtonian time (time One) is only a thin abstraction as one descriptor of occasion. Nor is Priestly unaware of the implications of this position for the education of children:

Because most children are highly imaginative, it is supposed by some to reach maturity we ought to leave imagination behind, like the habit of smearing our faces with chocolate. But an adult in whom imagination has withered is mentally lame and lopsided, in danger of turning into a zombie or a murderer. It is the creative imagination that has given our ruthless bloodthirsty species its occasional gleams of nobility, its hope of rising above the muck it spreads.[34]

Priestly's observation, based on his literary sensibilities and intensive study of dream-time, are now supported by the speculation of philosophy-minded physicists. Bohm[35] (see quote from Bohm for his specific language), for example, posits an underlying reality he calls "ground," which process theory would translate as 'occasions within the extensive continuum.' Process theory suggests that there is a primitive apprehension of concrescing occasions which gives humans (and all beings) the sense of occasion coming into being and passing as we participate in them. Here again arises the opposition between process thought and modern cosmology. While process thinkers such as Wallack, Priestly, and Bohm are willing to speculate about the deeper sense of time that cannot be quantified in absolute or universal units and to further speculate that it is associated with varying qualities of human consciousness, the modernist can only vaguely designate such experience as "imagination" or "creative moments," then impatiently ask for hard evidence of such realms and experiences.[36] (We have, of course, not even discussed the predominant importance of cyclical time for many cultures or the planet.)

Given this background in alternative ways of understanding and experiencing time (depending on one's cosmological orientaton), we ask about their implications for teaching. It is clear that modern teaching and learning are designed to be experienced within the framework of absolute physical time. Just as with space, time is the backdrop against which we measure events as the movement of physical and substantial activities. Teachers' and children's schedules are made out to represent such events within time and space.

	M	T	W	TH	F
9:00	Math				
9:50	Soc. St.				
10:45	Hist.				
11:30	English				
12:15	Lunch				

It is important to emphasize again that such schedules as well as the time frameworks they define, are abstractions rather than factual dimensions of reality. A similar illusion of abstraction-as-reality carries further into the construction of curriculum itself. Mathematics is construed as a set of problems to be solved, corrected, put on the board, and handed in as homework. The unit of reality, again, is some rough match between numbers-of-pages-of-text-covered, number-of-problems-done, and number-of-minutes or class-periods-required to 'cover' the problems and pages. We are all aware that there is a deeper level of reality moving beneath these abstractly stated events. Recent studies of 'hidden curriculum' and school ethnographies are primitive efforts to describe this deeper reality. Given these conceptions, it is relatively easy to conclude that within a given framework of time and space, each person (student) experiences very different events. Even within highly structured tasks, such as doing ten problems in long division, strategies of problem-solving differ radically from child to child. But these understandings are still not the essence of the process insight. Process teaching sees the student and teacher as a *movement*, a rhythm that should move harmoniously between memory and new experience, and between tradition and change, between old knowledge and novel insight. There must be allowance for activity in the presence of knowledge (Whitehead's favorite recommendation to education) such that all participants discover their own meanings and form unique viewpoints. Above all, the essence of process teaching is to develop a sense of the shared pursuit of knowledge (which of course involves a teacher's risking failure in front of students).

Process teaching thus leads to important time considerations. First, the teacher plans for occasions only in more general ways. It is possible, even likely, that a planned occasion will never emerge; some other occasions might. In this mode, one sees oneself only generally as a math teacher or a reading teacher. The teacher attempts to encourage significant math or reading occasions to emerge. The teacher cannot *make* them happen, any more than she or he can compel an aesthetic experience. Moving within the multiplicity of complex and unpredictable events (prehensions) that constantly occur in the teaching situation requires that the teacher relinquish long-held notions of control, control of time and control of knowledge.

Second, occasions emerge from potentiality, which is, perhaps, most closely translated in human terms as imagination, imagery, fantasy. The relationship between time and imagination is novel and unexplored territory. But we have the sense that significant teaching occasions burst forth from convergent imaginations—when a text or a scribble on the blackboard combines with the fragment of a sentence by a student or the teacher into a bubbling conversation and exciting insight. As teachers, perhaps the most destructive thing we do is consider time for imagination and fantasy as wasted time, or as indulging students' whims, or, more constructively, as only 'motivation' for the real lessons.

Finally, we should, perhaps, attend more to the relationships between the initial sparks of imagination and the disciplined practice guided by our modern sense of machine time. Discipline here becomes the basis for a deeper connection with ground or grounded occasion. Educational programs which move in this direction abound: the discipline of yoga; the discipline of the Eastern martial arts; sports programs; music; drama; and so forth. The major significance here is that the student, because of some inarticulable inner need (drive?), maintains a regime (often mechanistically defined in terms of time and energy) that moves him or her in the direction of experiencing the deeper reality wherein conventional clock-time and absolute space fall away.

When this genuine thirst for learning springs forth, the student is often admonished for not keeping up with the full range of activities or 'subjects' required in a conventional educational setting. Again the culture of fragmentation dominates. There seems to be something dangerous about becoming fully engrossed. We wonder at the magic of requiring four or five subjects five times a week for thirty-six weeks. This kind of schedule seems least likely to move students from the fragmented moments of clock time to the deep involvement of grounded occasion.

Continuity and Change

In our presentation and elaboration of process cosmology, we have stressed the idea of occasion—i.e., the entity's experience of change and movement toward novelty. This allows us to bring into sharp relief the distinction between the premise of modernity, in which being is construed as enduring particles, versus the process view, in which being is construed as the flow of concrescing and perishing occasions. One can easily challenge the process sense of being by asking how one is to deal with the obvious and pressing sense of reality presented to us by the solid objects all around us (people, books, rocks, cars). Process thinking can, of course, respond with examples such as the water in the brook that consistently looks the same but is obviously changing. It is, however, more difficult, even for process people, to truly experience a stone or a human being as being in a state of constant change and motion. We know from the construction of reality presented by postmodern theoretical physics, as well as modern biology, that both living and non-living 'things' are constantly changing, even though they apparently remain the same, as does our experience of the brook passing us by. But we should perhaps work through in somewhat more detail the language of process that deals with this issue.

The two central process ideas that express continuity (endurance) and complexity and connectedness are *societies* and *nexus*.

In brief, society is a technical construct that explains the appearance of seemingly enduring objects. As far as we know there are no enduring objects; all are novel occasions in transitional process. However, we as humans, in order to cope with and adapt to our environment, apprehend and remember recurring patterns, occasions succeeding similar occasions. The human *umwelt* requires that we deal with nature, not as a quantum micro world nor as an astrophysical macrouniverse, but rather as a common-sense world in which our senses and being evolved. Nexus is the construct that describes our understanding that different occasions have different size, complexity, and quality. There are very brief, small, perhaps timeless electromagnetic occasions; there are larger molecular occasions; there are mineral, vegetable, and animal occasions; there are more complex ecosystem occasions. It is important to understand that nexus means more than an aggregate of occasions, like piles of stones on the landscape. Nexus implies an internal connectedness among occasions, much like Koestler's idea of holons. In common sense language, humans understand the process term 'society' as an enduring thing, person, object. We understand nexus as connectedness and community, and understand the term occasion as the set of unique relationships which defines in an ultimate sense the underlying basis of transitory, seemingly enduring things, or communities.

Cosmology, as we are using the term, describes the depth and extensiveness of a belief system. An essential characteristic of an adequate or positive cosmology is the balance and complementarity with which it describes the logical or paradoxical polarities that define the human common-sense world. One of our major misgivings about the cosmology of modernity is its stress on enduring material substance as the essence of reality. Classical science leads us to understand material substance as essence and to understand technology as our ability to consciously control, manipulate, and transform our material world. Mind is the external intelligence that ultimately understands materiality and makes the choices required to manipulate the world. In this kind of science, the internal organic connections (community of occasions) which define the complex world are reduced to the simplest units in order to allow for control and reconstruction of the material world in terms of these units. The unit of the inorganic world is the atom; the unit of the organic world is the cell (or perhaps subatomic particles and genetic material). As modern people, we assume that science and technology will eventually be able to reconstruct any connection or communal form from these building blocks.

Likewise, modernity looks upon novelty or creativity as 'error' or that which we do not yet fully understand. This assumes that the nature of the universe is one of substantial continuity. There are really no ultimate natural surprises; only the unforeseen that comes from lack of human scientific knowledge.

In these terms, modern education/teaching/curriculum places a primary emphasis on the continuity of substantial units (individual human organisms) which are to be serviced and developed in systematic ways into mature adults. The larger unit to which the 'student' is to be connected is not an organic community, an ecosystem consisting of land, air, friends, kin. It is a corporate team or bureaucracy, another predictable material thing. (We call them 'corporations' because they are substantial legal *bodies.)* Our 'maps', tables of organization, or 'lesson plans' are modeled after other forms of technology, where surprises or the novelty inherent in the process sense of occasion is unwelcome.

Process cosmology, on the hand, sees continuity (society, enduring objects), connectedness (community, nexus) and creativity (novelty of occasion) as three core experiential possibilities of the human *umwelt,* possibilities which themselves constitute a balanced and necessary view of nature. From this point of view teaching begins with nexus, with the connection among less complex occasions into a more complex occasion. The teacher and the student enter into a common moment, share a common satisfaction, and thus change. The teacher stands within a set of relationships; the teacher does not stand outside the student's world as one who would control or manipulate that world for those in it. But teacher and student alike recognize that there *are* quasi-stable patterns of continuity in terms of the definition of the individual organisms, the culture within which humans live, and the stable patterns that repeat in nature. And finally all understand that there is a potential in the setting for altering both the people and the relationships based not simply on scientific laws or technological manipulation of variables, but rather based on the fact that the underlying quality of being is in fact both novelty and continuity and the underlying unit of that reality is the emerging set of relationships we call occasions.

One might well maintain that in our effort to communicate across cosmologies we are simply rephrasing the old modern construction of the world with new language. Our only response is to reaffirm our vision that the world is different when we begin a cosmology with the profound sense that 'natural' and cultural pattern is a secondary expression of the novelty and potentiality of emerging occasions, and that the wise person (teacher) is one who is sensitive to the tensions between continuity and connection on the one hand and the potentiality for novelty on the other.

Modernity calls on education to improve, ameliorate, develop, or assist someone to mature. The 'one' varies, depending on one's ideology. In a liberal modern society, the one is a 'person,' a human individual. In a utopian communitarian society, the one that is supposed to develop and be perfected is both individual and commnity. In a socialist state one must think of stages. First the state or the society is to develop; later the state withers away, leaving individual personalities free to perfect themselves after the yoke of oppressive fascistic or capitalistic structures have been shrugged off. These kinds of ideological superstructures stand over the teacher when she or he thinks about what is to happen when she or he is teaching. But the great problem with these broader conceptions is that they all construe the appropriate unit of being which is to be developed, whether it be society, community, personality, culture, as if there were some substantial thing or permanent pattern that exists in time and space (i.e., 'principles,' 'values,' 'objectives,' 'models') whose quality of existence will be measured and perfected over time.

Our initial thrust into this problem is to imagine that there are three central constructs that define our reality: (1) enduring objects (personalities, people, culture, societies); (2) complex dynamic communities of people/things; and (3) occasions which are constantly rearranging themselves. As teachers we move into occasions that affect persons, recognizing that persons are both in some degree stable but dynamic societies; and recognizing that people are defined by a multiplicity of connections (their community of being) including their own self-perceptions, their families and friends, their talents and callings, their aspirations, and so on. But there may well be no authentic, permanent center of being for anyone, no ultimate perfection toward which one is moving. There is more likely a multiplicity of relationship that one is constantly engaged in building, repairing, extending. And it is plausible to construe 'people' as a network of relationships, because the underlying quality of being is a dynamic changing or becoming. In sum, therefore, humans need some sense of stable personality; they need some sense of continuity in culture and nature. In process terms these are historical societies, given the sense that being replicates itself in close approximation to its past. But at a deeper level humans, like all nexus and societies, are dynamic occasions which not only have potential for change but are inevitably involved in it. The great challenge for education is to teach with the awareness that change is both in some degree controllable and in considerable degree uncontrollable. To the extent that it is controllable, it is guided by the teacher to maintain a quality of reverence and consideration for the being, the intent, the potentiality of that learning moment. To the extent that it is uncontrollable, the teacher flows with the occasion to respect the feelings, the joys and sufferings that accompany the inevitable change that makes each of us a little different as we pass through each new occasion.

But the notion that there are somehow specific rules or dogma that will tell us, as teachers, how to respect the feelings that move into the intentions of a new occasion—how much to hang on to the continuity of old personality and culture and how much to let go—this notion seems simplistic in the extreme. We need less guidance here from experts in the field of psychological development and more guidance from the historical record that comes from listening to our neighbors and our inner ear that is tuned to some underlying ground of being.

We would conclude by adding that the stress we place on novelty and creativity is not without its negative consequences. As beings who have the experience of duration yet face the self-conscious inevitability of both becoming and perishing, humans live on the edge of a metaphysical-emotional precipice. Whitehead states the problem in eloquent terms:

> The world is thus faced by the paradox that, at least in its higher actualities, it craves for novelty and yet is haunted by terror at the loss of the past, with its familiarities and its loved ones. It seeks escape from time in its character of "perpetual perishing." Part of the joy of the new year is the hope of the old round of seasons, with their stable facts—of friendship, and love, and old association.

> . . .the culminating fact of conscious, rational life refuses to conceive itself as a transient enjoyment, transiently useful. In the order of the physical world its role is defined by its introduction of novelty. But, just as physical feelings are haunted by the vague insistence of causality, so the higher intellectual feelings are haunted by the vague insistence of another order, where there is no unrest, no travel, no shipwreck . . . .

This is the problem which gradually shapes itself as religion reaches its higher phases in civilized communities. The most general formulation of the religious problem is the question whether the process of the temporal world passes into the formation of other actualities, bound together in an order in which novelty does not mean loss.[37]

We would affirm with Whitehead that any adequate cosmology inevitably deals with religious, spiritual, or "mystical" issues, and an adequate educational theory must similarly face such issues. All teaching is essentially religious in that it carries with it, to some degree, an answer to the question: How does the world pass beyond itself and yet satisfy (or leave unsatisfied) the longing within us for continuity and permanence? We believe that process cosmology, which faces this issue with directness and integrity, can lead to a more adequate culture and more adequate educational practices by which such a culture can be maintained than does the modern cosmology or the various subcultures, ideologies, and societies that we associate with modernity.

Chapter Ten

The Current Context of Process Education

How does one move from here to there? The unpredictable nature of paradigmatic shifts in culture is characterized by Koestler as "sleepwalking."[1] As one looks back at such historic shifts the underlying reasons seem baffling, fatefilled, irrational. The central problem in proposing educational practices that require basic changes in culture is that we commonly live in a world of institutions or social structures—schools, workplaces, families, clubs, churches—suffused with activities and information that reinforce the old cosmology. In order to move to a new subconscious understanding of culture, we must reconstruct deliberately, and hence superficially, the social structures, the language, and the media of the old paradigm through which information is selected and shaped.

When we think of the games we play with ourselves attempting to disengage from the limits of the staid modern paradigm, we might compare it with the way Latin, French, and German were taught for many years in the classical high school. We would go to class for an hour each day, learn a little grammar, construe a couple of pages of translation from 'great literature,' discuss in English what had been translated, receive a new assignment, and then return to live in the world of our mother tongue for the next twenty-three hours. We know that few students ever learned either to speak or think in the new lanugage under these circumstances, but the hour each day was relatively painless and one learned a few cliches and phrases that gave one the illusion of cultural enrichment and progress. We all intuitively know this: that it is one thing to read books, to attend workshops, to discuss intellectually the idea of significant shifts in philosophical or cultural orientation; it is quite something else to take such change seriously, to take the risk of immersion (like intensive language learning), to try thinking and feeling in a different way.

One may ask: If paradigmatic change is so difficult, even painful, why move away from one's current view? Different cosmologies beckon with different incentives. For the Christian such a basic change, conversion, includes the promise of everlasting life in paradise—a substantial inducement. For the village person from the 'developing' Third World, modernity is the promise of independence from encumbering family and folk as well as the thrust forward into the stimulation and potential affluence of urban life. For the process person, perhaps the main incentive is the compelling sense that process cosmology leads toward a broader, deeper, and more coherent quality of experience and consequent knowing. The distortions required for the modern person to continue to 'make sense' become increasingly difficult. One might simply look, for example, at the many cataclysmic and mindless tragedies of the modern era: the genocide committed by European settlers against the native Americans on much of the North American continent; the American Civil War; the exploitation and poverty that have attended the countless economic depressions that arose from industrial change in the West; the Nazi Holocaust; the poverty, underemployment, and dislocation that attends 'modernization' in Third World nations; the nuclear terror that currently grips the planet. We wonder how modernity can hold to its unshakable faith in the progressive nature of history. We would prefer to believe in the process view—that we participate in the novelty of continuously unfolding occasions, with no particular guarantee (faith) that we are moving toward salvation or destruction, as a species, a planet, or a universe. One might note, as we learned earlier, that the Hopi have passed through three historical epochs, all of which were blind alleys, before entering a fourth, somewhat more hopeful, world. There is probably no reason for modern Western peoples to be more or less optimistic. (They may well be only in the third of six worlds.)

But aside from any rational or philosophical persuasiveness of process cosmology or the basic decency that we intuit from a process culture like the Hopi, the stark fact remains that we are in a transitional world in which the dominant cosmology is modernity dragging behind itself the semi-attached afterbirths of the archaic European and Middle Eastern religions and their philosophic traditions. In the midst of such a cosmological heritage, how does the process person find his or her way through hazards such as the secular dualism of mind–matter or the sacred dualism of God–man? In the scattered debris of this transitional postmodern world, who and where are the friends and relatives of process?

Programs and Movements Related to Process Education

We do, in fact, find friends of process education within established academic fields designated as process philosophy and process theology. They not only publish a scholarly journal, *Process Studies*, but also support an academic center[2] for process research and reflection. More recently, in 1987, a spinoff from this center established the Association for Process Philosophy

of Education, which, at its initial meeting, celebrated the substantial contributions of Robert Brumbaugh to this field.[3] Unlike earlier socio-
philosophical visions, however, which have had a profound effect on our
contemporary view of education—e.g., those of Dewey and the Pro-
gressives, Skinner and the behaviorists, Bruner and the cognitivists—the
actual application of Whiteheadian thinking to educational practice seems
to be just now emerging.

Part of the problem has undoubtedly been the difficulty in Whitehead's
writing style, in the effort he makes to go beyond the linearity and focused
message implicit in the structure of our language and his violation of the
conventions of philosophical/technical discourse required for easy translation into education as a practical professional field. He tends to insinuate
poetical and semi-mystical phrases into what appears to be expository
philosophical text. He penetrates (and in so doing brings into question) the
'obvious' barriers between nature, perception, and thought, between being
and cognition, and, more basically, between metaphysics and (social)
science.

Strangely enough, however, the harmonic chords of process are now
floating in, as it were, from the edges, via journalistic accounts of something
called "the new age." A major strand of this thinking has evolved in
popularized versions of quantum physics,[4] which has recently been joined
by some of the more academically inclined process philosophers.[5] New Age
thinkers share our critical assessment of modernity for many of the same
reasons, yet often offer a more optimistic prognosis, believing that humans
may have reached some significant and positive turning point in our global
evolution.

Writers like Ferguson in *The Aquarian Conspiracy*[6] go so far as to
suggest that the tendrils of a positive new age are sprouting all across the
landscape. Schumacher, however, in *A Guide for the Perplexed*, written
shortly before Ferguson's optimistic book, reaches a more mixed conclusion.
He asks:

> Can we rely on it that a "turning around" will be accomplished by enough
> people quickly enough to save the modern world? This question is often asked,
> but no matter what the answer, it will mislead. The answer "Yes" would lead
> to complacency, the answer "No" to despair. It is desirable to leave these
> perplexities behind us and get down to work.[7]

However one feels about the prospects for a successful shift to a more balanced, process-based culture, there are a good many teachers and other
social change activists "getting down to work." It would, in fact, be useful
to have a critical guide to what one might call 'transformative' or 'New Age'
education so that we could compare the broader range of praxis with

theoretical visions such as the one presented here. Such a guide is obviously beyond the scope of this book. It does seem useful, however, to place our view of process education within the spectrum of a limited set of efforts to create various modes of postmodern education. This review, although of necessity brief and superficial, is meant to suggest issues that will inevitably arise as we seek to move the process vision and imaginative experience into the realm of concrete culture and lived community.

HOLISTIC EDUCATION AND THE HUMAN POTENTIAL MOVEMENT. There is a substantial movement now underway perhaps best designated 'holistic' or 'human potential' education. The movement has found homes in both colleges and universities[8] and in special centers. Interface, a major center in the Boston area, lists in its 1985 catalog workshops and courses in such areas as health and healing, critical life issues (divorce, dying, abortion, alcoholism), family relationships, body awareness, spiritual development, and outdoor programs. Community events sponsored by Interface run the gamut from Tibetan Concert and Sacred Tantric Rituals to Reinventing the Corporation, Whale Watches, and Finding the Balance Between Love and Work. There is a similar institution in New York City called the New York Open Center. Such centers trace their recent lineage back to the Esalen Institute in Big Sur, California, which came into prominence some fifteen years ago. One of the 'Esalen books' most directly related to schooling was George Brown's *Human Teaching for Human Learning: An Introduction to Confluent Education.*[9] Brown uses the term "confluent education" to designate the flowing together of affective or feeling aspects of learning with the more cognitive or intellectual aspects. Stuart Miller, in the editor's introduction to the book outlines the novelty and significance of the Esalen approach.

> *Human Teaching for Human Learning* is a book about affective education and its relation to current educational practices. Dr. Brown and his colleagues have schooled themselves in a variety of techniques and disciplines that have started to cluster, that seem to provide the raw materials for a new affective education—one that is appropriate for our age and can be combined with cognitive concerns. These techniques and disciplines derive from the humanistic psychology of such figures as Abraham Maslow and Carl Rogers, as well as from developments in such disparate and often unlikely fields as modern dance, the contemporary theater, Eastern religions, new group therapies, physical education, and the creativity training used by certain large corporations. Indeed, the strength of this new beginning is its ecclecticism, its lack of orthodoxy, and its willingness to experiment. (p. xvi)

Moving beyond weekend workshops and limited experiments in schools and institutes, the movement is now commonly publicized through the mass media in such magazines as *New Age* and *Whole Life Times,* and in books such as Ferguson's *Aquarian Conspiracy* and Houston's *The Possible Human*[10] as well as in countless paperback books. Ferguson sees the scattered and diffuse nature of the movement as representing the beginning stages of a worldwide transformation of culture and consciousness. She uses, in fact, the language of Kuhn, as have we, when she talks about the world being in the midst of a "paradigm shift." We believe the human potential vision, at least at this point, to be more an extension of modernity than a shift toward any radical reformulation of modern cosmology. It assumes that the great archaic religions or philosophical systems of East and West will somehow become integrated with radical new discoveries in the natural sciences (from relativity and quantum physics to genetic engineering) and create an almost totally positive progressive reality for the future. It often goes beyond efforts simply to create holistic educational experiences to a hope, if not a promise, that there is extended, perhaps unlimited, potential for human development.

As Ferguson quotes Prigogine, "We are at a very exciting moment in history, perhaps a turning point." She notes that Prigogine won the 1977 Nobel Prize[11] "for a theory that describes transformations, not only in the physical sciences but also in society—the role of stress and 'perturbations' that can thrust us into a new, higher state." Ferguson affirms that not only scientists but poets and philosophers were right in their intimations of an open, creative universe. "Transformation, innovation, evolution—these are the natural responses to crisis."[12]

She then adds as authoritative evidence the conclusions of de Chardin, who talks about an advancing spiral of human progress—as well as Einsten's special theory of relativity, which "proves that we have outgrown Newton's clockwork universe" and have moved to an uncertainty paradigm, from the absolute to the relative. An essential characteristic of the human potential vision is the discovery (or rediscovery, in perennial philosophical terms) of various forms of extended consciousness. It is commonly asserted that humans are on the verge of an historically new broadening and deepening of their understanding of what it means to be human. While it may be conceded that this broadening and deepening has been available in limited ways in the past, Ferguson maintains that a qualitative change has come about in the past ten years.

> Quite suddenly, in this decade...the riches of many cultures are available to whole populations, both in orignial form and in contemporary adaptations. Drugstore racks and airport newsstands offer the wisdom of the ages in paperback. University extension classes and weekend seminars, adult education courses, and commercial centers are offering techniques that help people connect to new sources of personal energy, integration, harmony.[13]

Houston uses similar language, but carries the positon further:

> As we have seen, previous cultures have tended to deny some areas of development while acknowledging and encouraging others. With the present convergence of the findings of anthropology, cross cultural studies, psychophysical research, and studies into the nature and function of brain, we are beginning to have in hand a perspective on human possibility as profound as it is provocative. This perspective allows us to turn the corner on our humanity, exploring and experiencing the astonishing complexity and variety of the world of the possible human. It is virtually a new introduction to the human race.[14]

There is little doubt that among human potential enthusiasts one finds a sense of ecstatic excitement. At this point, however, we would conclude that these experiences are well within the contemporary cosmology of modernity for a number of reasons. First is the emphasis on individual perfection. One can easily transform the new human potential person into a consumer. A 1985 advertisement for *New Age* lists a series of consumer buzzwords: recycling, intimacy, self-healing, megatrends, Jean Houston, herbs, meditation, Gandhi, networking, ecology, natural childbirth, spiritual, yoga, Findhorn, natural food, solar, holistic health, fathering, acupuncture. By way of contrast, the emphasis of process reality is away from the consuming individual toward occasion, on threads that pass from individual 'things' or people to create a continuously transforming reality. The term 'change' or concrescence does not refer to some fundamental shift in the *quality* of humanity but rather in the way we understand or experience our humanity in relationship to the flux of unfolding events. In human potential thinking there is a kind of Faustian promise that humans have the potential of the gods. We regard this promise as the familiar old Western 'trip': that humans are uniquely God's creatures and can in some way participate with him/her/it in heaven, Eden or New Jerusalem.

A second distinction between the human potential variation of modern cosmology and process relates to the acceptance of the limitations inherent in the concept of culture. Human potential people assume a universality in the worldwide transformation of consciousness. They assume that humans will come to stand outside culture, outside the process of change, to control and guide it in the interest of a perfected (or at least maturing) humanity. We would suggest that the distinction between the more universal sense of cosmology or metaphysics and its cultural expression in a specific society never disappears. We would, in fact, argue that an essential arrogance, growing out of our Western enculturation, leads people to believe that there are two kinds of people—those who live in a world of universal truth and those who are closed or trapped in parochial or "cultural" beliefs. We have consistently stated that modern people are enclosed within a cosmology fundamentally restricted by limiting metaphors and language. The driving sense of progress, of destiny beyond the present, of linear history are hallmarks of the culture of modernity and especially of human potential modernity.

An area of overlap and relatedness between process and the human potential movement certainly does exist in the importance each places on artistic experience, creativity, and its relationship to both intellectual and bodily experience. As Houston affirms,[15]

> In our programs, the child is taught to think in images as well as words, to learn spelling or even arithmetic in rhythmic patterns, to think of his or her whole body, and to actively use both hemispheres of the brain. As a rich arts program is always essential to multimodal education, we helped develop and even restore arts-related learning in schools throughout the United States and Canada.[16]

Another area of overlap between human potential and process thought is the emphasis each places on reality as a continuously creative becoming, as a process of unitary occasion evolving from both the conceptual and the physical. Ferguson's *Brain/Mind Bulletin* quotes and elaborates Bohm[12] on this point:

> "I wish to bring out a new way of thinking, consistent with modern physics, that does not divide mind and matter or subject from object," Bohm said. This link is indivisible, like two sides of a continuous mobius strip. Information contained in one thought, on the "mental" side, is at the same time a chemical activity on the "material" side.[18]

This sounds very much like a process cosmology. However, for human potential advocates the implications of the mind–matter integration become extended far beyond the process position. A romantic leap takes us down an alchemist's path: since mind and matter are both aspects of the same reality, then thought (including imagination) can, in fact, create its own material reality. Since there is presumably no limit to what humans can imagine (obviously there is), there is no limit to what humans can make of the universe. The distinction between the old mechanistic dualism and the romantic New Age unity is expressed by Ferguson and Bohm as follows:

> Modern biology treats life as a material, mechanical process, he (Bohm) said. Peptides, hormones, amino acids and DNA are considered separate entities, like "parts of a machine."

> In human beings strong distinctions prevail between emotions, thoughts, and acts. "This underlying fragmentation expresses itself outwardly as a lack of care for life on the planet."

As long as the significance of the finite which is implicit in the machine metaphor dominates consciousness, he said, "the individual will actually *be* this finite significance. But when we truly see the new meaning that humanity need not be limited in this way, we will actually cease to be limited. We will begin to be open to the infinite, able to act creatively in every phase of life."[19]

We would add that to act creatively has no obvious value. One can act creatively for good or ill. In process thought the creative becoming of relationship *is* reality. In the conception of the Tao or the Hopi Way (as the Hopi refer to the positive thrust of their culture) the purpose is to bring one's being or the becoming of human life and culture into continuity and harmony with the rest of the naturally occurring creative process. But for the Hopi (and presumably for many human cultures) this search for a generous and open heart that will lead one down the 'right' path is a difficult one, requiring meditation, reflective living, being in tune with nature of which one is a part. For the human potential enthusiast, however, there is a profound shift in logic in the way she or he views creative imagination. It is not to find the way of harmony with nature; it is to create the way, much as the scientific technologist seeks to create his own way. As Bohm asserts:

If people could sustain a perception of the world as an unbroken whole, with a multiplicity of meanings, some of which are harmonious and some not, a very different state of affairs could unfold. There could be an unending creative perception of new meanings that encompass the older ones in broader and more harmonious wholes, which would unfold in a corresponding transformation of the overall reality.[20]

It is as if the human *umwelt* were capable of first apprehending the ground of causal efficacy in one overall holistic image, and then imagining how to move forward to create maximum harmony for the whole. Human imagination is used not to find its place in nature (as with the Hopi), but rather to create a new reality that is most congenial for humans, or for all being. This is, indeed, an arrogant implication from what would now seem the rather modest premise that reality was composed of a unitary integration of mind and matter. As Bateson would ask, what is the connection between human mind, eco-mind, and universal mind?

In process terms, human mind participates in creative activities that certainly extend beyond the physical units we call "persons," but the notion that persons can somehow synch with, and thus control, the broader universe of mind and thus control our physical world rather resonates with the cosmology of modern technology.

STEINER'S HOLISTIC EDUCATION. While the human potential movement has had its major impact on relatively stressed, affluent, middle-class adults searching for some meaning behind a consumer-driven hedonistic economy, there is an earlier prophet whose concern was holistic education for children and adolescents. Rudolph Steiner started the first Waldorf School in 1919 in Stuttgart, Germany, where he personally put into practice his particular theories of "holistic" personality and human development. This was, in fact, the beginning of a substantial educational movement: there are now Waldorf or 'Steiner' schools and teacher training institutions all over the world.[21]

Steiner saw clearly the restricted consciousness implicit in the linear scientific thought characteristic of both modern schooling and work, and he proposed to develop a fuller sense of knowing for children. Teachers, he said, should teach from a "penetrating knowledge of man."

> If we have a growing human being before us, a child, it is not enough. . . to have certain rules of how he should be taught and educated, and then just conform to the rules as one does in a technical science. This will never lead to good teaching. We must bring an inner fire, an inner enthusiasm, to our work; we must have impulses which are not intellectually transmitted from teacher to child according to certain rules, but which passes over from teacher to child in an intimate way. The whole of our being must work in us as educators, not only the thinking man; the man of feeling and the man of will must also play their part.[22]

He then goes on to talk about the limitations of scientific thinking which addresses itself only to the physical body and to the senses. He says that the human is made up of the physical body, the soul, and the spirit; that the world is "permeated by spirit, and true knowledge of the world must be spiritual knowledge."[23] It seems clear that Steiner wishes to extend modernity's meaning of "knowing" but still maintains the dualism between humans and the human sense of being and other processes of being. He is searching for a broader range of scientific concern which will allow humans, as the ultimate knowers of the planet, to understand and come into harmony with nature. He therefore develops a 'science' of human development. He goes to considerable lengths to show how man *is* like other aspects of nature—he shares the temperaments of the 'lower' animals, for example; he sleeps and wakes like the winter and summer of the seasons. These analogies are taken as more than poetic indications; they are often used as the basis for a new holistic science. So Steiner says:

> If the teacher can acquire a true knowledge of man, then he will notice how, when the etheric body is freed at the change of teeth, the child has an inner urge to receive everything in the form of pictures. In his own inner being he himself wants to become "picture."[24]

Steiner's vision of nature and the human relationship to nature reveals an intense search for deeper connectedness between human consciousness and experience and what he calls the spirit of the world. His educational ideas also include a highly integrated sense of knowing—wherein music, painting, language, and movement are seen as expressions of a common human development, rather than as the fragments portrayed in academic disciplines.

But we also see, quite contrary to process thought, the drive for the formulation of relatively specific and corrrect theories of the human condition, education, and society, in much the same way as modern New Age thought. The result is that little distinction is made between science and metaphysics, between broader areas of speculative philosophy and immediate fact. We believe that the importance of metaphysics is that it gives us an intellectual linguistic arena within which to think systematically about adequate and comprehensive theories of reality, and to test these theories against common experience. It then becomes possible for us to imagine, describe, and identify a great range of cultural practices, including science, that might express a more or less adequate sense of reality; there need not be only one. Contrary to this view, Steiner creates specific "correct" educational–cultural practices. Eurythmics, for example, is a particular art form and educational technique developed by Steiner, consisting of a set of body movements and gestures which express the relationships among movement, human vocal sound, poetry, and story. We have little doubt that this technique commonly creates a rich and holistic educational experience for children, but, as process teachers, we would say that it is certainly not the only technique by which children might have such an experience.

All in all, Steiner seems to assume that there is a specific philosophical–scientific construction of the world which can be used to direct us toward effective educational practice that will maximize full human development. He sees these practices as extending to many forms of human expression—dance, the use of color, relationships with plants and animals, musical activity, and spiritual development, all of which are major contributions to holistic education. Underlying Steiner's science, however, is the same drive for certainty and codification that is characteristic of the normal materialistic science he criticizes. So while holism, the vision of an interconnected world with more intimate relationships between humans and nature, brings Steiner's thought close to process thinking, the translation of this vision into somewhat firm, if not rigid, science-like generalizations and ritualized educational practices is more suggestive of archaic dogma and the 'laws' of scientific modernity. Moreover, not only does Steiner's style of thinking and approach to knowing reveal an effort to splice together the dogma of religiosity with the laws of science, but much of the ideological substance of his curriculum deals uncritically with Western history as the story of mankind's progressive climb toward perfection. When discussing his participation in the Theosophical Society (a quasi-religious society founded to integrate Eastern and Western thought), for example, Steiner says:

> Continued successful development in the Western countries is depending on how far it proves able to assimilate the principle of Western initiation. For Eastern initiations must, of necessity, leave untouched the Christ-principle as the central cosmic factor of evolution. Yet without this principle the Theosophical movement must remain without any decisive effect on Western culture, which has the life of Christ as its point of origin. In the West, the revelations of Oriental initiation would have to live as a mere sectarian alongside the living culture. Their only hope of affecting evolution would be if they could eradicate the Christ-principle from Western culture. This, however, would be identical with extinguishing the essential meaning of the earth, which lies in the knowledge and realization of the intentions of the living Christ.[25]

We would, at this point, note the sharp dividing line between those New Age thinkers who see an essential problem of modernity as requiring some kind of integration between science/technology and the great religious systems of the "civilized" world (as does Steiner) and other thinkers who are concerned more with the integration of primitive culture and experience with the insights of both the archaic religions and science. Our process position is clearly the latter.

PATRICIA CARINI AND THE PROSPECT SCHOOL. Carini is a contemporary educator whose major interest has been the observation and guidance of learning for children within her own school, the Prospect School in North Bennington, Vermont. Of the various figures and movements discussed here who have some intellectual or practical connection with process cosmology, Carini's work is probably most explicitly related to this thought. It is interesting to hear her speak of her transformation from modernity to process:

> My own philosophical orientation and early education and experience placed me in the mainstream of this so-called scientific thought. However, over the past 12 years, my work as an observer of children at The Prospect School has led me to a radical questioning of the applicability of this science to human events. In particular, the opportunity to observe children over long spans of time and through the rich variation of setting afforded by the Prospect School, has raised questions about observing itself (which I take to be the root of science), about the issues of objectivity and subjectivity central to it, and also about causation, past experience, and explanations, as these ideas are applied in the sciences of man.[26]

Carini's references very much overlap our own; they include Barfield and Whitehead. Her central conception of reality is process and relationship rather than physical or mental person or personality. It is in the mythic connection within a network of extensions (prehensions?) with the surrounding world that we are to find meaning, rather than in the careful description of physical substance, people, or "things." In Carini's words:

> The universal and transpersonal symbolism surrounding and permeating the individual quest is a time-honored source of perspective and guidance to the seeker for life and meaning. Myth and religion are its repositories, although in the West these sources have, for many, long lost their vitalizing power, leaving the person in a state of virtual isolation which brings in its train restlessness, confusion, and fragmentation. Collectively, and in concert with the natural world, however, we are the source of our own wisdom.[27]

This is, of course, close to our own assessment of the meaning crisis of modernity, although Carini assumes a universality beyond culture and myth which allows meaning-making to continue to happen in the light of inadequate cosmologies and shallow cultures. So we recognize each other by the nature of our search for and involvement in relationship:

> Thus it is the perspective of the universal and transpersonal which provides an integrating pattern for gathering the trends of meaning which compose the fabric of individual life. It is never so much the facts, circumstances, and literal occurrences that describe and portray the person as the *relationship* the persons make to those literal events, and the choices that follow from the mode of relating. The person is not rendered visible or understandable to himself or others by a factual account of his experience, but rather through the perspective he brings to bear on those experiences.[28]

It is exciting to find a practical educator construing her work within the process framework. Her conception of the imagination, for example, is expressed in full-blown process language:

> In imagining, the person's own spirit is united with the spirit of that in which he is immersed, and that in which he is immersed reveals back to him his own spirit. In imagining, detachment is abrogated and the merging of the viewer and the viewed brings a new meaning into existence, reflective of both moments, enhancing of each and the possession of neither.[29]

Bringing to bear one's own experience as a mode of relating is a major factor in Carini's work. Rather than simply describing a child in more holistic terms than usual, she is attempting to discover ". . .that unity that encompasses (even). . .seemingly opposite experiences are actually recognitions of our "shadow realms"—i.e., our own uncollected, ungathered thoughts—when we perceive others:

> When . . . the perception of other persons is based on direct access through the expressiveness of the body in its engagement with things-in-the-world, there is an assumption of co-existensive beings united through the shared world setting. From that assumption it can be derived that self-knowledge and knowledge of others are achieved reciprocally and intersubjectively.[30]

Our regret is that Carini's reciprocal and intersubjective knowledge (albeit an apt paraphrase of Whitehead's prehension) is apparently restricted to knowledge of other *persons.* As such, it falls short of acknowledging a unitary sense of being in which each of us is no longer fundamentally separated from and outside of everything else in the universe. Carini's monograph *The Art of Seeing and the Visibility of the Person* has the ring of the intuitive and the indeterminist, of understanding teaching more as an art than a science. She does want teachers to see individual children in their own terms, in some sense interacting with the teacher who is him- or herself part child. Yet the strongest proviso is to improve one's observational skills. In analyzing subtle gestures of the body, for example, Carini notes:

> This is a difficult undertaking. It requires of the observer a reengagement and strengthening of the perception of the value qualities underlying the more familiar, obvious, and nameable constant object traits. It also requires time in order that recurrent gestural patterns can be described and in order that the gestures through which the body's composition is made visible can be objectified.[31]

Although even here Carini acknowledges an intellectual debt to Whitehead ("The human body is that region of the world which is the primary field of human expression"),[32] trying to objectify gestures sounds more like a prescription for a new social science methodology than a call for moving beyond the researcher–subject dichotomy. Carini's emphasis is on being a sensitive observer toward the end of deeply understanding another *human being.* This is a different reading of Whitehead's cautions (". . . the body is . . . continuous with the external world . . . we cannot define where a body begins and where the external world ends")[33] from that which we would give. Like the attempts of humanists to have us refine our empathy skills, Carini's unmistakable assertion is that humans are entities worthy of extraordinary consideration. What we object to is the attendant implication that we may disrgard the context in which they tenderly coexist with *all* aspects of nature.

The Carini approach to both teaching and the science of pedagogy raises interesting questions about the possibility of integrating the insights of the process view of reality with normal scientific and professional practice. More importantly, such integration would relate to a problem left untouched in

Carini's work: the use of power and power relationships. The student/teacher duality brings with it a particular metaphysical and epistemological construction of the source and use of 'power.' Is power inherent in relationship and thus only to emerge out of relationship? Or is there power *over*—power of supervisor or researcher over teacher, power of teacher over student, power of student over environment? This issue becomes central when we deal with our next relative of process, liberation education.

LIBERATION EDUCATION. The holistic education of Steiner, with its effort to expand the conception of learning and maturation beyond rational or analytic thinking—to movement, feeling, will, and spiritual connectedness with nature—focused very much on the idea of individual fulfillment. It sought to expand the richness and quality of what it means to live in the natural world. One might well consider the human potential movement as a popular extension of these earlier roots planted by Steiner. In Waldorf schools today,[34] one sees the emphasis on the integration of art, music, movement, nature study and science that flows through the pages of Jean Houston's *The Possible Human*. We see this strand of process-oriented education as a product of polite and reflective, albeit radical, thought. Although a radical thinker, Steiner makes no mention of revolutionary confrontation. Similarly, in the human potential movement we are led to believe that social transformation will come about by means of the myriad decisions of millions of people, transformed through social networks, support groups, and quasi-religious conversions. One does not anticipate unpleasant conflict, except as it is planned and worked out in workshops. Likewise, Carini works within the framework of consultations, workshops, and university seminars.

Liberation education, on the other hand, is a stepchild of the turbulent 1960s, the era of strikes, demonstrations, sit-ins, demands for equal access to privilege, and even the burning of cities. It tends to stress reform and transformation at the societal neighborhood and personal level (note the slogan "think globally, act locally"). One of its earliest advocates was a Quaker-oriented group in Philadelphia called The Movement for a New Society (MNS). The Movement advocates a comprehensive systems view of the pathology of modernity. It sees politics, economics, environment, feminism, peace, and the need for communal cooperation and spiritual regeneration as interrelated issues. In its first major document, *Moving Toward a New Society*,[35] it lists a constellation of aspects required of a healthy society:

> physical security
> equality

non-exploitation
work
democracy
wholeness
community
freedom
positive conflict
ecological harmony
world community

Its program is summarized in Table 10.1. One should note that its advocacy of a simple lifestyle (communal living, the sharing of housing, furniture, etc.) reflects, in fact, the life that MNS members in Philadelphia actually live. As they describe themselves:

> The Philadelphia Life Center is a multigenerational support community for persons involved in fundamental social change training and activity. Beginning in 1971 as a group of about 35 persons, the Life Center has grown to about 125 persons, living in seventeen houses located in West Philadelphia and all within easy walking distance of each other. We tie in with a network of other communities, work collectives, and training centers across the United States and in other parts of the world.[36]

Table 10.1

What we now have: Our Ecologically Faulty System.	What we'll need for an Ecologically-orientated Economic System
	Values
Growth, "big-is-good," complex technology, maximum production and consumption, planned obsolescence.	Steady state, "small is beautiful," intermediate technology, adequate production and minimized consumption, equilibrium, conservation, frugality, durability.
	Lifestyles
"Keep up with the Joneses" conspicuous consumption, nuclear family, desire for highest possible income, eating meat and living off the top of the food chain.	Simplicity, communal living (with sharing of housing furniture, appliances), greatly reduced consumption, delight in living with minimal income and possessions, vegetarianism.

Planning

Mostly by business firms to maximize their profit and economic growth.

Developed through democratically-controlled bodies and aimed at governing production by social and ecological criteria.

Capital

Maximum accumulation of capital through search for maximum profit. Maximize GNP and *quantity* of capital stock.

Capital investment rate set equal to depreciation rate. Production for social use rather than private profit. Minimize GNP and maximize *quality* of capital stock.

Resources

Used in wasteful way—use rate increaing exponentially. Planned obsolescence leads to very high resource consumption. Unnecessary duplication leads to wasted material, time and energy resources, e.g., having many private insurance companies with enormous sales staff, rather than handling insurance through Social Security.

Drastic reduction in resource use per unit of industrial production. Products built for durability, repairability, recycling. Minimal "throughput." Goal of waste elimination, e.g., instead of several competing private drug companies making almost identical products with enormous advertising outlay, have few regional drug companies making standardized drugs.

Pollution

Ecologically faulty technology (about ½ of post-World War II productive enterprise) pollutes air, water, soil. Introduces synthetics (chemical pesticides and fertilizers, synthetic fibers, plastics, detergents, etc.) which require high inputs of energy in their manufacture and which cannot be recycled by the earth's natural mechanisms.

Replace ecologically faulty technology with ecologically harmonious one. Essentially complete recycling of all reusable metal, glass and paper products. Synthetic products replaced by natural ones, wherever possible (e.g., using biological pest control). Essentially complete containment and reclamation of wastes from combustion, smelting and chemical operations. Make smokestacks rare.

Technology

Wastes resources, creates high pollution products & non-biodegradable synthetics. Geared to maximizing business profits. Focus on quantity.

Seeks processes that conserve materials and energy, are non-polluting, durable, labor-intensive, intermediate. Geared to social needs and ecological efficiency. Focus on quality.

Services

So minimal and haphazard that people feel no real security from them. People feel they must struggle to achieve their own economic security by accumulating possessions and money.

Provide floor of guaranteed minimum universal services (free health care, job re-training, etc.) to entire population. Give people assurance that de-development will not mean loss of economic security.

Advertising

Accounts for about $18 billion of GNP. Aimed at getting people to purchase more and more, be dissatisfied with what they now have.

Eliminate private advertising industry. Public research agencies test and rate products, distribute consumer information to the public.

Autos

Account for $80-90 billion of GNP, highways for $15 billion. One-fourth of economy now dependent on them and their infrastructure. One-fourth to one-third of city land area devoted to streets and parking lots. Very high resource users and pollution creators. (Energy outlay for cement and steel in roadways estimated at 3 to 4 times greater than that required for building a railway, and uses 4 times more land.)

Largely replaced by widespread mass transit system, bicycles, walking. Build no more roads. Any remaining autos powered by steam, wankel, or other non-polluting, low resource-using engine. Cars available through public car-rental facilities. City streets and parking lots torn up and planted with gardens, grass, trees, bike paths, walkways.

Military

Approaching $100 billion of GNP.

Replace with nonviolent civilian defense force.

Consumers

"Consumer goods and services" accounts for about $400 billion of GNP—much is baubles and luxuries like electric carving knives and hair spray.

Elimination of luxuries and non-essentials. Focus on provisions of essentials of food, clothing, housing (in simple but adequate way) to whole population. Recycling clothing and furniture through large increase in second-hand shops.

Food and Agriculture

Agribusiness moving heavily into farming—family farms disappearing. Developers and speculators using farm land for industry, housing, commerce. Inorganic fertilizer and chemical pesticides polluting soil and water. 78% of grain harvest fed to livestock, wasting about 18 million tons of protein per year (which approaches the world's protein deficit). Government programs to reduce agricultural surpluses, even though half-billion of the world's people are chronically hungry.

End agribusiness and re-establish family farm. Rural new towns and other services (e.g., training programs in ecology, botany, entomology) to encourage "back to the farm" movement. Strict land use planning to prevent speculation; encourage farming, green belts, wilderness area preservation, protection of wetlands and estuaries. Greatly reduced use of inorganic fertilizers and chemical pesticides. Treated sewage and garbage transported to farms and used for fertilizer. Grain harvest used to provide vegetarian diet. (Feed raised on 1 acre of land and converted into beef will meet 1 person's protein needs for 77 days; soy beans on same acre can meet one person's needs for 6.1 years.) Diversion of capital into food production to assure sufficient food for the world.

Energy

Exponential increase in use, reliance on uses which pollute. Turning to nuclear power plants, with their lethal radio-active wastes.

Great reduction in use. Reliance on energy sources which cause minimal or no pollution, e.g., solar power, wind power, etc.

Population

U.S. population growing slowly, but high per capita use of resources and pollution impact means that each additional American has a much more damaging effect on the ecosystem than each person born in poorer countries.

Reduce U. S. population by setting birth rate lower than death rate until optimum size (measured by ecological impact) is reached. Then stabilize at "no-growth" level. Encourage adoption. Free contraception, mass education on population issues.

While MNS sees the crisis of modernity in the well-worked language of misplaced political, economic, technological, and military values, its remedies stress, in a refreshing way, the importance of changing not only one's values and world view but the way one actually lives. Its program for lifestyle changes has been codified in an educational book, *Resource Manual for a Living Revolution.*[37] It extends the theoretical concerns included earlier in *Moving Toward a New Society* to the level of practical application and deals with issues of community building and training for direct action to bring about social change. MNS is within the American tradition of pragmatic social action; it is not burdened with the heavy metaphysical or theoretical exercises in which we have engaged in this book. Rather than turning to extended philosophical, political, or social theory for guidance, it seeks inspiration and direction from positive historical examples in which direct action and nonviolence have successfully changed the course of events: Gandhi in India; Martin Luther King in Montgomery; the Quakers in colonial Pennsylvania; the Norwegian resistance to the Nazis.

A liberation position which focuses less on broadscale revolution in lifestyle and community development and more on the use of teaching and curriculum development to effect radical social change is developed by Shor and described in *Critical Thinking in Everyday Life*[38]. While Shor relies heavily on Freire's conception of critical consciousness as a rationale for his teaching, the context of his work takes place among poor and working-class young adults in New York City. He sees the oppressive qualities of modernity much as they are described in MNS, but develops a curriculum and teaching program within the constraints of school and college, using the contemporary structure of schooling itself to exemplify the nature of that oppression. He initially questions the irrationality and contradictions within everyday life and contrasts them with what is espoused by legitimate institutions as a "responsive" and "democratic" society.[39]

> The powerlessness and confusion in daily life can only be understood through critical thinking yet most people are alienated from their own conceptual habits of mind. How come? Why don't masses of people engage in social reflection? Why isn't introspection an habitual feature of life? What prevents popular awareness of how the whole system operates, and which alternatives would best serve human needs? Why is political imagination driven from common experience? Confronted by an "eclipse of reason" in mass culture, what can liberatory pedagogy do?[40]

He responds to his own question:

> Faced with this [situation], the designers of an empowering pedagogy have to study the shape of disempowering forces. As allies of the powerless, liberatory teachers need a working knowledge of the anti-critical field in which a critical pedagogy evolves. The systematic investigation of mass reality prepares the teacher for using daily life as subject matter. The teacher's own critical learning prefigures the knowledge that the class as a whole will gain.[41]

Shor then suggests a number of the major forces in the culture that tend to reinforce the false consciousness or "mass denial of reason" characteristic of the modern system. These forces include what Shor calls "vocational culture" or "the machinification of character". He stresses, as do we, the mechanistic metaphor as a central driving force of modernity which leads to the separation of one's inner sense of being from the instrumental work of the society.

> Dismembered and disintegrated, the workforce becomes dishabituated to its own critical, creative, and emotional potentials, which atrophy from lack of exercise. One consequence of not being allowed to think, to govern, to create, or to express deep feeling, is a defensive rigidity when confronted with the forbidden.[42]

And again:

> The vocationalization of character rests on a sturdy reality of corporate society: machines are the most reliable part of the production process. The "human factor" has emerged as a synonym for error and unpredictability. Humans are emotional and demanding.[43]

He sees vocationalization as trapping the mind into a world of the static and the contained, which he calls reification—resulting in a consciousness of our lives as pieces or fragments which seem omnipresent and immovable. They refer to the isolated pieces of labor that mysteriously add up to a 'product.' They include the institutions of public life which are accepted as 'just there': the Internal Revenue Service, the motor vehicle bureau, the public school, the banks, the social security office, the department of public works, the police.

> Reified culture achieves this disempowerment through related alienations: people are alienated from their own class-peers, lacking the solidarity needed to organize for power; people are alienated from a grasp of the system's whole operation and the mediating mechanisms which reproduce daily life.... Demobilized masses of people are channeled into spectatorism: sports, television, movies, followed by the glamorous lives of film stars and jet-setters, being activated by experts, authorities and opinion-makers from the mass media. One spectator activity, "window shopping,"registers the routine reification of everyday life, where the alluring given order freezes transcendent action.[44]

We would note that reification, which posits a static, frozen, fixed world, stands in stark opposition to process metaphysics. In the modern world, technology, jobs, and products rapidly change, but the fragmentary mechanized life that allows this to happen is reified and seemingly stays the same. Shor sees this inability to loosen ourselves from the static sense of institutional dominance as a loss of faith in commonsense rationality—it is in fact a resort to prescientific and even magical thinking. As he says, "For people raised with doubts about their ability to think, the big, quick, untestable truth of prescientism has the authority of being simple and certain" (p. 61). People thus end up with blind faith in Dodge trucks and Velveeta cheese.

Shor's solution to the obstinate hold of reification and the consequent blind faith of modern people in the opague, fragmentary, and seemingly magical political, economic, and educational system is what he calls the "re-experiencing of the ordinary," but with an enlightened and critical teacher. The "ordinary" includes one's view of work, family life, consuming, school. His book then contains a host of examples of how to do just this.

The intellectual tradition out of which Shor is working has familiar landmarks, from Marx and Freud to Habermas, Marcuse, and Freire.[45] Shor's contribution, as with Freire, includes the translation of a more general theoretical liberationist position into concrete educational programs for a specific audience. It is quite different from MNS in a number of important respects. First, Shor sees the central problem of modernity as the creation of fake or inauthentic modes of knowing as well as the stripping of oppressed peoples of their inherent capacity to see through these modes of knowing.

The illusion that things must always be like this (e.g., one must always put up with inequality; one must always lose in the meritocratic race for privilege; the genesis of authority and legitimate power is always from above) is reinforced by the large and seemingly stable institutions that constantly grind out the message. From the point of view of young, poor, and working-class people, the most destructive of these institutions is the public school. The way out of this bind, according to Shor, is critical consciousness or "seeing through" the culture of oppression.

Shor's analysis of the oppressive institutions in modern society is quite similar to that of MNS. Rather than using a broad-scale community action approach to reform, as does MNS, he chooses rather to remain within the framework of schooling and to change, in a fundamental way, its curriculum and the relationships among teachers and students. There is, however, a deeper difference between MNS and Shor than their strategy for change. It lies in the way MNS sees the core and genesis of knowing. The Quaker view of the world, implicit in much of the work of MNS, suggests that there is a transpersonal divine spark in all human beings. The problem with modernity is not simply one of hierarchical institutional structures wherein humans mislead and exploit one another with a false consciousness and with false values; it is deeper and more serious. It is that the special reverence due all humans is ignored, corrupted, or exploited by poverty, sexism, racism, and nationalism as these are expressed in political, economic and military institutions. Seeing the divinity in the human condition requires that we live a life of reverence wherein we can experience the unseen but guiding order of God and feel his or her presence. The MNS delight in living with minimal worldly goods is, we suspect, based at least partly on the example of Jesus as his life is recounted in the Gospel stories. The Quaker's critical consciousness requires more than lifting the veil that shrouds arrogant and corrupt institutions; it requires a sense of knowing rooted in a spiritual experience that connects one with a deeper sense of one's community. It cannot be done within the transitory environments of colleges and schools, as Shor proposes. Hence the creation of the Life Center by the Philadelphia group.

This distinction between the Shor brand of liberation which relies heavily on a simple change in the way one constructs or thinks about one's social reality, and the Quaker view of a kind of liberation that is linked to a spiritual quality in humanity itself is important. There is, of course, a movement called liberation theology, which makes explicit the connection between techniques and forces for liberation from various forms of oppression and the religious institutional base through which liberation is possible. Unlike Shor and the critical theorists of England, Europe, and North America, liberation theology has its roots in the efforts of the poor in Central and South America to move out of their existence of poverty and marginality. One of its early interpreters was Gustavo Gutierrez, a Jesuit and native of Peru, and author of *A Theology of Liberation*.[46] Gutierrez speaks of God's special love for the poor, the sick, and the broken. Because of widespread Marxist thought and politics in Latin America and the obvious association between Marx's workers and peasants and Jesus's downtrodden, the movement has brought about considerable controversy within the relatively conservative Catholic Church.[47]

What seems compelling about liberation theology is the effort to integrate the socioeconomic critique of modernity provided by Marx with the spiritual critique of modernity provided by radical Christians. It is presumably an effort to bring back into central focus the importance of 'this world' and the centrality of peace, justice, and universal compassion in the here and now, not as instruments for getting to the next world but as a common basis for a natural universe. Process, of course, posits a single world of nature, as does both Marxist and liberal humanist modernity. In our own experience, however, it is difficult to underestimate the deep and pervasive influence of the ancient Greek/Christian cosmology which moves one to experience reality as a multiplicity of domains, strung together as 'a great chain of being'—heaven with God and the saints, semi-heaven with angels and unfinished divinities, semi-corrupted earth with humans, animals, plants and minerals, limbo, purgatory, and hell. If modern people could, in fact, shake themselves loose from this fragmentary multi-cosmos and truly believe that there is here, now, in our shopping malls and toxic waste dumps, only one place to be, this might well generate a considerable apprehension and sense of alarm. For the Christian liberationist, Jesus is dramatically and profoundly present in this world, not simply as a personal or institutional bridge to the next but as a force for redeeming decency in our contemporary existence. From our vantage point it would seem that the great weight of sacred text, church history, liturgical rite, and institutional form is so fixed in the Christian cosmology, with the ultimate escape image—heaven—that it is most difficult to imagine any theological reformulation that would make the Christian meaning system and experience consistent with either a just secular world or a more comprehensive and coherent process world.

A general critique and commentary on liberationist education is difficult because its focus has become so diffused in recent years. Its most exciting aspect, perhaps, is that represented both by the Movement for a New Society and the liberation theologians in their effort to integrate critical Marxist and neo-Marxist theoretical formulations, in their dealing with the conception and use of *power* in modernity, with a more spiritual vision of the human condition.[48] One serious problem in liberationist thinking, however, rests in the universalistic conception of liberation itself. We can imagine the plausibility of liberation from specific institutionalized forms of oppression or specific reified beliefs that trap people into oppressive conditions of dependency and hierarchy—e.g., the myth that only medical doctors know the secrets of healing and can or should administer exclusively techniques of healing. Yet there is implicit in the very idea of 'critical consciousness' an assumption that it transcends one's 'entrapment' in culture. The suggestion is that the individual can move from cultural consciousness to a universal sensibility that makes culture obsolete. As a consequence, one should regard racism, sexism, and all forms of cultural stereotyping and roles as unnecessary in postmodern consciousness. For us the distinction between metaphysical and cultural cosmology is critical. We assume that one can search for a kind of universal discourse that transcends the specifics of culture, but that at best this discourse trails off into a poetical or mystical idiom. This was the limit that Whitehead self-consciously pushed. But we believe there is no real hope of *transcending* culture, for culture is carried within the communication process itself, which is required to talk about culture. (Metacultural conversation contains within itself the more specific cultural forms that are being discussed.) Earlier we included Whorf's discussion of this issue with respect to Hopi language. Dorothy Lee makes a similar observation about language, using the Wintu people of North America as her example.

> For the Wintu, then, essence or quality, is generic and found in nature; it is permanent and remains unaffected by man. Form is imposed by men, through act of will. But the impress man makes is temporary. The deer stands out as an individual only at the moment of his speech; as soon as he ceases speaking the deer merges into darkness.[49]

According to Lee, for the Wintu the world is made up of generic 'things,' that have and will always exist. Specific forms—specific types of animals or humans—are not essential reality. They are only formed from more basic things such as dawn and fire and earth, and they come and go. There is the whole of nature, with its permanence and stability, and the fragments of form that are with us only temporarily. For example:

> The premise of primacy of the whole finds expression in the Wintu concept of himself as originally one, not a sum of limbs or members. When I asked for a word for the body, I was given the term *the whole person*. The Wintu does not say *my head aches*; he says *I headache*. . . A Wintu girl does not say her *dress was striped* but *she was dress-striped*.[50]

This analysis is reminiscent of Barfield's discussion of figuration. Humans, through a process of cognitive focusing, objectify the world, make and name objects in the world; but the quality and syntax by which these objects are described differ, depending on the cosmology of the culture and more deeply on the language or communication system that portrays that cosmology. And although one may 'liberate' oneself from the reified themes in the language and generate new ones, one is still embedded in the syntax. In English, for example, one cannot excape the duality implicit in most of its syntax wherein subject acts on object, doing something to or for someone with or by means of something else. Action is outside object; object is outside causation. Within these terms the Whiteheadian conception of process, modern quantum physics, and much of Eastern philosophy are almost unintelligible.

We believe it is important to speculate about the adequacy of one's cultural cosmology, to test it against what seems to be more general standards of comprehensiveness, validity, and authenticity. Herein is our emphasis on studying and reflecting on the human cultural record, which moves toward a comprehensive cosmology. But as we search for more adequate conceptions of cosmology and culture, we always understand that we are in some ways still connected with the constraints of our own culture, for separation from one's mother culture could only result in the kind of radical rupture and social alienation we associate with insanity.

In process thought there is no ultimate liberation from nature or culture. In a sense the idiom of "liberation" itself becomes inappropriate, and we speak rather of apprehending our involvement in the concrescence of occasion. We are convinced that process 'consciousness' might well result in community and teaching programs strikingly similar to those suggested by liberationists such as Freire, Shor, and the Movement for a New Society. But there would be, in addition, a fundamental shift in concern —greater attention to apprehending the fullness of the immediacy of occasions on the one hand and less concern for transcending culture on the other. Neither liberation nor process, from our perspective, can transcend culture, for they are simply visions of new possible cultures or steps along the way. Liberation tends more than process to posit an ideal condition of being in the future toward which one is moving. For process there is no perfection, only continual change: the becoming, transforming, and perishing of occasions. All nature, including human imagination, participates in this process; all deserve the tender consideration of the most comprehensive and sensitive sort available to the human *umwelt*. In short, process is existentially oriented; liberation is apocalyptically oriented. However, within the framework of the actual institutions that oppress us in our contemporary human condition, the attainment of both process and liberation probably requires a traumatic letting go of the familiar. How education can promote the coming about of such a creative trauma is the search in which liberation and process are both engaged.

ECOLOGY AND PRESERVATION OF THE EARTH. Ecology is another social and educational movement related to process education. Ecology can be construed simply as a conventional academic discipline within the field of biology, meaning the scientific study of complex relationships among plants and animals, and their geological and climatic surroundings—how they interrelate with one another and the limits placed on individual species as well as ecological communities because of the broader environments within which they live. It is this last point that has led to our use of the term "ecology" to signify some kind of global crisis: the fear that we might push beyond the limits required by the planet to maintain an environment that is habitable for humans and other forms of existence which sustain our comfort, convenience, and even our survival. In this sense of the term, the ecological movement has been punctuated by such cries of alarm as Rachel Carson's *Silent Spring*[51] and the Club of Rome's landmark study *The Limits to Growth*.[52] As in our discussion of various movements above, we are constrained from presenting in any comprehensive way ecology's history, meaning, or educational significance. At most we can but mention one or two of its more important advocates or streams of thought and relate these to our own understanding of process education.

Murray Bookchin is a major spokesman for the ecology movement. His book *The Ecology of Freedom* brings together the thinking and work of over thirty years. In his own words:

> During these years I. . .concentrated on how a truly free society, based on ecological principles, could mediate humanity's relationship with nature. As a result, I began to explore the development of a new technology scaled to comprehensive human dimensions. Such a technology would include small solar and wind installations, organic gardens, and the use of local "natural resources" worked by decentralized communities. This view quickly gave rise to another—the need for direct democracy, for urban specialization, for a high measure of self-sufficiency, for self-empowerment based on communal forms of social life—in short, the nonauthoritarian Commune composed of communes.[53]

Bookchin became increasingly troubled at the extent to which people tended to subvert the unity, coherence, and radical nature of his focus. This concern is reminiscent of our own characterization of modernity as a tremendously fragmenting cosmology. Bookchin was trying to put together such disparate fields as community development, social hierarchy, and alternative technology with the idea of "human scale" into a single plausible world; yet this concept of ecological holism itself was the most difficult to communicate. As he says:

> Combined in a coherent whole and supported by a consistently radical practice. . . these views challenge the *status quo* in a far reaching manner—in the only manner commensurate with the nature of the crisis. It was precisely this *synthesis* of ideas that I sought to achieve in *The Ecology of Freedom*.[54]

Bookchin assumes that if an analysis were appropriately rooted in the historical circumstances of the planet, one might well imagine a different future for the planet and feel compelled to act on that vision.

> What *should* be could become what *must* be, if humanity and the biological complexity on which it rests were to survive. Change and reconstruction could emerge from existing problems rather than wishful thinking and misty vagaries.[55]

The essential nature of this change rests, according to Bookchin, on the application of three central principles: The first of these is *usufruct*, referring to "the freedom of individuals in a community to appropriate resources merely by virture of the fact that they are using them"[56]—as opposed to value associated with ownership, proprietorship, work, and even mutual aid or reciprocity. The idea of usufruct is related to process in important ways.

Static property cannot be separated from its use for fulfillment and enjoyment—action, event, occasion become more central than possession of commodities. Usufruct also emphasizes collective (as opposed to personal) relationships among aspects of 'things' in action, in use, rather than the association of reality with concrete personality. The second and third principles are what Bookchin calls "complementarity" and "the equality of unequals." These principles refer to unconditional and freely given consideration among peoples of each other's needs, quite apart from issues of power or the determination of objective economic value. In summarizing the significance of these principles and their relationship to the broader principle of freedom, Bookchin says;

> I have tried to pierce through the layered membranes of freedom from its outward surface as the inequality of equals, probing through its various economic layers of equivalence, to work with its core as a caring sensibility, a supportive domestic life, and its own rule of the equality of unequals. I have found residual areas of freedom in communities where the world simply does not exist, in loyalties that are freely given without expectations of recompense, in systems of distribution that know no rules of exchange, and in interpersonal relations that are completely devoid of domination. Indeed, insofar as humanity has been free to voice the subjectivity of nature and meanings latent within it, nature itself has revealed its own voice, subjectivity, and fecundity through humanity. Ultimately, it is in this ecological interplay of social freedom and natural freedom that a true ecology of freedom will be fashioned.[57]

Bookchin suggests that his community of social reality transcends the Western duality of subject/object—human/nature and enters an arena where nature and culture are no longer seen in opposition. As in our own thinking, this sensibility is strongly influenced by studying so-called primitive peoples, who have, in fact, as much to teach us as the great civilizations which attract so much scholarly attention.

> "Civilization," with its claim to be the cradle of culture, has rested theoretically on the imagery of a "stingy" nature that could support only elites, whose "freedom" and "free time". . . has been possible historically by exploiting the labor of the many.

> Preliterate societies never held this view; ordinally they resisted every attempt to impose it . . . Rarely did the "savages" even try to "wrestle" with nature; rather, they *coaxed* it along slowly and patiently with chants, songs, and ceremonials that we rightly call dances. All this was done in a spirit of cooperation within the community itself, and between the community and nature. "Necessity" was collectivized to foster cooperation and colonized by "freedom" long before preliterate communities verbalized any distinction between the two. The very words "necessity" and "freedom" had yet to be formed by the separation and

tensions that "civilization" was to create between them, and by the repressive discipline "civilization" was to impose on nonhuman and human nature alike.[58]

Bookchin's position, like our own interpretation of process, requires the comparative perspective of modern/primitive. What was once an unconscious and spontaneous connection between humans and the larger ecological context now requires conscious and deliberate effort. The self-consciousness in archaic and modern thought that leads us to celebrate such categories as 'humanity,' 'individuality,' 'personality,' and the notion of the 'conquest of nature' forecloses any return to an easy acceptance of the deep and important qualities of being implicit in usufruct and complementarity. As Bookchin says:

> On this qualitatively new terrain, we cannot—and should not—rely on the power of custom, much less on traditions that have long faded into the past. We are no longer an inwardly oriented, largely homogeneous group of folk that is untroubled by a long history of internal conflict and unblemished by the mores and practices of domination. Our values and practices now demand a degree of consciousness and intellectual sophistication that early bands, clans, and tribes never required to maintain their freedoms as a lived phenomenon.[59]

There is obviously no return, even if one were genuinely to want it. There is now a constant interplay between the universality of philosophy and science on the one hand and the effort to build specific, subconsciously based, decent, authentic culture on the other, recognizing that such universalistic philosophy and science are to some degree always culture and that culture is always subject to the critique of reflective consideration.

Very few spokespeople for the ecology movement have as comprehensive and well-developed positions as Bookchin, especially in their ability to relate scientific and technical issues with the broader social-theoretical issue. We would add a note to Bookchin's work. There is a growing distinction (controversy?) within the field centered around the term 'deep ecology.' Deep ecology is, it would seem, primarily an attack on the conception of humans as stewards for the planet. The deep ecological position assumes (as does both process and Bookchin) that there is a more authentic quality of being for humans than is understood by either humanistic modernists or the Christian stewards which would see all forms of being as having as sacred and legitmate right to exist as do humans themselves. Naess formulates the principles of the movement as follows:

1. The well-being of nonhuman life on Earth has value in itself. This value is independent of any instrumental usefulness for limited human purposes.

2. Richness and diversity in life forms contribute this value and is a further value in itself.

3. Humans have no right to interfere destructively with nonhuman life except for purposes of satisfying vital needs.

4. Present interference is excessive and detrimental.

5. Present policies must therefore be changed.

6. The necessary policy changes affect basic economic and ideological structures and will be the more drastic the longer it takes before significant change is started.

7. The ideological change is mainly that of appreciating life quality (focusing on situations involving inherent value) rather than enjoying a high standard of life (measured in terms of available means).

8. Those who subscribe to the foregoing points have an obligation directly or indirectly to try to implement the necessary changes.[60]

We should add that there are two other extremely important threads in our discussion of educational movements related to process and ecology which require consideration. First is the feminist movement, which has already been introduced in the selection by Susan Griffin on comparative cosmology. The radical feminist position represented in the writing of Mary Daly[61] as well as in Griffin's work points clearly to a postmodern cosmology that is close to the spirit of Bookchin's ecology of freedom. The particular insight of the feminists that contributes, perhaps most, to a process cosmology is the stress placed on the destructiveness of an almost exclusively male conception of significant knowing—a knowing in modernity that relies on linear thought and expository writing, from philosophy to jounalism, from history to science. Western forms of knowing characterized as 'fiction', such as poetry, drama, movement, sports, music, painting, and liturgy, have been associated with recreation, entertainment, and superstition, rather than with authentic statements of the world around us. Newspapers, for example, set politics, economics, and science on the front page; editorials and commentary (theory and philosophy) at the end of the first section; and the expressive arts and sports somewhere in the second half of the paper. Formal schooling is, of course, even more blatantly guilty of this denigration of the intuitive, expressive, dramatic, or creative quality of knowing, as opposed to the more superficial type of 'hard' knowledge. Feminists have been among the most vocal to insist that knowledge cannot be separated from the person—there is no clear distinction between subject and object; knowing is generated in the flow of living occasions and reconstructed by living beings.

Second is the new peace movement. Global alarm over the potential catastrophe of the use of nuclear weapons has brought with it a sustained educational movement. Two groups might be mentioned: Physicians for Social Responsibility and Educators for Social Responsibility (ESR). The latter group has published considerable curricula on peace education and generated a grassroots organization of teachers to create new curricula and teach not only peace issues, narrowly construed, but also issues associated with the political and social empowerment required to affect the policies and actions of centralized government and unresponsive bureaucracies. In a paper on the distinction between "power over" and "power with," based partly on his experience with ESR, Kreisberg,[62] for example, is clearly moving in the direction of a cosmological shift from modernity to process.

GROUP PROCESS AND COOPERATIVE LEARNING. One of the most practical areas of teaching related to what we have called process education are the fields called variously group dynamics, group process, and cooperative education. Within the group process framework, the unit of consideration is dramatically shifted from individual learning to group behavior. Here knowledge is not only seen as private personal experience; it consists also of responsive interactions among various people appropriately construed as 'occasions.' This conception of teaching also suggests that the fullness of one's knowing depends upon the authenticity or honesty of the total group experience.

There have, of course, been prodigious efforts to describe and assess the nature and educational possibilities of group dynamics or group process since the classic experiments carried out by Lewin, Lippit, and White in the late 1930s, comparing the effectiveness of what they called authoritarian, democratic, and laissez-faire leadership styles guiding the activities of boys' clubs. These efforts have been carried out by social psychologists and sociologists and have had broad application to the fields of industry, social service, and education.[63] A central effort in this work has been to teach students to experience learning on several different levels; for example, group members and leaders learn to distinguish between 'task' behavior and socio-emotional or expressive interaction, and then to cope explicitly with the tensions and conflicts that emerge when socio-emotional or group maintenance issues are left unattended.

Although the use of group process techniques in education has lagged behind its application in industry and the social service professions, more recently a substantial movement has emerged in a field called 'cooperative education.'[64] The major thrust of this work is to organize classroom-size groups of children into small discussion or task groups that work together (sometimes competing against other groups through games and various forms of simulation) to achieve specific instructional goals. Organized efforts to develop, promote, and evaluate cooperative learning have gained considerable momentum in recent years.

Teaching within the context of group process or in cooperative groups has, in our opinion, important significance as a possible approach to what we have called process education. The significance is related to our conception of dialogue or conversation not only as a medium through which one can learn some final knowledge or skill but as the setting within which a creative educational/social/cultural event is actually developed and expressed. In this latter sense, the quality of a conversation carries its own significance. From this point of view, new culture emerges, comes to life, and finds expression, not only in individual people but (more importantly) in group settings. The point here is perhaps best illustrated in the way we see a chorus preparing for a concert or a drama group preparing a play. In both instances, the participants are learning individual skills and knowledge (diction, sight reading, vocal projection); they are learning the actions required to perform; but more importantly they are participating in a series of significant cultural occasions, both in rehearsals and performances. (Unfortunately, we often see the rehearsal as only instrumental in preparing for the performance, which is what 'really counts.') Yet it is the subtle relationships that happen all through the rehearsals and which culminate in the performance that are, perhaps, the most important qualities of learning. It would be absurd to construe the essential learning as singing the right musical notes or saying the right lines from the play. What one learns is to participate in a creative disciplined occasion. Habermas has persuasively argued along these lines for what he calls "communicative action," which differs fundamentally from instrumental action, the latter being oriented more toward focused purposeful goals. In "communicative action," underlying qualities of trust, community, truthfulness, and common intentionality come to transcend the individual egocentric purposes of participants; they rather become part of an intersubjective or deeply shared experience.

We believe that discourse and the group experience can be instrumental in teaching the knowledge and skills related to almost any subject matter area. Like the song or the play, however, group life has a life of its own. This life includes the imaginative moments that lead us into the conversation, the quality of feelings and personal relationships that emerge, our willingness to deal with both the 'objective' content and the 'subjective' feelings, and our understanding of the significance of the whole event called 'today's class.'

Postscript

THE VILLAGE AND THE CITY AS CONTEXTS FOR PROCESS EDUCATION. In this chapter we have been comparing various individuals and educational movements as they relate to our conception of a process philosophy of education. These ideas and programs, as well as our own view of postmodern education, have been presented as happening, either actually or potentially, within a variety of relatively conventional modern settings. The human potential people tend to teach in workshops, in weekend retreats, in evening courses with adults. Liberation teachers work in schools and colleges, in communities and neighborhoods, in churches, and most often with adults. Ecologists, feminists, and peace educators commonly work within the workshop framework, most often with adults, but increasingly press to have their programs included in formal school curricula. One could speculate that the range and diversity of settings in which the many relatives of process education have found the opportunity to work reveal the marginality of the movement. There is, however, a sense in which all modern education is marginal, and is meant to be; for embedded within the modern cosmology is the notion of functional specialization as the most efficient way of delivering commodities to clients and customers. So education is easily 'delivered' into specialized places called 'classrooms' which are then considered as separate both from 'real work' in the corporate setting and from coping and child-rearing associated with family. This marginality of education, we would suggest, is the result of a fundamental structural defect in modernity itself: the fact that it is limited to two central social forms, the nuclear family and corporate workplace, the latter of which is really inappropriate for what we have called process education.

There is, of course, another form of association, another social concept that is older than either the nuclear family or the corporation: This concept is that of the village or community, inhabited by a band, a tribe, or a set of related clans who live in close geographic proximity and who carry out the full range of human functions associated with human survival: child bearing and raising, hunting and gathering, horticulture and agriculture, tool- and craft-making, worshiping, celebrating, and so on. The Hopi, for example, would be characterized as a communal society.

We believe that the communal village or neighborhood setting is most likely to give one a comprehensive or grounded view of the human condition—where people do meaningful work, argue and gossip, love and care for one another, educate one another, redeem each other's failings and affirm each other's achievements, and celebrate their sense of connectedness to some broader realm of time and space out of which creative being emerges. The functionally differentiated social structure of modernity finds little room for such inefficient and anomalous places as communities, except perhaps as governmental units to regulate the actions of families and corporations. Small political jurisdictions (which we commonly call communities) now manage educational settings or 'schools' which are ordinarily construed as quasi-work places where people are prepared for more efficient and competent corporate work, or at least cared for until they are old enough to engage in such work. Likewise, teachers in schools, whether they are workshop facilitators or first-grade teachers, are considered as paid employees or consultants in a corporate setting.

It is our position that significant process transformation for both person and culture requires a deeper and more comprehensive experiential base than either the nuclear family or the work place can provide; for process requires that we transcend the fragmented conception of knowing in which the learner and the teacher and the subject matter are all seen as more important than the occasion they share. Knowing involves participation in uniquely created occasions which emerge and come together in a common event. The understanding of such events is always from the 'inside,' from the point of view of all who contribute prehensions to the occasion; it is thus always intimate and personal. This intimate and creative quality of knowing demands that one go beyond the sentimental ties that organically connect parents and children; it also requires more than the calculated instrumental relationships that connect professionals and clients, supervisors and workers, teachers and students. It requires an environment of sustained intimacy where people and things are genuinely known to one another, yet where there is the diversity and complexity necessary for spontaneity and creativity.

As Christopher Alexander has maintained about space and architecture, social context has knowable and stringent requirements for one to experience *living* occasions. One cannot build a process culture in an IBM plant, at an auto assembly line, in an office building, at a MacDonald's fast food dispensary, or in the semi-isolation of a two- or three-person family. It requires a setting that allows for a fuller expression of nature, a fuller range of humanity a more generous understanding of human/nature possibility.[65]

Our vision of the future society would thus include the familiar urban structure—the *polis*, the city—but would contain within and around it the face-to-face contact characteristic of villages, communites. We should remind ourselves, moreover, that this vision of an urban/multi-village society is not new in human history. This was, in fact, the state of affairs from the dawn of what Western people call 'civilization.'[66] Redfield and Singer describe the evolution of village or folk societies as they made the transition from separate or autonomous places to their inclusion within the preindustrial city. What they describe as "primary urbanization" is the expansion of a folk village and culture into a full-blown urban society. What they call "secondary urbanization" is the development of pluralistic cultures *within* a much more complex urban environment. This leads to what we have referred to as the monolithic dynamic of modernity—the effort to create a single meaning system wherein technical universalistic knowledge and habits of coping dominate and overwhelm village cultures, which then come to see themselves as separate and marginal, or simply wither away. Their argument is elaborated below:

> In the primary phase a pre-civilized folk society is transformed by urbanization into a peasant society and correlated urban center. It is primary in the sense that the peoples making up the pre-civilized folk more or less share a common culture which remains the matrix too for the peasant and urban cultures which develop from it in the course of urbanization. Such a development, occurring slowly in communities not radically disturbed, tends to produce a "sacred culture" which is gradually transmuted by the literati of the cities into a "Great Tradition." Primary urbanization thus takes place almost entirely within the framework of a core culture that develops, as the local cultures become urbanized and transformed, into an indigenous civilization.
>
> This leads to the secondary pattern of urbanization: the case in which a folk society, pre-civilized, peasant or partly urbanized, is further urbanized by contact with peoples of widely different cultures from that of its own members. This comes about through expansion of local cultures, or by the invasion of a culture—civilization by alien colonists or conquerors. This secondary pattern produces not only a new form or urban life in some part in conflict with local folk cultures, but also new social types in both city and country. In the city appear "marginal" and "cosmopolitan" men and an "intelligentsia"; in the country various types of marginal folk: enclaved-, minority-, imperialized-, transplanted-, remade-, quasi-folk, etc., depending on the kind of relation to the urban center. . . .[67]
>
> The general consequence of secondary urbanization is the weakening or suppression of the local and traditional cultures by states of mind that are incongruent with those local cultures. Among these are to be recognized:
>
> 1. The rise of a consensus appropriate to the technical order: i.e., based on self-interest and pecuniary calculation, or on recognition of obedience to common impersonal controls, characteristically supported by sanctions of force. (This is in contrast to a consensus based on common religious and non-expediential moral norms.) There is also an autonomous development of norms and standards for the arts, crafts and sciences.
>
> 2. The appearance of new sentiments of common cause attached to groups drawn from culturally heterogeneous backgrounds. In the city proletariats are formed and class or ethnic consciousness is developed, and also new professional and territorial groups. The city is the place where ecumenical religious reform is preached (though it is not originated there). It is the place where nationalism flourishes. On the side of social structure, the city is the place where new and larger groups are formed that are bound by few and powerful common interests and sentiments in place of the complexly interrelated roles and statuses that characterize the groups of local, long-established culture. Among social types that appear in this aspect

of the cultural processes in the city are the reformer, the agitator, the nativistic or nationalistic leader, the tyrant and his assassin, the missionary and the imported school teacher.[68]

From our reading of Redfield and Singer, what is new in our proposal above is *not* the idea of a pluralistic multi-village–urban society containing both emerging village cultures and a cosmopolitan culture.This was apparently a common state of affairs before the completion of "secondary urbanization" and the advent of the modern city, based on the development of massive technology as the detemination of virtue, wealth, and value in the market place. What is new is this model as a vision for the postmodern world. This presents us with the challenge of integrating the universalism associated with science and technology, philosophy, literature, and the arts—those human creations we consider as high cultural achievements— with the deeper sense of being and knowing that we associate with a more local 'primitive' village existence. The vision assumes that humans cannot 'get over' or outlive, historically, alienation from kin, nature, ground, and the experience of or search for unconscious connectedness. And it is these characteristics that we see as nurtured by the culture of sustained village life.

The multi-village–urban society would, in fact, give the individual and the nuclear family a very different perspective on the focus of "home" and the possibility for building a sustained process culture. For while one might look outward and be included in the great marketplace of modernity where one sells one's labor and buys the commodities that make profits for their makers, one can also look inward, toward a more permanent sense of home than is afforded in an isolated single-family house, apartment, or condominium. Home, embedded in village life, would require an intimate and personal participation in the being of a substantial variety of people, animals, vegetables, and 'things.' Home would become not simply a physical or geographic place, but participation in an emerging process that would include elements of stability as well as elements of novelty and fate-filled excitement associated with the complexity of a village.

There are, of course, people who share this communitarian vision of social transformation. Foremost is Bookchin's ecological commune. There is the Philadelphia Life Center in the Movement for a New Society, which is explicitly communitarian. There are the kibbutz and moshav movements in Israel, examples of the oldest and most successful postmodern villages of contemporary times, motivated by a combination of Zionist–Socialist fervor and the desire to build and live in a more intimate connection with authentic work and nature. There are fundamentalist Christian villages such as those of the Amish, Mennonites, and Hutterites in the United States and Canada. There are the Mormons, who represent perhaps the largest effort to build a neo-archaic bi-level society including both cosmopolitan centers of technology, education, art, and religion and connections with far-flung local communities. There is a substantial number of new age communal groups such as Twin Oaks in Virginia and East Wind in Missouri.[69] There are educational communities and retreats, such as Findhorn in Scotland. There are quasi-spiritual movements such as the Society of Emissaries, which maintains communities worldwide, both as places to live and as retreats from the crassness of the modern corporate world. There are conservative Christian groups adding schools and retirement homes to their parishes as a basis for more sustained community life.

It is obvious from our litany of examples that communal cultures are not necessarily process cultures. But our vision of postmodern society is not one that is exclusively process. Rather it is one that is genuinely pluralistic, in the cosmopolitan "high culture" sense as well as the village-tribal sense. It is one in which high priests and scholars of all shapes and varieties can work through possible cosmologies and compete in the marketplace for an audience, for adherents. But it is also a place where room is made and incentives provided for village culture building; where abstract cosmology and the art, literature, theology, and drama that portray such cosmology, can be transformed into a practice of living as well as absorbed in the application of abstract mind and electronic media which permeates the core of creative community life. For the experience of wholeness (and the holy) is not attained or attainable only within the framework of abstract human communication, but requires, we are convinced, the act of creative participation in making new culture come alive among one's relatives and friends—which, for process people, means friendly occasions.

Notes

Chapter One   *Prologue and Introduction*

1. From Walker Percy, *The Message in the Bottle* (New York: Farrar, Straus & Giroux, 1954), pp. 25–27.

2. The use of "man" and "men" by Percy to refer to persons generally is, we believe, an anachronism.

3. See Alex Inkeles and David H. Smith, *Becoming Modern* (Cambridge, MA: Harvard University Press, 1974), for the systematic confirmation of these paradigmatic differences.

Chapter Two   *Modernity, Fragmentation, and Cultural Balance*

1. Peter Berger, Brigette Berger, Hansfried Kellner, *The Homeless Mind,* (New York: Vintage, pp. 97–113, 1973.

2. *Note:* Functionalists commonly argue that the sense of coherence or wholeness in a culture is developed by yet another specialized function, meaning-making, which is executed by a range of institutions: schools, press, churches, media, etc. We would observe that these meaning-making institutions, in fact, reflect the same fragmentation that we experience in the specialized environments of our vocational life. Aside from the most generalized and diffuse of symbols (God, country, family, freedom, the Constitution, Social Security, and full employment) we see little effort by such institutions to provide any overall vision of what culture or society are to mean. Any deeper quality of meaning is left to one's private associations and moments, which, in some sense, is a contradiction, for culture is inherently "public". In short, we would argue that the fragmented nature of the society is reflected in rather than held together by the messages, images, and visions which confront us in the schools, the media, and other "cultural" institutions.

3. The term "ontological" suggests that the process of knowing flows from the process of occasions coming into being.

4. Zuesse has developed a similar dual theory of knowing, both aspects of which he relates to qualities of religious experience within the African context. He maintains that "together they comprise each person's entire universe, although different cultures may emphasize one or the other". The theory, summarized below, is from Evan M. Zuesse, *Ritual Cosmos* (Athens, OH: Ohio University Press, 1979), p. 135.

"Every moment of awareness is really the synthesis of two forms of cognition, not just one. There is the deductive type that starts from the abstract and general and 'descends,' so to speak, in increasingly concrete 'refractions' into the actualities of early life, building up a symbolic hierarchy linking the One and the Many. This we have already seen. And there is another, inductive kind of systematic network of symbols, that starts from the concrete and "ascends" from the Many to the One. The two types together create a complex grid, balanced and infinitely extending around each person; together they comprise each person's entire universe, although different cultures may emphasize one or the other.

"Ascending symbolisms, which we can also call 'orectic' symbolisms, are based on sensory physical complementaries, such as hot and cold, left and right, darkness and light, and so on—elemental sensual experiences—which in their repetition and interlacing correspondences weave an inclusive and organized sensory–motor order. Psychological studies have documented the slow refinement of the perceptions and organic responses that continues from the first days of infancy and finally produces the vivid, differentiated experiental world of maturity. This tacit cognitive structure, rooted as it is in the sensory–motor apparatus, is an entirely different kind of symbolism from that which moves from rationally deduced, systematically and consciously focused principles to the multiplicity of things. The later exults in clear meaning, but clear meaning is often in danger of lacking depth and persuasiveness, or even the sense of living reality. Ascending symbolisms, however, are mainly preconscious, sensory, even aesthetic and intuitive in nature. Yet the systematic abstract and therefore more often noticed system, and in fact the inductive and the deductive structures need each other to find completion. The abstract cognitive structures that descend from One to Many lack the specificity and rootedness that only the concrete 'ascending' symbolisms can bestow. It is the latter that determines on the precise form of shrines and ritual gestures, for only the latter organizes experiential reality systematically, engaging emotions directly."

5. Robert Redfield, *The Primitive World and its Transformation*. (Ithaca, NY: Cornell University Press, 1953).

6. "In Search of Scope and Sequence for the Social Studies", *Social Education*, 48, No. 4, 260.

7. For a systematic treatment of the concepts of "quality of life" or "positive culture", see Donald W. Oliver, *Education and Community*, McCutchan, Berkeley, CA, 1976.

8. Susanne K. Langer, *Philosophy in a New Key* (Cambridge, MA: Harvard University Press, 1941), p. 281.

9. Benjamin S. Bloom, ed., *Taxonomy of Educational Objectives* (White Plains, NY: Longman, Green, & Co., 1965).

10. This impatient and restless tendency to short-circuit the effort required for building the sense of mutuality necessary for deeper communication has been much discussed in the work of Habermas. See, for example, Jurgen Habermas, *Knowledge and Human Interests* (Boston; Beacon Press, 1971).

11. We would note, for example, the arguments made by Roger Fisher of the Harvard Law School extolling the advantages of technical negotiation as a means of conflict resolution. See Roger Fisher and William Ury, with Bruce Patton, *Getting to Yes Without Giving In* (Boston: Houghton-Mifflin, 1981).

12. The notion that the dance provides a unitary center for other metaphors—e.g., "work/labor/machine as well as body/nature/organism—is expressed persuasively in stanza VIII from Yeats' "Among School Children":

Labour is blossoming or dancing where
The body is not bruised to pleasure soul,
Nor beauty born out of its own despair,
Nor blear-eyed wisdom out of midnight oil.
O chestnut-tree, great-rooted blossomer,
Are you the leaf, the blossom or the bole?
O body swayed to music, O brightening glance,
How can we know the dancer from the dance?

W. B. Yeats, "Among School Children"' *Selected Poems and Two Plays of William Butler Yeats* edited by M. L. Rosenthal, (New York: Macmillan, 1962).

13. Alfred North Whitehead, *Adventurers of Ideas* (New York: The Free Press, 1933), p. 158.

14. We note the following news item: "Crash Award Reduced by U. S. Appeals Court," *Boston Globe*, 13 August 1985.

Crash award reduced by US appeals court

Associated Press

, NEW ORLEANS – The US Court of Appeals for the 5th Circuit yesterday ordered a reduction in a $2.7 million award to a man whose wife and three sons were killed in the 1982 crash of a Pan Am jetliner in Kenner, La.

Robert Giancontieri is entitled to about $1.5 million for the deaths of Sandy Giancontieri, 26, and Robbie, 7; Ryan, 4; and Christopher, 4 months, the court said. The original judgment. included $1.5 million for the loss of Mrs. Giancontieri's love and affection, and $400,000 for that of each child.

The maximum allowable would be $500,000 for his wife's love and affection and $200,000 for loss of her services, and $250,000 for the loss of each boy's love and affection. the appeals court said.

A new trial will be held on the matter unless Giancontieri agrees to the figures outlined in the appeals court opinion.

Mrs. Giancontieri and the boys were at their home when a Boeing 727 carrying 146 people cartwheeled through a Kenner subdivision July 9. The Giancontieris's house was among the first hit. and was torn apart.

The crash killed everyone on the plane and the Giancontieris and four other people on the ground.

15. Gregory Bateson, *Steps to an Ecology of Mind*, Ballantine, 1972, p. 462. Note: Relative to Bateson's prediction, see Ian Steele, "Slash and Burn Practice of Poor Dooming Forests," *Montreal Globe and Mail*, 26 November 1985.

16. Daniel Bell, *The Coming of Post-Industrial Society* (New York: Basic Books, 1973), p. 478.

17. Lewis Henry Morgan, ed., Ancient Society, or Researches in the Lines of Human Progress from Savagery through Barbarism to Civilization (1877) (Cleveland: Eleanor Burke Leacock, 1963).

18. We would point out here Trevor-Roper's negative connotation for the idea of "dance" as a central and integrating feature in primitive society.

19. Hugh Trevor-Roper, *The Rise of Christian Europe* (London: Thames and Hudson, 1965), p. 9, with thanks to Francis Jennings in *The Invasion of America*, (NY: Norton, 1975) for leading me to this quote.

20. We would note, for example, the work of Edward Sapir, Robert Redfield, Dorothy Lee, Paul Radin, Stanley Diamond, Laura Thompson, and Francis Jennings.

21. Stanley Diamond, *The Search of the Primitive* (New Brunswick, NJ: Transaction, 1974).

22. *The Novel and Feelings*, 755–759, in *Phoenix: The Posthumous Papers of D. H. Lawrence*, (edited by Edward D. McDonald, New York: the Viking Press, 1936).

23. Pitrium A. Sorokin, "Three Basic Trends of Our Times", in *Main Currents in Modern Thought*, Vol. 16, no. 3, (New York: 1960).

24. While we have our reservations about "new age education" (see Chapter Ten,) it does provide excellent examples of creative curriculum ventures along these lines. We would note, for example, a "sacred psychology seminar" taught by Jean Houston and associates in the spring of 1986 based on the theme: "Egyptian Myths of Transformation." In the words of the conference brochure:

> Staff and participants alike will join in the unfolding of an intricate tapestry comprised of the multicolored, multitextured threads of philosophy, mythology, psychology, religion, history, anthropology, physics, neurology and other sciences, and creativity. These universal strands are artistically interwoven with the more individual strands of personal experience found in music, dance, drama, high play, varied states of consciousness, and mutual empowerment.

Although such seminars seem to proimise the total bounty of human wisdom packaged in a week-long or weekend retreat, they are at least an effort to go beyond the fragmentation of experience and the academic pigeonholes that characterize most "legitimate" schooling. See *The Myths of Transformation: The New Sacred Psychology Seminar*, (Arlington, VA: NTL Institute, 1988).

Chapter Three   *Categories of the Whole*

1. We would note the careful work exemplified in Wildred Cantwell Smith's *The Meaning and End of Religion* (New York: Harper & Row, 1962), as suggesting what an elaborated discussion of academic categories of the whole might include.

2. Charles T. Tart, *States of Consciousness* (New York: E. P. Dutton, 1975), pp. 40–41. Bidney elaborates the same point:

> Actual positive, or historical, culture differs markedly from one another in the selection of possible forms of activity and organization, and every society, therefore, has the defects corresponding to its cultural vitures. This cultural selection and integration is manifested by the ideal type of man which the members of a given society prefer and by the social institutions they provide to make it possible for the average individual to approximate this ideal. Thus, one society idealizes the warrior type; another, the man of wealth; a third, the scholar; a fourth, the cooperative individual who performs his social duties easily. Each ideal type calls for the development of some human potential-

ities and the suppression and restraint of others. As there are a limited number of natural human propensities and basic impulses, there are necessarily a limited number of cultural configurations and cultural personality types.

(David Bidney, *Theoretical Anthropology* [New York: Schocken Books, 1967,], p. 146).

3. Clifford Geertz, *The Interpretation of Cultures* (New York: Basic Books, 1973), pp. 49–50.

4. Marshall Sahlins, *Culture and Practical Reason* (Chicago, IL: University of Chnicago Press, 1979), p. 55.

5. Morris Freilich (ed.), *The Meaning of Culture* (Lexington, MA: Xerox, 1972), p. 287.

6. Robert Wuthnow, James Davidson Hunter, Albert Bergeron, and Edith Kurzweil, *Cultural Analysis* (Boston: Routledge and Kegan Paul, 1984), p. 259.

7. Stanley Diamond, *In Search of the Primitive* (New Brunswick, NJ: Transaction Books, 1974), p. 122.

8. As we noted earlier, since human experience is conditioned by the limited range of potentiality allowed by our physical equipment and also by the extent to which that potentiality has been "taught" to express itself within culture, the assumption that we are outside either nature or culture is something of an epistemological fiction. While there is no obvious way out of this fiction, we can treat metaphysics and science as appropriate ways for speculating both about answers to the most universal questions *and* about the relationship between these generalities and the cultural and natural background which must color the way we view them.

9. Alfred North Whitehead, *Process and Reality* (corrected edition) edited by David Ray Griffin and Donald W. Sherburne, (New York: Free Press, 1978), p. 3.

10. Abraham Kaplan, *In Pursuit of Wisdom* (Beverly Hills, CA: Glencoe, 1977), p. 227.

11. Karl R. Popper, *Objective Knowledge* (New York: Oxford University Press, 1972).

12. The Museum of Comparative Zoology at Harvard University represents an interesting example of an effort to bring science and metaphysics together. The collection in the Museum makes an almost religious statement about the meaning of the Darwinian revelation. The breadth and scope of knowledge represented by the exhibits and the physical size of the museum give it a cathedral-like aura.

13. See, for example, Arthur Koestler, *The Sleepwalkers* (New York: Macmillan, 1963), for an elaboration of this point.

14. F. S. C. Northrup, *The Meeting of East and West* (New York: Macmillan, 1946).

15. Christopher Norris, *The Deconstructive Turn* (London: Methuen, 1983), pp. 1–2.

16. From "Death and Image," by Philip Sherrard, in *Orthodoxy, Life and Freedom*, edited by A. J. Philippou, (Oxford: Studion Publications, 1973), pp. 49–50.

17. Paul Wiebe, "Search for a Paradigm," *The Journal of Religion* 84, no. 3, (July 1974): 348–362.

18. Walter A. Nelson, "Religion in the Social Studies Curriculum," *Social Education* 45 no. 1 (January 1981): 28–31.

19. Wilfred Cantwell Smith, *The Meaning and End of Religion* (New York: Harper and Row, 1962), pp. 130–131.

20. Ibid., p. 134.

21. We could, of course, discuss additional categories—such as the arts, literature, and sports—commonly taught in schools and universities.

Chapter Four   *Cosmology*

1. The term cosmology has, more recently, been partially preempted by the natural sciences, especially astrophysics, to connote the scientific study of the history, shape, size, and future behavior of the universe (especially the heavens). Chaison, for example, defines it as "the study of the origin, evolution, and destiny of the aggregate of all matter and all energy known as the Universe." Nothing is said of the metaphysical or religious questions concerning what was here before (or after) matter and energy. Koestler, in the vein of Whitehead, however, continues to use the term in a broader way. Koestler's first hero, Pythagoras, attempted to find some balanced unity in the relationships among mathematics, music, astronomy, and philosophy. Carl Sagan's popularization of the term cosmos, meaning astronomy, has, of course, somewhat undermined the broader use of the term suggested by Whitehead and Koestler.

We should also mention Stephen Toulmin's *The Return to Cosmology: Postmodern Science and the Theology of Nature* (Berkeley: University of California Press, 1982) as an effort very much along the lines we are pursuing here. The major part of Toulmin's work deals with recent cosmologists, two of whom are central to our thinking: Arthur Koestler and Gregory Bateson. Toulmin suggests that conditions are ripening for a more unitary view of knowledge that will bring together natural science and natural religion. It is interesting that Toulmin makes only marginal reference to Whitehead, who pioneered efforts toward such a unitary vision.

2. Alfred North Whitehead, *Process and Reality* (Corrected Edition), edited by David Ray Griffin and Donald W. Sherburne (New York: The Free Press, 1978), p. xii.

3. Ibid., pp. 15–16.

4. Manfred Halpern, "A Redefinition of the Revolutionary Situation," *Journal of International Affairs* 23, no. 1 (1969): 59–60.

5. Carl G. Vaught, *The Quest for Wholeness* (Albany, NY: SUNY Press, 1982), pp. 3–4.

Chapter Five   *Cosmology as Curriculum*

1. R. S. Brumbaugh, "Prolegomena: Metaphysical Presuppositions and the Study of Time", in *Voices of Time*, edited by J. T. Fraser, N. Lawrence, and D. Park (New York: Springer-Verlag, 1976).

2. Regarding the generality of Brumbaugh's system, he notes (p. 7): "with very modest modification and translation, my set of systems resembles that of Richard McKeon (e.g., in *Freedom and History*), Paul Weiss (e.g., in *Modes of Being*), Stephen Pepper (his root metaphors), and Newton Stallknecht (e.g., in Stallknecht and Brumbaugh, *The Compass of Philosophy*)."

3. Susan Griffin, *Woman and Nature* (Harper & Row, New York: 1978).

4. Gary J. Coates, ed. *Resettling America* (Andover, MA: Brick House 1981), pp. 24–27.

5. There are, of course, difficult practical questions regarding the acceptance of such a curriculum by modern people, who are habituated to the incoherence characteristic of their own fragmented cosmology—and who often carry, as well, a defensive posture toward the fragments of their own partially understood cosmological inheritance, e.g., Catholicism, Puritanism, Judaism, humanism. One must ask whether we, as modern people, can be persuaded to search for a more comprehensive and coherent way of thinking. We are certainly aware of the suspicion with which comprehensive world views are often seen. Those who work out of or come to believe in a systematic cosmology are frequently accused of being true believers or ideologues. Unfortunately, their critics often fail to realize that they carry within themselves the same level of 'irrational' commitment—only in their case to modern fragmentary eclecticism—of which they seem to accuse their more integrated neighbor.

6. Benjamin Lee Whorf, "Time, Space, and Language", chapter 8 in *Culture in Crisis*, Laura Thompson, (New York: Harper and Brothers, 1950).

7. Owen Barfield, *Saving the Appearances: A study of Idolatry* (New York: Harcourt Brace Jovanovich, 1957).

8. Ibid, p. 32.

9. Alfred North Whitehead, *Adventures of Ideas* (New York: The Free Press, 1933).

Part Three   *Process Cosmology*

1. Our use of the term "process " comes from Whitehead's *Process and Reality*, [Alfred North Whitehead, *Process and Reality*, edited by David Ray Griffin and Donald W. Sherburne, The Free Press, New York, 1978] as well as from the scholarly tradition and applications that have evolved from that work. We note here, however, that the term has had wide use in education and group dynamics. Most notable we think of the terms "group process" and "discussion process" and their connection to the broader idea of "democratic process." While all of these uses imply participatory involvement in the creation of new occasions—and in this sense are related to Whiteheadian process—their lineage is more directly traceable to liberal democratic theory and the search for a better understanding of the underlying conflicts and strategies for their resolution that play a part in group decision-making. Discussion process research, for example, usually assumes that there are a variety of individual actors competing for leadership and group control, which can be used to promote ideas and procedures by which the group and/or individuals within it might better adapt to the socio-emotional or task conditions within which they find themselves.

"Process" has also been commonly used in educational circles to distinguish between "product" and "process", especially as these terms relate to instructional objectives. "Products" usually refers to the learning of specific data, while "process" connotes learning procedures for further learning. In this sense, inquiry or group interaction skills would be seen as process goals while learning textbook data or the findings of research would be seen as product goals. The same distinction is used pejoratively in the analogy between schools and factories: we process raw materials to create products much as students, construed as raw materials, are processed to become finished (educated) products.

2. p. 342 in Ralph Wendell Burhoe, "The Human Prospect and 'The Lord of History,' *Zygon* 10, no. 3 (Sept. 1975): 299–375.

Chapter Six   *From Scientific Modernity Toward a Process Universe*

1. J. T. Fraser, *The Genesis and Evolution of Time* (Amherst, MA: University of Massachusetts Press, 1982), p. 20.

2. Lorenz maintains, for example, that physiological research has discovered the mechanisms that contribute to the human idea of three-dimensional space. The sense organs and the nervous system function together, allowing our eyes to calculate the size and distance of objects. Contributing to a clear image of space are touch spots on our body which themselves communicate information about the body's position in relation to objects. Research on the physiology of the inner ear, with the utricle and its three membraneous semicircular canals, shows that the ear registers movement of the body in space and its responses to speed and rotation. Clearly our three-dimensional Euclidian space has its foundation in the human's physiological capacities.

We would agree with Lorenz who says that, in a certain sense, these capacities *are* this particular form of ideation. Mathematicians have created models postulating multi-dimensional space; physicists have demonstrated a space that has at least four dimensions. Humans are able to visualize only that simpler version which the organization of our sense organs and nervous system enables us to apprehend. Lorenz goes further:

> . . .organisms often construe the world in a substantially *distorted way* in order to make information more appropriate, intelligible, and usable for their comfort and survival. If one looks at a piece of white paper reflecting different colored lights, humans will usually see the paper as a constant white, even though it does in fact change colors in the eye. Or one will look at the shape of an object, and even though it changes form on the retina as the object is seen from different angles, the organism will see the object as having a constant form. Or, finally, we see objects as roughly the same size, even though, as we move away, their size becomes smaller on our retina. (p. 11)

Conrad Lorenz, *Behind the Mirror* (New York: Harcourt Brace Joranovich, 1973).

3. Patricia F. Carini, *The Art of Seeing and the Visibility of the Person* (Grand Forks: University of North Dakota Press, 1979), p. 15.

4. Arthur Koestler, *Janus* (New York: Vintage, 1978), p. 34.

5. Lewis Thomas, *The Lives of a Cell* (New York: Bantam, 1974), p. 2–4.

6. Gregory Bateson, *Steps to An Ecology of Mind* (New York: Ballantine, 1972), pp. 460–462. For an elaboration of the radical significance of Bateson's work see Morris Berman, *The Reenchantment of the World* (Ithaca, NY: Cornell University Press, 1981).

7. For an excellent discussion of process philosophy and its relative historical independence from earlier progressive evolutionary cosmologies (as seen, for example, in the works of deChardin), see George R. Lucas, Jr., "Evolutionist Theories and Whitehead's Philosophy", *Process Studies* 14, no. 4 (1985): 287–300.

8. Fraser, "Genesis."

9. Carl Friedrich von Weizsacker (Francis J. Zucker, trans.), *The Unity of Nature* (New York: Farrar, Straus, & Giroux, 1980).

10. Earlier von Weizsacker suggests a concept he calls the postulate of ultimate objects. He argues that all objects consist of ultimate objects with n=2. "In German I called them Urob-

jekte, and their alternatives Uralternativen; as a whimsy, I proposed the abbreviation *ein Ur*, 'an ur', for such an object, which I will use here, too" (p. 216).

11. Whitehead concurs: "This realm [of alternative entities] is disclosed by all the untrue propositions which can be predicated significantly of that occasion. *It is the realm of alternative suggestions whose foothold in actuality transcends each actual occasion. . . .* An event is decisive in proportion to the importance (for it) of its untrue propositions: Their relevance to the event cannot be dissociated from what the event is, in itself, by way of achievement." (emphasis added) *Science and the Modern World* (NY: Macmillan, 1925), p. 158.

12. Note other writers in the same vein: Fritjof Capra, *The Tao of Physics* (New York: Bantam, 1976); and Gary Zukav, *The Dancing WuLi Masters* (New York: Bantam, 1979).

13. It is interesting to note that in the new field of "cognitive science" scholars still struggle with the distinction between the organic (biological) and mechanical basis of mind.

Gardner, for example, in the quotation below talks about the necessity of maintaining connections both to neurobiology and computer intelligence, thus keeping intact the mind–body dualism of modern cosmology. He assumes that mind is somehow to be explained partly as a set of logical mechanical operations and partly as an historically evolved organ (the brain?). The broader issue of using the organic metaphor to show connections between human mind and *other forms of being* to which we are intimately related is essentially avoided. Gardner is clearly a modern thinker.

> My other reservation about the computer as model centers on the deep difference between biological and mechanical systems. I find it distorted to conceive of human beings apart from their membership in a species that has evolved over the millennia, and as other than organisms who themselves develop according to a complex interaction between genetic proclivities and environmental processes over a lifetime. To the extent that thought processes reflect these bio-developmental factors and are suffused with regressions, anticipations, frustrations, and ambivalent feelings, they will differ in fundamental ways from those exhibited by a nonorganic system. Note that it did not *have* to be this way — biological systems might have been just like inorganic (mechanical) systems. But it is clear that they are not. I therefore believe that adequate models of human thought and behavior will have to incorporate aspects of biological systems (for example, processes of organic differentiation or fusion) as well as aspects of mechanical systems (the operation of electronic circuits). The very comparisons between organic and mechanical structures and processes may be among the most instructive aspects of the science. All told, cognitive science will have to incorporate (and connect to) neurobiology as much as to artificial intelligence.

Howard Gardner, *Toward an Integrated Cognitive Science* (New York: Basic Books, 1985), p. 388.

14. Alfred N. Whitehead, *Science and the Modern World* (New York: Macmillan, 1925), p. 155.

15. William E. Hocking, "Mind and Nature'" in *The Philosophy of Alfred North Whitehead*, ed. by Paul Arthur Schilpp, (Evanston and Chicago, IL: Northwestern University Press, 1941), p. 394.

Chapter Seven   *Whitehead's Process Cosmology*

1. In strictly Whiteheadian terms, an actual occasion or entity is a micro event that happens within a split second. The more complex events and "things" we associate with our

common sense perception of the everyday world are thus constituted of connections among these micro events (nexus) as well as the reiteration of similar events so as to give the appearance of stable, solid reality. The world is thus seen as ultimately constituted of quantum happenings.

2. Alfred N. Whitehead, *Adventures of Ideas* (New York: Free Press, 1933), p. 176.

3. Alfred N. Whitehead, *Modes of Thought* (New York: Free Press, 1938), p. 166.

4. Whitehead, *Science*, p. 54.

5. Ibid, p. 72.

6. Ibid, p. 69.

7. Harold Conklin, "Hanonuo Color Categories," in *Language, Culture, and Society: A Reader in Linguistics and Anthropology*, edited by Dell Hymes (New York: Harper and Row, 1964), p. 189-191.

8. Victor Lowe, *Understanding Whitehead* (Baltimore, MD: Johns Hopkins University Press, 1962), p. 52.

9. Ibid.

10. Owen Barfield, *Saving the Appearances: A Study of Idolatry* (New York: Harcourt Brace Jovanovich, 1957), p. 68.

11. Alfred N. Whitehead, *Process and Reality* (corrected edition) edited by David Ray Griffin and Donald W. Sherburne, (New York: Free Press, 1978), p. 339.

12. Whitehead, *Adventures*, p. 181.

13. Victor Lowe, p. 39.

14. Alfred North Whitehead, *Religion in the Making*, New York: Free Press 1926, pp. 88-90.

15. Whitehead, *Process and Reality*, p. 24.

16. Ibid., p. 24.

17. Harold B. Dunkel, *Whitehead on Education* (Columbus, OH: Ohio State University Press, 1965), p. 39.

18. Whitehead, *Process and Reality*, p. 228.

19. Ibid., p. 59.

20. Robert S. Brumbaugh *Whitehead, Process Philosophy and Education*, (Albany, NY: State University of New York Press, 1982), pp. 43-46.

21. Whitehead, *Adventures*, p. 203.

22. Whitehead, *Science*, p. 152.

23. Whitehead, *Process and Reality*, p. 24.

24. Whitehead, *Modes of Thought*, p. 156-57

25. Lowe, p. 349.

26. Whitehead, *Modes of Thought*, p. 156.

27. Note here the difference between Whitehead and Fraser.

28. Dunkel, Op. Cit., p. 56.

29. Whitehead, *Modes of Thought,* p. 11.

30. Ibid., p. 12.

31. Ibid.

32. *Process and Reality,* p. 15.

33. Ibid.

34. Whitehead, *Modes of Thought,* p. 27.

35. Ibid.

36. Ibid., p. 28.

37, Alfred N. Whitehead, *Essays in Science and Philosophy* (New York: Philosophical Library, 1947), p. 109.

38. Ibid., p. 130.

39. Robert Benedetti, *Seeming, Being and Becoming: Acting in our Century,* (New York: Drama Book Specialists, 1976), p.87.

40. J. T. Fraser, *Of Time, Passion and Knowledge,* (New York: George Braziller, 1975), p. 382.

41. Rollo May, *The Courage to Create* (New York: W. W. Norton Company, 1975), p. 31.

42. Whitehead, *Process and Reality,* p. 21.

43. Henry W. Homes, "Whitehead's View on Education," in *The Philosophy of Alfred North Whitehead,* edited by Paul Arthur Schilpp (Evanston and Chicago, IL: Northwestern University Press, 1941), p. 622.

Chapter Eight   *The Moral Basis of Process Education: Intimacy, Intensity, and Balance*

1. The notion of reflective ethics and law is such a commonplace modern assumption that it requires little discussion. For a clear statement of its premises one might refer to John Dewey and James H. Tufts, *Ethics,* (New York: Holt, 1936).

2. For elaboration of this point see Morton G. White, *Social Thought in America: The Revolt Against Formalism* (New York: Oxford University Press, 1976).

3. Benjamin S. Bloom, *Taxonomy of Educational Objectives* (New York: Longman, 1965).

4. We note the recent work in moral reasoning and moral development by Lawrence Kohlberg and colleagues, who associate the ability to exhibit increasingly abstract statements with educational and moral progress.

5. In this and subsequent chapters we are using the term 'occasion', as distinct from 'actual occasion', in a more common-sense and metaphorical way than the strict Whiteheadian

cosmology requires. We think that it is important to distinguish between the highly technical dialogue required to justify specific premises and claims embedded in Whitehead's process metaphysics and the broader spirit and significance of the process paradigm.

6. Whitehead, *Science*, p. 50.

7. See David Bohm, *Wholeness and the Implicate Order* (London: Routledge and Kegan Paul, 1980).

8. See for elaboration Harold Oliver, *A Relational Metaphysic* (The Hague: Martiuus Nijhoff, 1982).

9. Koestler, p. 34.

10. To use Whitehead's terms.

11. It is important to note at this point that the other cosmologies with which we have been comparing process have been expressed in specific human societies and cultures. Process cosmology certainly has its cultural and societal exemplifications, one of which was presented in our brief description of the Hopi in Chapter Five.

12. We might note here the ancient meaning system of China described in the I Ching, which has both metaphorical richness and complementary balance.

13. Martin Heidegger (translated by Albert Hofstadter), *Poetry, Language, Thought* (New York: Harper Colophon Books, 1971), pp. 147–148.

14. Jeffrey S. Stamps, *Holonomy: A Human Systems Theory* (Seaside, CA: Intersystems Publications, 1980), pp. 46–47.

Chapter Nine   *Teaching and Learning Within the Occasion:*[1]
                          Notes on Process Education

1. We are here using the term *occasion* as a metaphorical extension of Whitehead's notion of 'actual occasion'.

2. Whitehead, *Process and Reality*, p. 349.

3. Lucien Price, *The Dialogues of Alfred North Whitehead* (Boston, MA: Little, Brown, 1954), p. 368.

4. John Dewey, *Art as Experience* (New York: Minton, Balch & Co., 1934), p. 294.

5. Monroe C. Beardsley, "On the Creation of Art," *Journal of Aesthetics and Art Criticism* 23, no. 3 (1965): 291.

6. Alfred North Whitehead, *The Aims of Education and Other Essays* (New York: Free Press, 1929) p. 57.

7. Whitehead, *Adventures*, p. 271.

8. Ibid., p. 272.

9. Michael J. Reddy, "The Conduit Metaphor. . . a Case of Frame Conflict in Metaphor and Thought," In *Language and Metaphor*, edited by Andrew Ortony, (New York: Cambridge University Press, 1979), p. 288.

10. Reddy, pp. 292–296.

11. This, of course, harks back to the central point made by Walker Percy at the beginning of the book.

12. Whitehead, *Science*, pp. 115–116.

13. Douglas Sturm, "Process Thought and Political Theory: Implications of a Principle of Internal Relations," in *Process Philosophy and Social Thought*, edited by John B. Cobb Jr. and W. Widicks Schroeder (Chicago: Center for the Scientific Study of Religion, 1981), p. 87.

14. Ibid., p. 88.

15. Ibid., p. 90.

16. Alfred North Whitehead, *Adventures*, p. 63.

17. Laura Thompson, *Culture and Crisis* (New York: Harper's, 1950), p. 176.

18. Whitehead, *Process and Reality*, pp. 162–163.

19. Evelyn Fox Keller, *A Feeling for the Organism* (New York: W. H. Freeman, 1983), pp. 148–149.

20. David Keane, "A Composer's Approach to Music, Cognition, and Emotion," *The Musical Quarterly* 68, no. 3 (July): 328–329.

21. George Arkell Riggens, "Quantum Physics and Freedom in a Whiteheadian Perspective," *Zygon* 17, no. 3 (September 1982): 261.

22. F. Bradford Wallack, *The Epochal Nature of Process in Whitehead's Metaphysics* (Albany, NY: SUNY Press, 1980), p. 289.

23. Christopher Alexander, *The Timeless Way of Building*, New York: Oxford University Press, 1979), p. 101.

24. Ibid., p. 106.

25. Ibid., p. 107.

26. Ibid., p. 112–113.

27. Ibid., p. 123.

28. Ibid., p. 118.

29. Ibid., pp. 119–121.

30. For a scholarly elaboration of the metaphor of the garden and its connection with modern thinking one is referred to Yi-Fu Tuan, *Dominance and Affection: The Making of Pets* (New Haven, CT: Yale University Press, 1984).

31. Wallack, pp. 135–136.

32. J. B. Priestly, *Man and Time* (London: Aldus Books, 1964), p. 292.

33. Ibid., p. 298.

34. Ibid., p. 297

35. "First, it is well known that, as directly sensed and experienced in consciousness, time is highly variable and relative to conditions (e.g., a given period may be felt to be short or long by different people, or even by the same person, according to the interests of the different people concerned). On the other hand it seems in common experience that physical time is absolute and does not depend on conditions. However, one of the most important implications of the theory of relativity is that physical time is in fact relative, in the sense that it may vary according to the speed of the observer. . . . What is crucial in the present context is that according to the theory of relativity, a sharp distinction between space and time cannot be maintained. . . .Thus, since quantum theory implies that elements that are separated in space are generally non-causally and non-locally related projections of a higher-dimensional reality, it follows that moments separated in time are also projections of this reality.

Evidently, this leads to a fundamentally new notion of the meaning of time. Both in common experience and in physics, time has generally been considered to be a primary independent and universally accepted order, perhaps the most fundamental one known to us. Now, we have been led to propose that it is secondary and that, like space . . . it is to be derived from a higher-dimensional ground, as a particular order. [We thus live in] multidimensional reality that cannot be comprehended fully in terms of any [single] time order, or set of such orders. . ." (David Bohm, *Wholeness and the Implicate Order* London: Routledge and Kegan Paul, 1980, p. 210).

36. Modern science writers rarely mention the possibility that there is *any other* conception of time. Asimov flatly states, for example, that "the universe is four-dimensional, with time one of the dimensions. . . ." ([Isaac] Asimov's *New guide to Science*, Basic Books, New York, 1984), p. 390.

37. Whitehead, *Process and Reality*, p. 340.

Chapter Ten   *The Current Context of Process Education*

1. See Arthur Koestler, *The Sleepwalkers* (New York: Macmillan, 1959).

2. The Center for Process Studies, 1325 North College Avenue, Claremont, CA.

3. See, for example, Robert Brumbaugh, *Whitehead, Process Philosophy, and Education* (Albany, NY: State University of New York Press, 1982).
   See also, Harold B. Dunkel, *Whitehead on Education*, (Cleveland, OH: Ohio State University Press, 1965; also the special issue of *Educational Theory* which commemorates the centennial of Whitehead's birth: Vol. XI, No. 4, 1961.

4. As suggested earlier, there are many books in the field now, but we have noted two of the more important earlier ones: Frijtof Capra, *The Tao of Physics* (Boulder, CO: Shambala Publications, 1975 and Gary Zukav, *The Dancing WuLi Masters* New York: Morrow, 1979).

5. The reader is referred to a special issue of the journal *Zygon*, Vol. 20, No. 2, June 1985, which has a major section devoted to "David Bohm's Implicate Order: Physics, Philosophy, and Theology."

6. Marilyn Ferguson, *The Aquarian Conspiracy*, (Los Angeles: J. P. Tarcher, 1980).

7. E. F. Schumacher, *A Guide for the Perplexed* (New York: Harper's Colophon, 1978), p. 140.

8. There was a holistic education program for a time, at least, at the University of Massachusetts at Amherst, as well as a master's degree program at Interface in Newton, Massachusetts.

9. George Isaac Brown, *Human Teaching and Human Learning* (New York: Viking Press, 1971).

10. Jean Houston, *The Possible Human* (Los Angeles: J. P. Tarcher, 1982).

11. Human potential advocates tend to search out "scientific" bases for their metaphysics and thus stress legitimating titles such as Nobel laureates and biologically based mind–brain connections.

12. Ferguson, p. 25.

13. Ibid., p. 31.

14. Houston, xvii.

15. It should be noted not only that this approach to learning and knowing was advocated much earlier by Steiner (see below), but that he and his followers built substantial curricula to implement these goals well before the human potential movement emerged.

16. Houston, Op. Cit., p. xx.

17. Again we would note the connections among human potential advocates, philosophically oriented scientists such as Bohm, Capra, and Prigogine, and academics who publish in scholarly journals such as *Process Studies* or *Zygon*.

18. Marilyn Ferguson, *Brain/Mind Bulletin* 10, No. 10 (May 27, 1985): 1.

19. Ibid., pp. 1–2.

20. Ibid., p. 2.

21. Steiner's writings are broad and voluminous, touching on such subjects as education, architecture, religion, psychology, and history.

22. Robert A. McDermott (ed.), *The Essential Steiner* (San Francisco: Harper & Row, 1984), p. 316.

23. Ibid., p. 327.

24. Ibid., p. 354.

25. Ibid., p. 22.

26. Patricia F. Carini, *The Art of Seeing and the Visibility of the Person* (Grand Forks, ND: University of North Dakota Press, 1979), p. 1.

27. Ibid., p. 6.

28. Ibid., p. 7.

29. Ibid., p. 22.

30. Ibid., p. 29.

31. Ibid., p. 39.

32. Compare Whitehead, *Modes of Thought*, p. 30, with Carini, p. 35.

33. Ibid., p. 263, cf. Carini, p. 37.

34. See David Marshak's "An Investigation of Rudolf Steiner's Vision of Human Development and Education" for a description of Waldorf school daily practice [Qualifying Paper, Harvard Graduate School of Education, Cambridge, MA, 1984].

35. Susanne Gowan, George Lakey, William Moyer, and Richard Taylor, *Moving Toward a New Society* (Philadelphia, PA: New Society Press, 1976).

36. Ibid., p. 284.

37. Virginia Coover, Ellen Deacon, Charles Esser, and Christopher Moore, *Resource Manual for a Living Revolution* (Philadelphia PA: New Society Press, 1977).

38. Ira Shor, *Critical Thinking in Everyday Life* (Chicago, IL: University of Chicago Press, 1980).

39. For additional references on liberation education we would note the special issue of *Social Education*, Vol. 49, Number 5 (May 1985) on "New Criticism and Social Education," edited by Jack L. Nelson.

40. Shor, p. 47.

41. Ibid.

42. Ibid., p. 50.

43. Ibid., p. 52.

44. Ibid., p. 57.

45. In political and social theory terms it is the territory that has been worked over recently and perhaps most helpfully by Richard J. Bernstein in *The Restructuring of Social and Political Theory* (Philadelphia, PA: University of Pennsylvania Press, 1976; and *Beyond Objectivism and Relativism: Science, Hermeneutics, and Praxis* (Philadelphia, PA: University of Pennsylvania Press, 1983). The focus of much of Bernstein's analysis is the relationship between human community, knowledge and power. While this may seem superficially alien from Whitehead and process thought, we would note that Whitehead was centrally concerned with the problem of coercion versus persuasion. One of the more constructive efforts to move process toward a consideration of the issue of power is presented in the article by Sturm referred to in chapter 9 of this book.

46. Gustavo Gutierrez, *A Theology of Liberation* (Maryknoll, NY: Orbis, 1973).

47. An interesting papal response to liberation theology, which defends a more sacramental view of the Catholic Church, is the *Instruction on Certain Aspects of the 'Theology of Liberation'* (Boston, MA: The Daughters of St. Paul, 1984).

48. It might be noted that Steiner and the human potential movement likewise share the deeper vision of human spirit, but seriously underplay problems of power and oppression associated with the centralized hierarchical structure characteristic of so many modern institutions.

49. Dorothy Lee, "Linguistic Reflection on Wintu Thought," pp. 12–23, in Edmund Carpenter and Marshall McLuhan, editors, *Explorations in Communication* (Boston, MA: Beacon Press, 1960).

50. Ibid., p. 15.

51. Rachel Carson, *Silent Spring* (New York: Fawcett Crest, 1962).

52. The Club of Rome, *The Limits to Growth* (Washington D.C.: Potomic Associates, 1972).

53. Murray Bookchin, *The Ecology of Freedom* (Palo Alto, CA: Cheshire Books, 1982), p. 2.

54. Ibid., p. 3.

55. Ibid., p. 3.

56. Ibid., p. 50.

57. Ibid., p. 318-319.

58. Ibid., p. 320.

59. Ibid., p. 319.

60. Arne Naess, "A Defense of the Deep Ecology Movement," *Environmental Ethics* 6, no. 3 (Fall 1984): 265-270.

61. Mary Daly, *Beyond God the Father: Toward a Philosophy of Women's Liberation* (Boston, MA: Beacon, 1973), and *Gyn/Ecology: the Metaethics of Radical Feminism* (Boston, MA: Beacon, 1978).

62. Seith Kreisberg, *Transforming Power* Ed.D. dissertation, Harvard Graduate School of Education, Cambridge, MA, 1986.

63. For an excellent introduction to the field, the reader is referred to Richard A. Schmuck and Patricia A. Schmuck, *Group Processes in the Classroom* (Dubuque, IA: 1983). Wm. C. Brown Company.

64. For more information on the cooperative education movement, the reader is referred to the International Association for the Study of Cooperative Education, 136 Liberty St., Santa Cruz, CA. Also for an excellent review of research on cooperative learning in secondary schools, the reader is referred to the National Center on Effective Secondary Schools, University of Wisconsin-Madison, Madison, WI.

65. We would concede that there are special places where one might live a monastic life and experience the depth of process as reality—e.g., as Thoreau did at Walden—but we see these as exceptional circumstances inhabited by exceptional persons who were able to create a community truly within nature.

66. Robert Redfield and Milton B. Singer, "The Cultural Role of Cities," in *Peasants and Peasant Societies,* edited by Teodor Shanin (Middlesex, England: Penguin, 1971). pp. 337-365.

67. Ibid., pp. 344-345.

68. Ibid., pp. 349-350.

69. For more information on such intentional communities, see Corinne McLaughlin and Gordon Davidson, *Builders of the Day* (Walpole, NH: Stilepoint Publishing, 1985).

INDEX

actual occasions, defined, 113,
116–118, 137
Alexander, Christopher, 158, 188–193, 237
alternative objects; defined, 109
animism, 146
Association for Process Philosophy of
Education, 206

Barfield, Owen, 88–91; figuration, 120,
228; qualities of human thought, 88–91
Bateson, Gregory, 106, 107, 212; notion of
mind, 146; relation of humans to nature,
21
Beardsley , Monroe, 166
Bell, Daniel; antinomianism, 22
Benedetti, Robert, 128
Berger, Peter; components of reality, 22;
six themes of modernity, 13
Bloom, Benjamin, 18, 133
Bohm, David, 137, 211–212; ground as
reality, 196
Bookchin, Murray, 230, 239
Brown, George, 208
Brumbaugh, Robert S.; cosmologizing,
68–70; patterns of change, 123
Burhoe, Ralph Wendell, 95

Carini, Patricia F., 101, 215–218
Carson, Rachel, 229
Christianity, 87
Club of Rome, 229
Coates, Gary J., 75–81
conscrescence, 26
cooperative education, 234
cosmology, 34; and curriculum, 85, 94;
comparative, and communication, 89;
defined, 94; Hopi, 84; Judeo christian, 82;

metaphysical, 60; modern humanistic,
83; platonic, 82; process, 95
creativity; Whitehead, 121
culture; and potentiality, 38; aspects of a
positive, 19; authentic, 145; balance, 22;
cosmological comparisons, 85; dangers
of, 21; defined, 20, 37; development, 4;
Geertz, Clifford, 38; metaphors, 19;
process, 185; Sorokin's three types,
27–29;   specialization, 11, 12; theory,
94; time, 197
curriculum; time, 197; process, 185

Daly, Mary, 233
Dewey, John, 166
Diamond, Stanley, 3; features of primitive
societies, 23; fragmentation of
anthropology, 43; primitive existen-
tialism, 26
Dunkel, Harold B., 126
Durkheim, Emile, 88, 89

education; change, 30; cooperative, 234;
evolution of societies, 23; examples of
integrated societies, 22; fallacy of simple
location, 21; features of primitive social
life, 25; specialization, 12, 29
Educators for Social Responsibility, 234

Ferguson, Marilyn, 207, 209, 211
Fraser, J. T., 128; levels of the physical
universe, 108; umwelts, 100
Freilich, Morris, 40
Freire, Pablo, 229

Geertz, Clifford, 39
God; in process thought, 122, 138
Griffin, Susan, 70–74, 233